PROFIT AND THE EFFECTIVENESS OF HUMAN RIGHTS

Paula Marcilio Tonani de Carvalho

PROFIT AND THE EFFECTIVENESS OF HUMAN RIGHTS

1st Edition
POD

K

KBR
Petrópolis
2014

Translation **Amanda Morris**
Text Edition **Noga Sklar**
Cover **KBR**

ISBN 978-85-8180-245-9

KBR Editora Digital Ltda.
www.kbrdigital.com.br
www.facebook.com/kbrdigital
atendimento@kbrdigital.com.br
55|24|2222.3491

LAW009000 - Law / Business & Financial

Printed in USA

Paula Marcilio Tonani de Carvalho has a PhD in Business Law and a Masters in Civil Law by Pontifícia Universidade Católica de São Paulo — PUC/SP and teaches at both bachelor and graduate level law school. She is a member of IASP — São Paulo Lawyers' Institute, is a practicing attorney and has been a partner at a law firm since 1997.

E-mail: paula@tonaniadvogados.com.br

Sumário

To Julia and Gustavo, once more and always.

PREFACE

Intuitively and historically, mankind has always spurned financial gain, which is often known as profit. Negative reactions to such advantages are not recent — the Bible itself referred to profiting from interest as sin.

Up to the mid-11th century, almost all goods were produced for personal consumption; the concepts of property and commerce differed from our current understanding. People then produced their own food, clothing and furniture.

In the Middle Ages, lords received the product of labor of their unremunerated serfs. Occasionally, there was barter of goods and services, but mostly, the Church and fiefdoms accumulated all wealth in gold and silver — but that cannot be considered capital in the modern sense.

At this point in history, the word profit was not normally used. In fact, it was seen negatively, as undue spoils; the barter system would only flourish after the decline of feudalism. Additionally, profit would only become common usage when money (currency) began to be traded in exchange for goods.

In this context, Prof. Octavio Gouvêa de Bulhões notes that:

> [...] although selfishness had always existed, in the 19th century it became widespread, due to the absence of institutions that imposed ethical behavior, as in the early Middle Ages,

which would make the concept of "profit spoils" (from the appropriation of labor-costs excess) accepted. Historical documents of that time demonstrate this frame of mind, which helps explain the opposition to private property contained in two essays with otherwise diametrically opposed views: the "Communist Manifesto," published in 1848 and the encyclical "*Rerum Novarum*," issued in 1891. Premises and conclusions are antithetical in these works, but both assume, wrongly, that profit comes from retaining the fruits of labor.[1]

Currently, it can be said that the term profit is closely connected to the establishment of capitalism as the dominant economic system in Eastern Europe. Capitalism has, undoubtedly, ruptured old social and economical relations between people. However, establishing the capitalist system was not instantaneous or peaceful.

Capitalism will exist in a society when people realize that goods needed for living, previously shared and assumed to be communal, should belong to one person.

When a man builds a fence around his crop so his neighbor cannot access his field and, especially, when he declares ownership of land, either because he took or traded it for something of value, the first notions of the capitalist system are born.

At this point, some goods will then be considered more valuable than others and supply and demand will influence bartering, because people will then decide what they need and will realize, with a capitalist mindset, they can save, have more economic power and accumulate what is known as "wealth."

Once wealth is accumulated by the few, issues caused by income inequality and its damaging effects come to play, which is a problem savage capitalism cannot solve.

Therefore, at first, profit was connected to capital accumulation, with the sole intention of creating more and more

---

1BULHÕES, O. *Dois Conceitos de Lucro.* Rio de Janeiro: Apec Editora, 1969.

capital. Speculation became the capitalist's sole purpose, without a thought to anything else.

People's value began being measured by what they owned, not who they were; the capitalist system instituted the worth of goods over people, directly and indirectly demeaning human existence.

The law does not support a free market economy and is seen by capitalists as a hindrance to their goal of ever-increasing profit. Thus, a capitalist will only use the rule of law when it is useful to sustain their position in the market.

The end of the 18th century sees the British Industrial Revolution and, shortly thereafter, the establishment of liberalism and industrial capitalism by the French Revolution.

Paul-Eugène Charbonneau noted, about economic liberalism, that:

[. . .] this economic system is not based in any philosophy, nor was it born from any other system. It is, by nature, an economic system created by historical circumstances that uses liberal philosophy to its own benefit. Economic liberalism comes, historically, from the mercantilist direction of post-feudal economy and the technical advances that created huge and expensive machinery [. . .] Its keys are liberalism (from the libertarian wave originated by the French Revolution) and the resultant individualistic view of the world. As Joyce stated, it can be said the 18th and 19th centuries left only one choice: to eat or be eaten. This is the background in which the capitalist system established its main structure. [. . .] Liberal philosophy was adopted by capitalism because it was convenient. It remained, however, parallel and extrinsic. Unlike Marx, who first built a philosophy to then create an economic system, capitalism is its own philosophical system; it is accidental and cannot be considered intrinsically evil. As liberalism, its first concrete historical form, it must be fully condemned. But in itself, seen apart from liberal philosophy, the capitalist system could be viable, even though its current iteration seems unacceptable.[2]

Indeed, the French Revolution is one of the most important chapters of the long historical transition from the feudalistic to capitalist system. Additionally, the English's 17th century revolution, the Industrial Revolution in the 18th century and the American Revolution in 1776 also had crucial influence in the change in social and economic relationships and, consequently, in the definition of profit itself and its way of obtention through private enterprise.

The French Revolution overthrew the aristocracy that lived off feudal privileges and ended serfdom, bringing down the system that supported Louis XVI's absolutist regime. At this time, the hierarchy instituted by a society organized into the three estates of the realm — nobility, clergy and commoners — was coming to an end, creating conditions for the development of capitalism in France, since one of the founding principles of the new regime was freedom, including the freedom of enterprise and to gain profit.

Undoubtedly, the French Revolution gained strength from popular movements, both urban and rural. Peasants were driven into extreme poverty, due to the economic crisis, which made their world unsafe and caused a rural exodus. The revolution was, then, a product of poverty, hunger, unemployment, lack of basic goods, population growth and bad harvests from 1788-89.

The French Revolution had several stages: (i) National Constituent Assembly (1789 to 1791); (ii) end of the feudal system and construction of a constitutional monarchy; (iii) constitutional monarchy (1791 to 1792). Clearly, there was a conflict between monarchists, who wanted the king's independent power preserved, and the Assembly's majority, that maintained that the people should have power to supervise and control the government.

---

2 CHARBONNEAU, P. *Entre Capitalismo e Socialismo: a Empresa Humana*. São Paulo: Pioneira, 1983, p. 72.

The urban and rural popular movement had a decisive role in the revolution; workers and artisans had the power to assemble and denounce the regime; the bourgeoisie's leaders used their strength to bring down nobility and gain political power.

Within the French Revolution, several other revolutions occurred, which had enormous influence in creating new definitions of not only profit, but also of fraternity. The concept of profit was disfigured by the liberal economic model, which created artificial, unguaranteed currencies.

In fact, even by mid-19th century, the word profit was still defined by two different concepts, used interchangeably: the appropriation of labor-cost excess and financial investments.

Change was brought by the worldwide economic downturn of the early 1930s, which resulted in the Great Depression; it was proposed that there could be a solution to the crisis by increasing consumption, to generate new jobs and put old factories back into business. Profit began to be seen as a source of wealth, whether to increase productivity or investments in the business. Reinvested profit became valuable and a positive concept for capitalism, not to be confused anymore with profits generated by financial investments.

Incidentally, Prof. Octavio Gouvêa de Bulhões notes that "[...] investment profits are generic and unconnected to the owners of the means of production. Investment profits, such as interest from a savings account, which is part of the investment, are not capital profits."[3]

However, other economic systems, such as socialism, were opposed to any kind of profit. In fact, the socialist system believed, generally speaking, that profit must be contested, seeing that the value of labor was directly connected to consumer needs so, conversely, production should focus on primary, secondary and tertiary human needs, concentrating on the appropriate use of resources, not on profit.

Nevertheless, the government tried to allocate prof-

---

3 *Op. Cit.*, p. 41.

its gained through private enterprise, by collecting taxes as a way to share them indirectly and ensure benefits to those who helped gain said profits.

Financial gain, however, was not only seen adversely. In 1794, Albert Gallatin shared profits from his glass factory, New Genève, with his employees. It was one of the first historical instances in which profit was destined to the greater good of the community.

There are several historical instances of financial gain from private enterprises used for good. Presently, legal solutions were created to harmonize profit that benefits a community with private profit.

For example,

[. . .] in 1812, Napoleon Bonaparte granted by decree that artists from the Comédie-Française were entitled to part of the company's profits (feux), along with their salaries. The artists received part of the net profit, based on fame, age and seniority. [. . .] In 1842, Monsieur Edme-Jean Leclaire, owner of a small painting workshop, Maison Leclaire, after drawing its balance sheet and calculating profit, gave his employees, with no explanation, a considerable portion of his earnings. In 1844, Edmond-Larouche Joubert, of Angoulême, established profit sharing at his stationery store. John Stuart Mill and John Bright asserted that profit sharing was a way to prevent strikes and for employees to have access to company stock and, eventually, become part of the management. [. . .] In Scotland, in the early 19th century, Robert Owen also experimentally shared profits with his employees. Around 1847 in Prussia, profit sharing became more common. In 1850, it was adopted by England as well and, in 1869, by the United States. Charles Robert was also a pioneer, around 1848, writing about profit sharing plans in his study *Le Partage des fruits du travail* (Paris, 1878). [. . .] in 1917, the Mexican constitution established compulsory profit sharing (article 123, VI and IX) for factories, agricultural, commercial and mining companies, a provision that was duly regulated several years later. [. . .] in Germany, H. Bohmerto observed profit sharing and the equalizing of employees and employers at Ernst Abbe's Zeiss Optical Shop. [. . .] Cardinal Mercier's social studies were embraced by Pope Leo XIII's encyclical *Rerum Novarum* (1891), which also claimed profit sharing was a social justice imperative.[4]

The growing complexity of social relations made lawmakers rely less on legal formalism, especially in the 20th century, and move towards a new, more substantial view of profit accrual. These relations went through deep changes in our days, by virtue of closer economic connections between people and cultures all over the world.

When production started to rely more on machinery, which became more common after the Industrial Revolution, and less on human labor, large-scale production became possible. This fact, along with the rural exodus that happened during the same period, allowed urban centers to flourish and changed the way business was conducted.

In this new economic environment, the government created new laws to deal with the ramifications of legal and economic relations and to interfere in private transactions.

According to Carlos Alberto Bittar,

[. . .] economic interventionism is effected through measures taken by the government to control the economy. It implies market interference, transaction delimitation, economic sector domination, lawmaking and, generally, tampering with the economy. It is an observable fact that, historically, there has always been state intervention in economic dealings; from tribal formations to enlightened absolutism's princes and monarchs, from primitive societies to the century of lights' democracies.[5]

---

4 MARTINS, S. *Participação dos Empregados nos Lucros das Empresas*. São Paulo: Atlas, 2009, pp. 05/06.
5 BITTAR, C. *Direito Civil Constitucional*. São Paulo: Revista dos Tribunais, 2003, p. 116.

The establishment of a new economic order and drastic change in labor relations altered the way the government intervenes in the economy and private transactions. In this regard, it is understandable that common law countries instituted, right after World War II, constitutional courts to oversee the direction taken by economic and legal relationships relating to economic issues and public interest.

The values guiding several constitutions must, inevitably, be confronted with principles of solidarity and humanitarianism, as well as the protection of natural and imprescriptible rights, all contained in several legal systems created after the French Revolution and the Declaration of the Rights of Man and of the Citizen in 1798, which prompted Vicente Ráo to affirm that:

> [...] this document asserts the existence of natural, inalienable, imprescriptible and sacred human rights. The Declaration lays these rights, which condense and encompass freedom and equality principles, at the base of the democratic state. However, in the relationship between society and the individual, the person must prevail, for two main reasons: a) the political and social meaning of the French Revolution, which was a reaction against the government's absolute power, magnified by privileges granted to certain social classes and the actions of artisans and workers, that held a monopoly on their activities; b) the economic circumstances of the time, based on small-scale production.

Large-scale legal transactions became more common in the shape of, for instance, standard-form or adhesion contracts. Thus, the creation of legal mechanisms to regulate power imbalances within legal transactions became imperative to protect and keep the main focus on individuals.

Despite the above-mentioned changes, the government increasingly intervened in the economy, affecting private industrial and commercial activities that had received tax benefit stimulus for occurring in areas in which the government couldn't operate directly.

In this context of technological advances and changed legal transactions, excessive formalism exacerbated the risk of supporting totalitarian regimes, such as those in Italy (fascism), Spain and Germany, for instance.

To illustrate said interventionism, Prof. Bittar points out that:

> [. . .] noted: periodically creating specific interventionist and planning laws in which the reach of said control would be established; converting supplemental laws into mandatory laws for the public interest (in fields such as transportation, commercial and residential rentals, insurance, real estate, etc.); granting regulatory powers to interventionist organizations within or supervised by the Executive branch (for instance, social security institutes, professional associations, controlling or supervising institutions such as reserve banks, securities and exchange commissions and others); charging fees to subsidize intervention services and expenses (within, for example, social security, unions, professional associations, economic regulatory agencies and others); the use of taxes as incentive and to help develop regions and activities (tax benefits, such as exemptions, reductions and abatements, and other forms of taxation to finance special programs); creating control and supervision laws of activities and transactions [. . .]; submitting private transactions to intervening institutions for approval (like in financial market transactions, technology transfers and others).[6]

It is, thus, noteworthy that the mid and late 20th century were the stage in which solidarity economics were reinvented: workers gained rights, including shorter work hours, higher sal-

---

6 BITTAR, C. *Op. Cit.*, p. 121.

aries and comprehensive and universal access to social security. The solidarity economy program is based on the premise that capitalist traditions create opportunities for the development of economic organizations rooted in logic that opposes the dominant mode of production.

Furthermore, solidarity economy theory understands that the way to make economy grow is to be part of competitive markets; it shall only become an alternative better than capitalism once it offers opportunities to achieve self-sufficiency to all and provides a structure of production and distribution of merchandise as efficient as the capitalist system's.

Nonetheless, freedom and equality, principles that reinforce rights to individuality and liberation, are insufficient to protect diffuse and collective interests, which must be tempered by fraternity. Hence, the French Revolution ideals are expressed by a symbiosis of liberty and equality, balanced by fraternity, destined to fulfill common interests.

Until the French Revolution, fraternity distinguished legal transactions and its consequences. Later, it was gradually replaced by the concept of solidarity, which amplified the acknowledgment of human rights and of the need to protect collective and diffuse interests.

Either way, fraternity is connected directly to efficacy and, thus, within a framework based on solidarity and humanitarianism, the law regulates capitalism and inserts the need for socialization and humanization in a social and legal context, whether by interpreting or implementing laws and, therefore, influencing life in society.

The legal system and its principles have the instrumental role of balancing human relations, creating checks and balances to the capitalist market system and harmonizing capital and labor, so capital works in service of people and not the other way around.

In turn, reframing some of the law's main linchpins, such as giving a new perspective on profit obtention, for instance, attempts to find a balance between individual and collective interest that is required, currently more than ever, for life in society. This aspired social parity is achieved by cooperation between living beings and establishing a new reality, built on people's individual and communal roles, along with economic and commercial activity.

Individual interest will then, inevitably, produce social effects accepted and desired by the community. Profit, a major market economy booster and invigorator, is among these effects. For instance, according to the social function protected by Brazilian law, an individual's actions should not be motivated only by their own personal benefit, but by the common good.

Guilherme Calmon Nogueira da Gama asserts, in this vein, that:

> [...] The social function must be understood as a standard or general clause, to be contemplated and built on a framework of ethical, economic and social values. A jurist's understanding of the law cannot remain unaffected by transformations occurring in society, especially when this standard has been set in the constitution by the legislators themselves [...] The social function doctrine affects several branches of the law, such as property, contract, commercial and family law and has influenced several nonconstitutional laws.[7]

Building a society based on equality and respect to fellow human beings is more necessary than ever, both within social relations and each human being's personal projects. Solidarity means accepting that, although human beings are essentially unique, growth, improvement and dedication to life projects must, inescapably, take place in a healthy community.

---

7 GAMA, G. *Função Social no Direito Civil*. São Paulo: Atlas, 2007, pp. 16/17.

Chapter I - Legal Aspects of Profit

Profit is the cost of production of a good or service, subtracted from the value of production. To subsist, a company must gain profits and reinvest, largely to renovate equipment and production; it must also raise labor productivity, as a cost-reduction measure.

Profits are a badge of success that shows the company has been managed competently; profits are synonymous to economic efficiency. Economic loss takes away the company's credit and even its reason to exist, unlike what happens in a profitable enterprise.

Profit is also a means to achieving new goals, since it is the most important way capital is accumulated — profit must, after all, become new capital. It is demanded, within a company, from all ranks of merit and responsibility, offering workers an opportunity for so-called career advancement.

The definition and scope of the locution are broad, as it will be demonstrated.

1.1 - General Concepts about Profit

It is impossible to define or construe the word profit in a categorical way, and not because it lacks clarity, but due to its several possible meanings, both within and without the legal system.

The word profit means gain, acquisition, accumulation, benefit — it has, therefore, a positive connotation.

Rubens Requião, for instance, defines profit as:

[. . .] The surplus a company can produce, as a result of investment of capital and other resources into its activity. Economists must define the term, no matter if defending or opposing its legitimacy. From a legal standpoint, profit can be classified as final assets or dividends. Final assets are distributed to shareholders when a company is being shut down, after all liabilities have been paid off, and invested equity and remaining results have been returned to the shareholders. The net product, an expression favored by erstwhile physiocrats, is the profit generated by the company while it was active. Dividends are paid as distribution of balance sheet profits, at the end of the fiscal year. Article 191 of Brazil's Corporation Law states that the fiscal year's net profit is calculated periodically and corresponds to the amount remaining, after losses from previous years, taxes and the profit sharing mentioned on article 190 are subtracted.[8]

As Sérgio Pinto Martins notes:

[. . .] The concept of profit is not completely indeterminate. The Brazilian constitution doesn't define it, nor it should; other laws can very well delineate the definition. [. . .] The Social Sciences Dictionary (1987) affirms "the word profit has no specific technical meaning in the social sciences sphere, except within economic theory — where it is usually used in the plural form." In the economic field, it is possible to roughly group the concept of profit into three main categories that overlap partially: (a) profits from income received by categories institutionally allowed to receive income; (b) profits (positive

---

8 REQUIÃO, R. *Curso de Direito Comercial.* São Paulo: Editora Saraiva, 1988, vol. II, p. 203.

or negative) of an abstract, residual, non-functional income; (c) profits as revenue (positive or negative) from business activity. [. . .] Profit, in economic theory, is the remainder of productive activity, after all factors of production have been paid for: capital (interest), land (rent), labor (salaries) (Harold A. Sloan and Arnold J. Zurcher, 195: 256) [. . .] The concept of profit is related to a company's economic activity, minus its expenses. Profit is, therefore, intrinsic to a company's economic purpose, which is to provide a market with goods or services. [. . .] Consequently, profit is the business owner's remuneration; employees receive a salary. [. . .] It seems that profit, in a constitutional context, refers to net profit, which is a company's profitability after accounting for all its costs. It isn't gross profit, which is the difference between the good or service's purchase price, minus taxation. The overhead is not deducted from the gross profit calculation.[9]

It can be understood, from the above-quoted jurists' definitions, that the concept of profit is directly connected to its given purpose.

To the ordinary person, profit is what is left over from a company's activity, exceeding the operating costs in the balance sheet.

Accounting theory defines profit as the difference between revenue and costs (assets) that will generate an increase in the net assets. Profit is, then, the result of a fiscal year's activity. In this context, accounting profit reflects a process that measures and identifies revenue and costs occurred in a certain period, according to accepted conventions of accounting; it represents the positive or negative balance of a company's transactions' loss or gain in the pursuit of its corporate purpose.

Legal science adopts the economic definition of profit, since in corporate law, for instance, what matters is asset in-

---

9 MARTINS, S. *Participação dos Empregados nos Lucros das Empresas. Op. Cit.*, pp. 62/63.

crease; civil law deals with property and goods, which will, necessarily, have a measurable economic value. For legal science, a company's profit is also an economic issue, which will be discussed in this treatise's final chapter.

As a general rule, economists make a distinction between business profit — the difference between revenue and explicit costs — and pure profit — the difference between revenue and both explicit and implicit costs; the latter includes, for instance, interest from invested capital and executive compensation.

Either way, a corporation differs from other private law entities in that it not only may obtain profit, but also can distribute said profit among its members.

Manuel Meireles notes:

[. . .] Profit can be understood as the capital owner's earnings, considered as the residual and arbitrary difference between revenue and explicit or implicit costs, within a certain time frame. In the context of this study, the time frame will be the time necessary to process a certain number of items. Konrad Mellerowicz (1936) remarks that the total lifespan of a company should be considered, and the difference between the capital invested and the final results will equal that company's real profit. "This is the safe and absolute way to measure profit, as it is calculated in a perfectly correct way. Any other profit will always be relative."[10]

As Gregory Lewis states:

[. . .] Profit is not only necessary to provide dividends to stockholders or financial returns to the owners of capital; it is essential to finance the substitution or addition of assets, such as equipment and vehicles, and to provide funds for the

10 MEIRELES, M. *O Lucro. Esboço para uma Teoria do Lucro como fruto da Alavancagem Tecnológica do Capital.* São Paulo: Arte & Ciência Villipress Editora, 2000.

business' expansion. Business expansion or growth is always a very costly endeavor. [. . .] Invested capital corresponds to the amount in a bank, loans from that institution and the company's assets and stock. If it has not been reinvested in the business, this amount might be deposited in a bank account or invested to accumulate interest. Investments are a way to generate revenue and possibly capital increase without business risks.[11]

Profit is also seen as the fruit of capital. In fact, Adam Smith established the connection between capital and profit in his work *The Wealth of Nations*, in which the extent that profit is accrued is related to the capital's value and the assets employed in the company's activities. In his work, Smith claims that profit is not just salary with a different name, for instance, but a completely separate issue, regulated by the value of the capital invested in the company. In this context, to clarify, the word "capital" means a body of assets destined to aid production and commercializing of the company's goods or services.

Considering its origin is, or could be, related to the capital's physical productivity, profit can also be understood as the fruit of the capital's gained interest. However, it doesn't explain why some capital may yield more than others, nor does it clarify how profit occurs.

A modern example of profit from interest is earned by real estate developers; it is the difference between the interest rate paid to investors that loaned the money to finance a land purchase and the construction's outset or until the sale of the building, and the amount earned by investing the borrowed capital.

However, the theory that profit equals fruits of capital has its dissenters. José Luiz de Almeida Nogueira Porto asseverates that:

---

11 LEWIS, G. *O Preço do Lucro*. Lisboa: Lyon Multimédia Edições, 1995, pp. 44/46.

[. . .] The theory of profit as fruits of capital doesn't seem enough to elucidate why some capital will yield more than others and doesn't explain how profit is accrued; both issues are integral to the understanding of the subject. Why would some capital only yield the bare minimum, which is interest, and others have higher returns? How this excess amount is named is irrelevant; it exists and, as such, must be explained. However, it is not enough to state that profit is a consequence of the capital's productivity.[12]

Profit is also related to the size of the risk associated to the venture; therefore, there is an element of uncertainty. In this case, the capital investments are made based on expectations of profit, but no guarantees are given.

José Luiz de Almeida Nogueira Porto states that:

[. . .] There is one situation, however, in which profit results from risk taken and unverified: profit from occasional speculation. Although it would be possible to characterize said profit as "interest from risk," that would be a stretch; due to the lack of a better option, then, it is acceptable to classify it as profit. But this kind of profit is like gambling: "like winning a bet" — writes Davenport (19) and doesn't have much in common with the subject of this work, profit obtained by companies. However, if a corporation's regular activity included speculation or gambling, then there would be no question; said risk would have to be included when figuring the company's revenue, as "interest from risk." For instance, if the business in question were a casino, in which there is always a chance of loss, this risk, then, must be acknowledged as part of the company's capital remuneration.[13]

---

12 PORTO, J. *Contribuição para a Teoria do Lucro.* São Paulo: Edição Própria, 1954, p. 73.
13 *Op. Cit.*, pp. 80/81.

Therefore, it can be said that, even to those that relate risk theory to the structure of profit accrual, profit is related to the fruit of capital. Profit is also connected to the company manager's performance; thus, the manager's competence has a crucial influence in obtaining profit or not.

As José Luiz de Almeida Nogueira Porto states:

> [...] Most economists attribute profit gain, to a major or lesser degree, to the manager's work and capacity. Among them are Stuart Mill, Walker, Marshall, Cassel, Schumpeter, Taussig, Davenport and, more recently, Gino Arias. The latter claims that profit "is the real remuneration of labor," in two ways: as the "businessperson's activity" helming the company and as a compensation for risk, that is, "initiative work." [...] However, in this writer's opinion, the manager's activity is a condition for profit, not a cause; the causes are much more complex and include several other elements beside the company's executive chief's effort and competence. Various examples could be mentioned to demonstrate that profit not always results from the manager's actions, nor is it proportional to their work; sometimes, it comes from accidental or conjectural causes. It is not possible to credit only the manager's work and personal abilities as profit generators. Capital, risk, uncertainty and the business cycle are factors that cannot be ignored.[14]

The concept of profit is also related to the company's capacity for growth and its investments' financing. As Adrian Wood points out:

> [...] The chief object of a typical firm in a capitalist economy is to cause its sales to grow. This entails the expansion of its productive capacity, which in turn requires investment in fixed assets and stocks. The firm must, of course, be able to

---

14 *Op. Cit.*, pp. 85/86.

finance this investment; that is, it must be able to obtain the funds needed for expenditure on its capital projects. In practice, ploughed-back profits are necessarily the main source of finance for investment. The central principle of the present theory, therefore, is that the amount of profits which the firm sets out to earn is determined by the amount of investment that it plans to undertake. [...] The reason for its willingness to devote its retained profits to such a project, rather than obtaining a better return by lending the money to someone else, is that this sort of loan (and indeed the acquisition of financial assets in general) while it would increase the non-trading income of the firm, would add nothing to its sales revenue.[15]

Manuel Meireles, divergently, considers profit as a fruit of technological capital leverage:

[...] Profit comes from technological advances that, when adopted, allow the capitalist to have the lowest competitive price (LCP) and obtain a higher return margin than the market's regular competitive price (CP). [...] Capitalists act in different competitive fields and the technological status specific to each of these spheres generates different technological leverage factors. Even within the same competitive field, each capitalist has a technological leverage factor that their capital can provide. This diversity of competitive prices (CP) in their fields is challenged by the several lowest competitive prices (LCP) of each capitalist and, ultimately, determines the profit per unit (PPU) of each item and, in its turn, the total profit (TP) of each capitalist.[16]

Currently, costs, expenses, taxing and profit compose a product or service's price. Therefore, the analysis of profit allocation can be related to short, mid or long-term invest-

---

15 WOOD, A. *A Theory of Profits.* pp. 4/8.
16 MEIRELES, M. *Op. Cit.*

ments, without any need to search for external resources.

In this case, profit earned will be reinvested in equipment, machinery or even specialized labor; it will not be necessary to search for international funds or pay interest.

In the same vein, Adrian Wood states that:

> [...] The exact level of the gearing limit depends on two sorts of things: 1) managerial expectations of the future course of the company's profits with special reference to the chances of the company's profitability falling to very low levels (or, more precisely, with special reference to the lower tails of the subjective probability distributions of the company's profit rate in future periods). These expectations, in conjunction with expectations about the level of the interest rate (which will increase with the gearing ration, but which in other respects we will treat given) determine the subjective probabilities of bankruptcy and of financial difficulties of a lesser kind at each level of the gearing ratio. 2) Which level of the gearing ratio is chosen as a limit and as a target will then depend on the attitudes of managers and owners towards the risks and disadvantages of borrowing, and in particular on the degree to which they are risk averse.[17]

Of course, a possible profit level drop will create a need to obtain external resources to maintain the above-mentioned investments.

Francisco Araújo Santos defines profit as:

> [...] the total value of goods and services produced by a company; IC is the total cost of inputs and W, the entire amount needed to pay for salaries, in this way: PQ = TPV/(IC+W). The profit quotient will equal the total value of goods and services produced by a company, divided by the total cost of inputs (IC) plus cost of labor or salaries (W). The difference

---

17 WOOD, A. *Op. Cit.* p. 31.

(PQ-1) equals surplus value (SV). Karl Marx, in 1867, provided a similar definition in the first volume of his work, Capital.[18]

As Paul Singer explains:

[. . .] The capitalist owns the means of production, operated by hired workers; then, the resulting product is sold and the money earned is compared to the amount invested at the start. The goal is to have gained more; the difference between their startup and final capital is profit. Every activity aims for profit higher than the startup capital. Considering the relation between profit/capital is the "profit rate" in a certain time frame (usually a year), it can be said that its objective is to maximize the profit rate, that is, to obtain an annual profit as high as possible, for each million invested in a given business. The production cycle follows a D-M-D' formula: D is the startup capital, which is necessarily presented in cash (capital-money); M is the capital transformed into means of production and labor power (capital-merchandise); during the production process, workers transform the means of production into products to be sold. D' is the revenue from sales that rebuilds the startup capital-money (D), supplemented by its increase, that is, its profit (AD). Therefore, D' is usually larger than D, considering D'=D+AD; in other words, the capital at the end of the production cycle equals capital plus profit.[19]

From the several viewpoints quoted above, it can be concluded that the concept of profit is unquestionably correlated to an advantage, a benefit, a positive result and directly related to the fruit of capital, a fruit of the capital's volume that generates interest, to the amount of risk in the

---

18 SANTOS, F. *Lucro & Ética*. São Leopoldo: Editora Unisinos, 2003, p. 54.
19 SINGER, P. *O Capitalismo: sua evolução, sua lógica e sua dinâmica*. São Paulo: Editora Moderna, 1987, p. 24.

venture and even to its productive capacity.

Either way, the business activity's capacity to produce positive, or even negative, results, as well as its lawful distribution among shareholders are undeniable.

1.2 - Differences between Profit and Retained Earnings

In the context of properly defining profit, it must be said that the concept cannot be confused with "retained earnings," which are a reserve set aside for a specific purpose.

As Rubens Requião explains:

> [. . .] Erymá Carneiro, a jurist with a Master's degree in accounting, explains, "retained earnings, in legal terms, are nothing more than undistributed profits, a concept that has been acknowledged by judiciary and tax courts in Brazil. Brazilian law recognizes the accounting definition of retained earnings which means it has been incorporated into the legal system, as it has, by the way, in other modern legislations." The main purpose of retained earnings is, writes the jurist, to serve as a guarantee and reinforcement to the owners' capital and as a collateral to creditors. "It is an amendment," he states, "to the company's capital and serves as a reinforcement." Therefore, it is said that retained earnings belong to the company and not to the shareholders, which is true to a point, since it will depend on the type of company.[20]

Indeed, retained earnings are a portion of accrued profit that won't be distributed among shareholders or stockholders; the company will hold it permanently or temporarily. Retained earnings can be classified as: (i) legal — established by law; they shall be retained at the company as possible compensation for

---

20 REQUIÃO, R. *Curso de Direito Comercial. Op. Cit.*, pp. 203/204.

damages, for instance; or (ii) statutory — established by the company's articles of incorporation, a portion of the profits to be distributed will be retained for different purposes; they can also be (iii) voluntary — their purpose will be determined by a shareholder/stockholder meeting; and (iv) undisclosed — in this case, they do not appear on the balance sheet and must be approved by a shareholder/ stockholder annual meeting.

This chapter does not aim to be a thorough examination of retained earnings; the goal is only to clarify that their definition and legal aspects differ from the concept of profit. After all, retained earnings are just one of the purposes of profit; as such, although taken from a portion of profits, they are a form of insurance in case the business activity does not produce positive results, or for future and calculated investments.

Therefore, specific legal issues regarding solidary or fraternal retained earnings are irrelevant in this context.

1.3 - Differences between Profit and Dividends

Just as profits cannot be mistaken for retained earnings, neither can they be seen as a dividend. This, because retained earnings are a part of the profits that have not been distributed among shareholders or stockholders, and dividends are a portion of profit that corresponds to each share — therefore, if profits are distributed as shares among stockholders, they are called dividends.

As Rubens Requião expounds:

[...] within the allocation of shares. [...] The company may only distribute dividends from its fiscal year's net profits, accumulated profits or retained profits; never from the owners' capital. The owners' capital must be safeguarded, as demanded by the Brazilian legal system. Exceptionally, in case of shares of preferred stock, the law allows cumulative dividends to be paid from the capital reserve on a fiscal year in which profit is insufficient. [...] The stockholder that holds nominative shares and, on the day of the annual meeting to distribute dividends, is duly inscribed in the appropriate books as the stock's owner or usufructuary is entitled to dividends.[21]

Alberto Xavier adds:

[...] It is not enough, however, to be a capital company: there still must be a right to a share of the dividends. The type of participation is irrelevant — there are several in comparative law: fruition rights, negotiable securities, founders' shares, all types of capital shares and stock (common, preferred, fruition). But what must be clear is that dividends cannot be understood as the company's debt, even though these rights involve some participation in the profits. Therefore, beneficiaries' returns and interest on convertible debentures are not dividends according to treaties. Thus, the concept of dividends presupposes the existence of revenue that is subjected to similar fiscal treatment as the stock in the country of the company's head address.[22]

Dividends may be fixed or variable, according to the articles of incorporation, but cannot be paid out in case of owners' capital loss, since dividends represent a portion of the profit from each share.

1.4 - Differences between Profit and Surplus

The word profit also must not be confused with the surplus from cooperative activity. To understand the importance

---

21 *Op. Cit.*, p. 207.
22 XAVIER, A. *Direito Tributário Internacional do Brasil*. Rio de Janeiro: Forense Editora, 2007, pp. 726/727.

and legal implications of surplus, it is necessary to first provide a short history of the creation and expansion of cooperatives.

The Rochdale Society of Equitable Pioneers was the first of the consumer cooperatives. It was established in 1844 by a group of 28 laborers of different backgrounds, half of them owenites;[23] its founding might have been inspired by the failure of a weavers strike on that same year.

At that point, the cooperative's principles were: (i) one vote per proposal to each member, regardless of the amount of money invested in the cooperative; (ii) an unlimited number of members were allowed; the community was open to all who wanted to join; (iii) fixed interest rate on loaned capital; (iv) surplus would be shared by all members, proportionally to their purchases from the cooperative; (v) cooperative sales would always be paid in cash; (vi) goods sold by the cooperative would always have an unadulterated origin; (vii) cooperative education would be one of their main endeavors; (viii) religious and political neutrality.

From the principles listed above, it becomes clear that the cooperative's organization and the results of their production of goods and services were quite different from a company's profit.

The Society of Equitable Pioneers had a modest start in 1844, with a capital of only 28 pounds; five years later, after the Rochdale's Savings Bank's bankruptcy, several former clients of the bank were welcomed into the community, which, in the following year, had already 390 members and would later hold vast financial power. They were able to finance a reading room and a library, opened a wholesale department and created the Rochdale Cooperative Manufacturing Society; began to build their own weaving factory and cotton mill. Part of the funding came from the cooperative, its members and workers at the coop factories.

---

23 Editor's note: laborers at Robert Owen's cotton mill who, in 1817, proposed the creation of villages of cooperation, where people could live and work.

The cooperative store was the first step of the pioneers' project, in which goods produced by one cooperative could be exchanged by those produced by another. In Rochdale's instance, however, the number of members grew faster than available positions in the production cooperatives; thus, as the years went by, the village lost most of its members. Its expansion in the 1850s and 1860s was part of a movement that revitalized and made the cooperative movement grow strong.

Also in mid-19th century, the Schulze-Delitzsch credit union began to develop, adapting to the needs of artisans and small urban business owners, initially without their own capital, which was remedied a few years later. The group of artisans and business owners needed each other's savings to capitalize their respective businesses; through the credit union, they were able to obtain loans in the financial markets at a regular interest rate.

The expansion of the cooperative movement allowed the creation of second degree cooperatives, which operated in wholesale, providing the affiliated coops a dependable supply of necessary, quality goods at a decent price. In 1863, 48 cooperatives in the North of England merged to found the Co-operative Wholesale Industrial and Provident Society Limited; at first, the original coop buyers, who had good connections with wholesale distributors, refused to do business with the new society. However, the conflict did not last long.

Ten years later, they had already approximately 200,000 members and the capital had already grown and multiplied, along with all deposits and loans. The positive results of this activity were named surplus, not profit. Their history shows how important it was, at that point, to create legal regulations for cooperatives.

When coal prices went down, workers lost their discount for its purchase from consumer cooperatives, which later led wholesale cooperatives to rescind workers' bonuses.

By the end of the 19th century, consumer cooperatives were all around Great Britain; by 1881, there were 547,000 members and 1,707,000 by 1900. There were fewer cooperatives, but the remaining ones had a higher commercial activity.

This expansion was a result of industrial advances, urbanization and innovations brought by cooperatives to wholesale and retail commerce, impelled by the Rochdale pioneers, at a time in which British retail was trailing behind and cooperative wholesale was much more successful than conventional ones.

Cooperatives offered a starting advantage, in the form of a "guaranteed market" through their expanding member roster. The consumer cooperative system dominated wholesale and retail in British markets and, in the 20th century, also expanded to other countries, such as the United States, Switzerland and France, with the same wholesale and retail strategy, rounding off by creating a national cooperative association.

The cooperative system went through a crisis when, after World War II, automobiles started being sold in Western and Eastern Europe and self-service supermarkets and department stores opened. These innovations reduced costs, but this new business model was not easily adaptable to consumer cooperatives, which were community-based, formed by neighbors and only open to members; as such, they were destined to either lose clients to their competition that could offer lower prices, or abandon their values and merge with larger cooperatives, losing their communal nature.

In several countries, despite a large number of members, the cooperative's sales were lower than expected, seemingly because their members were shopping elsewhere. That resulted in losses, which were initially covered by their reserves.

The effort to lower prices caused their decline; they had to sacrifice the dividend margin, which was no longer distributed among members who, then, reduced their expenses even more, until the wholesale coops forced primary cooperatives to merge. Balance sheets were forged and schemes were made to purchase stock.

Credit unions were modeled in financial market loans, upheld by an unlimited liabilities guarantee, an association of small investors united to heighten their access to credit through mutual financing. Cooperative banks are important as depositaries and distributors of financial supernumerary, transferring the surplus to the cooperatives and reducing any risks to its members.

During the industrial boom from the 1960s up to 1973, English workers invested in new factories; however, these were not cooperatives: they just were often sponsored by cooperative leaders and had consumer cooperatives among their shareholders.

Paul Singer defines production cooperatives as:

[. . .] production cooperatives are workers' associations that might include managers, planners, technicians, etc., that aim to produce marketable goods and services. As in all cooperatives, their members are subjected to principles that establish democracy and equality among all: one vote per member, absolute authority of the members' assembly; all members own the same share of the cooperative's capital.[24]

Both in production and credit cooperatives, the fruit of the labor is called surplus, which is not the same as profit. Cooperatives are a grouping of people united for the common purpose of providing services to its members through self-management. Their source of revenue is an administrative fee, charged during the fiscal year, designed to finance the whole endeavor.

Thus, states article 3 of Law 5.764/1971: "A cooperative society contract's purpose is to obtain mutual benefits to members who contribute with goods and services to an economic, nonprofit activity.

At the end of each fiscal year, accounts are settled; the operating costs are subtracted from the total amount collected by the cooperative, named administrative fee. If the administrative fee is higher than the cooperative's operating costs in that

---

24 SINGER, P. *Op. Cit.*, pp. 89/90.

same period, it means there is excess that will be called surplus. Otherwise, if the operating costs are higher than the administrative fee, there will be a deficit.

It must be noted that after the net results are calculated, the legal reserves — that are indivisible and belong to the cooperative: not only to current members, but also future ones — will be deducted and cannot be nominally distributed. The existence of a surplus or deficit can only be determined after said legal reserves are set aside.

In this regard, Wilson Alves Polonio states that:

> [...] surplus, as the name itself implies, are the cooperative's unused resources, which must be returned to its members, proportionally to the cooperative services used. [...] It is important to highlight that surplus is not a capital increase, but the return of unused resources to the cooperative members [...].[25]

Also, João Vitorino Azolin Benato mentions that:

> [...] Operational results from a certain time frame might be positive or negative. That is to say, the cooperative might have a positive result; in this case, there will be a surplus, which in capitalist jargon would be called profit. When a cooperative has negative results, it is called a deficit; in capitalist jargon, it means loss. Why surplus or deficit instead of profit or loss? For a philosophical and doctrinal reason: a cooperative is a society composed of people and does not aim to make profit; therefore it cannot suffer an economic loss in the same sense as a company can. Every one the cooperative's actions, therefore, have two clear objectives above all: (a) to fulfill a member's need that cannot be explored by capital and lust for profit; (b) to fulfill the cooperative's needs as an entity with le-

---

25 POLONIO, W. *Manual das Sociedades Cooperativas*. São Paulo: Atlas, 2001, p. 82

gal, social, economic and financial commitments. Therefore, the main goal is to find a financial-economical and social balance.[26]

Therefore, even when a surplus is distributed among the members of a cooperative, its purpose is simply to return unused resources resultant from administrative fees in that period that were higher than expenses; it cannot be understood as profit.

1.5 - Differences between Profit and Fruits.

Fruits are an economic product derived from goods; to be considered as such, the goods must retain their specific purpose. The extraction of fruits cannot alter the substance or essence of the original goods. Depending on their provenance, fruits can be natural, civil and legal. Clearly, they are legally classified as assets, since they have monetary value.

As Pontes de Miranda asseverates:

> [...] It matters not that clay might be removed from a coffee, sugar cane or cocoa tree plantation; but if the clay removal decreases the land's value, it is not a fruit. Renewable sources like water are always fruits. So is natural ice. In Roman law, however, flowing water (*aqua profluens*) is not. Fruits are *lucrum ex re*, not *lucrum ex persona*: a worker's production is neither his, nor even the company's fruit; nor is my intellectual production a fruit for me or the publishing company. Handmade items are also not fruits, a *quaestos* (Proverbs 31:16) — like paintings, sculptures, and writings.[27]

---

26 BENATO, J. *ABC do Cooperativismo*. São Paulo: Cenacope, 2007, p. 46.
27 MIRANDA, P. *Tratado de Direito Privado. Parte Geral*. Tomo II. São Paulo: Bookseller, 2000, pp.116/117.

Fruits can also be classified, in legal terms, regarding their place in time and space, since they might still be growing, pending, reaped, separated or received. Therefore, they are clear an accessory to a certain asset and will only be seen as an autonomous good once separated.

Also, it must be noted that fruit, deducted the costs of its acquirement, might produce a net result that could be seen as one of the ways to accrue profit.

1.6 - Differences between Profit and Damages

Profits are related to earnings, and losses, to depletion. Clearly, the word profit has a distinctly positive connotation, unlike loss.

In several judicial decisions awarding damages, loss of profits have been included in the calculation of the amount owed. Even in this case, though, profit does not predate the damage suffered, much less qualifies it, but it is granted as a way to fully repair what was lost and, why not, to obtain an advantage.

However, profit cannot be seen as restitution; that would contradict its positive connotation. Furthermore, profit isn't compensation for loss, for, as it has been said, it represents a gain.

New perspectives on civil liability, such as patrimonialization of assets, punitive damages or class actions do not change the fact that damages awarded by a judicial decision are not comparable to accruing profit, even when compensating for loss of profits.

In fact, damages shall be awarded by the court if a causal connection is proven between an action or omission and the injury, through payment, reparation to the *status quo ante* or even by imposing an obligation to do or not to do. In none of these circumstances, reparation can be understood as a form of profit.

Historically, damages were redressed through repression, punishment and, maybe, prevention. In modern times, forms of redress are vastly different. Damages are awarded to compensate for injuries caused by wrongdoing or nonperformance.

Article 944 of the Brazilian Civil Code notes that damages are measured by the scope of the injury; the amount might be reduced or increased depending if the perpetrator was at fault or not (breach of obligation). In this regard, even when moral damages, which are non-patrimonial in nature, are awarded — through financial compensation, not reparation *per se*, as sometimes may happen with pecuniary injuries — the amount received is not considered profit. If it were, it would be a case of unjust enrichment. Reparation is not meant to generate profit, but to compensate for what was lost/not reasonably gained due to the perpetrator's wrongdoing.

Pontes de Miranda notes that:

> [. . .] In legal systems, a principle establishes that the reparation is not meant to leave the offended party in a better condition than what existed before the injury. The intention is solely to restore the previous existing conditions, at least monetarily. The offender must restore the state of affairs to how it would have been, had their wrongdoing never happened. In this case, reparation through profits to the claimant would qualify as unjust enrichment. After all, redressed the damage, the claimant should be neither richer, nor poorer, than he was before. (H.A. Fischer, *Der Schaden nach dem BGB*, 219) Whether damages were caused by wrongdoing or nonperformance, the rules are the same (Brazilian Civil Code, articles 188, I and II, 929 and 930, sole paragraph). However, to compensate obligations, the injury must have originated from the same incident. This is why jurists insist the adequate causality principle must be applied in practice.[28]

---

28 MIRANDA, P. *Tratado de Direito Privado. Parte Especial*. Tomo XXVI. São Paulo: Bookseller, 2003, p. 80.

Even though it might not be possible to fix what was broken, for instance, by handing over a new object or the pecuniary equivalent in place of old and very used goods, even so, profit is not the appropriate term in this context. What occurs is a mere compensation for damages and injuries suffered.

Naturally, a loss of profits must also be compensated; in this case, the goal is to redress profits that would have reasonably been earned, had it not been for the offender's wrongdoing or nonperformance, whether by their actions or omissions.

Therefore, in this case, even though there is a "loss of profits," it cannot be said the reparation equals a benefit or an advantage; after all, it is still compensation for damages suffered due to wrongdoing or nonperformance, not a gain.

Consequently, profits are not damages, not even those awarded for loss of profits, which, despite their name, are a form of compensation, not really profit.

1.7 - Profit Ownership

Profit is a means to an end, not the object of economic activity. After all, a legal entity might perform its duties during a whole fiscal year and not necessarily accrue profit in that time frame. Private legal entities or, more specifically, companies, are entitled to distribute profits.

As José Luiz de Almeida Nogueira Porto affirms:

> [...] A company's actions are conducive to production; these actions specifically promote or interpret the dynamic that leads to profit. It has been said that a capitalist corporation's only goal is to obtain profit but, we must reaffirm, profit is a means, not an end; it is merely a condition necessary for a company's survival and expansion, but not for its existence. Some companies subsist even without profits, as long as the factors of production are remunerated; even if one of those

factors (the capital) does not receive all remuneration it would want, due to current interest rates, it would still be within a minimum profit limit.[29]

However, who are the agents that might obtain and, consequently, distribute profit? It is not exactly the owner of the business, but the business itself that has an economic activity pursuing financial success. The business is the civilly competent agent.

In this regard, José Luiz de Almeida Nogueira Porto asserts that:

> [...] There are three prerequisites to gain profit: a capable agent, dynamic efficiency and a compatible legal system. The first condition demands that said capable agents fulfill a series of objective and subjective requirements, which limits the number of entrepreneurs. Not only must they have capacity in the legal sense, high energy and a fighting spirit, but also own capital in the necessary amount to reach their goal, whether they own or procure said capital from other sources. The second condition is dynamic efficiency. The instability that comes from dynamism also manifests itself in this economy, bringing along uncertainty about the future and unshaped factors, searching for a new equilibrium. [...] In a moment of economic static efficiency, there might even be an income from their product which could be added to profit, but is still to be considered as income. Lastly, the third condition is a legal system that permits and enables profit in its ordinances that establish what is legal regarding a company's activity or the economic environment itself.[30]

Any organized economic activity might gain profit. An *organized activity* presupposes the concurrent existence of four

---

29 PORTO, J. *Contribuição para a Teoria do Lucro. Op. Cit*, p. 128.
30 *Op. Cit.*, pp. 156/157.

basic elements for the production of goods and/or services: (i) capital; (ii) labor; (iii) input materials; and (iv) technology. A company is an organized activity that aims to produce goods and services for a market, designed to obtain profit in a market economy.

A business owner might be either a human being or a legal entity and should not be mistaken for the company itself. In this regard, article 966 of the Brazilian Civil Code (an innovation that had not been in the 1916 civil code) states that: "A business owner engages professionally in an economic activity organized to produce or distribute goods or services."

Furthermore, a business owner must have civil capacity and no legal impediments to engage in an economic activity; all laws regarding business owners, commercial and mercantile activities that have not been revoked by the civil code are applicable.

At last, the company should not be confused with its establishment, which is the place where economic activity is pursued and a collection of assets that have a measurable economic value, allowing the company to achieve its goals and, consequently, accrue profit or suffer losses. Gaining profit is essential to an organized business activity.

On this subject, Maria Helena Diniz states that:

> [. . .] A company is, therefore, an economic activity that joins capital, labor, inputs and technology to produce and distribute goods and provide services. A company needs, thus, a framework, an organized body, an institution composed by material and immaterial (such as the establishment) assets, capital, labor (employees), the management of all these factors by the business owner, be it an individual businessperson or a company, and the productive activity; basically, it needs all these components in motion. [. . .] Brazil's Civil Code also states, in its article 966, that organized economic activity must be pursued in a professional and habitual manner; isolated acts are not enough to constitute a company's activity.

Business activity must, therefore, be performed continuously, a succession of repeated, organized acts that shall constantly provide an offer of goods and services to a community.[31]

The author proceeds:

[...] A company has a certain complexity, that requires a) a business owner (either a person or a legal entity), a sole proprietor or a collective endeavor that has a duly registered legal personality and may, as such, exercise rights; and b) property, composed by a body of assets, employed to achieve the company's purpose, by a businessperson or a corporation (Brazilian Civil Code, article 1142) which is the establishment or goodwill.[32]

Indeed, continuous and habitual acts performed to obtain profit or even economic results and organizing labor are indispensable to the organized activity above explained. Profit is obtained, thus, by the company, a private legal entity that performs an organized economic activity, in pursuit of a previously determined business purpose.

The government cannot accrue profit, since it is not a company and its activity, although organized, is not geared towards this kind of gain. However, when the government interferes in the economic sphere through a commercial activity, it might be equated to a private enterprise and obtain profit.

In this regard, Sérgio Pinto Martins explains that:

[...] it is important to remember, however, that public companies and government-controlled companies that pursue economic activities are subjected to the same laws as privately held companies, including labor laws (article 173, item II,

---

31 DINIZ, M. *Curso de Direito Civil Brasileiro -. Direito de Empresa*. São Paulo: Editora Saraiva, 2009, p. 17.
32 *Op. Cit.*, p. 34.

paragraph 1 of the constitution of Brazil) This means that these companies must also distribute profits among its employees in case of positive fiscal year results. Some companies, such as small businesses, might be excused from sharing profits, since they qualify for legal incentives and benefits, such as simpler tax, social security and labor laws, according to article 179 of the constitution.[33]

Therefore, an enterprise is composed by a body of interests — such as profit, creation and recognition of new jobs, forming skilled labor and paying taxes — which fulfill a relevant socioeconomic role.

1.8 - The Antithesis between Profit and Losses.

An enterprise, i.e., the company's organized activity, does not have juridical personality; its purpose is to produce and/or distribute goods and services, in pursuit of wealth generation and profit, which is the barometer of vitality and efficiency. On the other hand, losses are negative profit, a manifestation of the enterprise's economic inefficiency in a market economy.

From the concepts explained in this chapter, one can conclude that the company's activity can generate profit, losses or neither.

A businessperson must seek dynamic solutions to improve the factors of production, in order to: boost production and reduce costs; figure a price per unit, considering the costs of production of goods and services; acquire raw material at a better price than the competition; and provide good consumer service to conquer new markets, among other possibilities.

All this activity and improvement might not generate profit, in the short or long term; after all, profit is not a mere

---

33 MARTINS, S. *Participação dos Empregados nos Lucros das Empresas. Op. Cit.*, pp. 99/100.

leftover from production of goods or services, but a positive development resulting from a combination of the above-mentioned factors. When this combination of factors does not generate positive results, losses are possible; just like profit, however, they may be temporary or not and are not just a residue of the production process.

As José Luiz de Almeida Nogueira Porto states:

[. . .] A businessperson's work with the combination of factors of production is, therefore, what creates temporary profit, in which there is an aspect of monopoly since, at this initial point, there are no competitors. This profit is certainly not a mere residue; it is the embodiment of the businessperson's contribution to production, just as salaries are the embodiment of the value produced by a worker.[34]

Profit might not be related to a positive or negative result, but to a neutral result — which does not happen in a sole instance, but in a series of satisfactory results — if, to reach this neutrality, that is to say, on the path to obtain profit, the activity did not harm the principle of human dignity.

It must be stressed that profits and results are different concepts. In accounting, profit is the result of the company's revenue, minus expenses and can be either positive or negative. Results are directly connected to reaching these goals, which must be pursued by all members of the company, from employees to employers.

On the other hand, the company has a social responsibility and also performs an important economic and social role, not only to its collaborators, but also to society as a whole. However, despite the importance of the social responsibility mentioned above, a company's value is calculated from its price index/expected profit.

A company's value appraisal is directly associated to in-

---

34 PORTO, J. *Op. Cit.*, p. 143.

terdisciplinarity, from all activities that determine its growth rate and profit, considering the factors employed in the production of goods or providing a service.

Traditionally, profit or loss are defined as the difference between the cost and price of the product or service in the market, represented by an economic currency.

1.9 - Nonprofit Associations

Several different types of legal entities might be qualified as "nonprofit associations" such as, for instance, associations, foundations, unions, cooperative societies, philanthropic and beneficent social welfare societies and some institutions devoted to philanthropy, recreation, culture and science. All have a common attribute, no matter the type: they do not pursue profit.

Companies, however, always intend to achieve an economic-financial result, even if not all companies aim for profit. Therefore, pursuing profit is not mandatory; just an indicator of an efficient organized economic activity.

Article 2, paragraph 3 of Law 10.101/2000 prescribes that:

> [...] The following entities shall not be considered a company, for the purposes of this law: I-a natural person; II-nonprofit organizations that do not, cumulatively: a) distribute results or dividends for any reason, under any name, even indirectly, to managers, officers or an associate company; b) invest all resources into its institutional mission and the country; c) if shutting down operations, assign its assets to a similar institution or the government; and d) keep accounting records to prove compliance with the other rules mentioned in this item and applicable tax, business and economic laws.

Brazil's Federal Accounting Council's understands that

the positive results in nonprofit associations are not intended to the equity owners and its profit or losses are named, respectively, surplus or deficit.

From the above-mentioned, two aspects become clear: (i) no distribution of positive results; and (ii) different nomenclature for results, that are not calculated in the conventional way.

The main sources of funding come from donations, subsidies and contributions and unrelated to costs and expenses, as in for-profit companies. However, this might often create a disparity between costs and expenses; there might be a surplus at some points and a deficit at others.

Surplus, not profit, is the goal of this kind of association, as a way to assure continuity and to fulfill its institutional mission. Members or sponsors are not entitled to any economic share of its assets or capital. A nonprofit association does not distribute results and assets, even when shutting down. Some of its peculiarities must be mentioned: its main sources of revenue and support are received (or promised) subsidies and donations, volunteer work and donations, tax immunities and exemptions, etc. Volunteers, who perform important services to reach a surplus, often aid these organizations. Volunteers may be people or legal entities, and the purpose is always to reach a surplus.

All institutions, however, even those that aim for profit, can and should effect relevant social change. In Brazil, Law 9.608, of February 18, 1998, regulates voluntary service. This law defines voluntary service as: "Non-remunerated activity performed by a person for a public entity of any nature, or a private nonprofit entity that has a civic, cultural, educational, scientific, recreation or social assistance objective, including mutual help."

Unlike a company's procedure, in which maximizing profits is essential, for a nonprofit, its equity represents its ability to keep afloat in a market, offering services to a community with efficiency and quality, without compromising its stability. Nonprofit associations also differ from companies because, for the latter, revenue is related to production of goods and services in a broad sense, and corresponds to the remuneration received from permanent or temporary sales of the company's assets or rendering of services or reduction of liabilities.

At last, it must be mentioned that a balance sheet is an important financial statement required from any kind of organization, whether it pursues profit or not.

1.10 - Constitutionality and Legal Aspects of Profit Obtention

Profit is protected by the constitution in Brazil's democratic state; that is, the legal system adopts a capitalist economy and does not forbid profiting from an activity.

Regarding the protection of human dignity, the Federative Republic of Brazil's economic order precepts include, among others, free initiative, free enterprise and freedom to pursue organized economic activity, within the boundaries of the social function and social values of labor.

Articles 5, XIII, 170, principal provision and items I to XI of the Brazilian constitution state that the economic order, including organized activity, is founded on the appreciation of the value of human labor and a life with dignity, in pursuit of the common good, well-being and social justice:

> Article 5. All persons are equal before the law, without any distinction whatsoever, Brazilians and foreigners residing in the country being ensured of inviolability of the right to life, to liberty, to equality, to security and to property, on the following terms:
> [...]
> XIII - the practice of any work, trade or profession is free, observing the professional qualifications, which the law shall establish;

[...]

Article 170. The economic order, founded on the appreciation of the value of human work and on free enterprise, is intended to ensure everyone a life with dignity, in accordance with the dictates of social justice, with due regard for the following principles

I - national sovereignty;

II - private property;

III - the social function of property;

IV - free competition;

V - consumer protection;

VI - environment protection, including by means of different treatments in accordance to the environmental impact of products and services and their respective production and rendering;

VII - reduction of regional and social differences;

VIII - pursuit of full employment;

XI - preferential treatment for small enterprises organized under Brazilian laws and having their head-office and management in Brazil.

In terms of civil and business nonconstitutional laws, the Brazilian Civil Code has not expressly adopted social function. However, even without explicitly mentioning it, the civil code has clearly acknowledged this principle, albeit in a different context, since it does mention two other institutes connected to business: property (article 1228, paragraph 1) and contracts (article 422).

In this regard, Statement 53, drafted by jurists during the 1st Convention of Civil Law promoted by the Federal Judicial Council, asseverates that:

Article 966 — although not explicitly mentioned, the social function principle must be considered, when interpreting corporate laws.

Brazil's Corporation Law (Law 6404/76) prescribes that the company's social function must be observed by the controlling stockholder, the manager and by the fiscal committee. To be clear, this social function principle is not to be confused with the company's social responsibility. That is because social responsibility comes from the company owner's awareness of social issues and their role in their solution. It is one of the company's ethical values and will be analyzed in its own chapter.

Furthermore, social responsibility is optional, while obeying the social function principle as it pertains to contracts and corporations is mandatory. Social responsibility is not necessarily connected to the company's purpose; social function is.

Observing the corporate social function principal does not mean the company or its owners should perform philanthropic actions; it means compliance with the constitutional principles prescribed by article 170 of Brazil's constitution. Also, the social function principle, when relating to corporate contract and property, must be always be entwined with good faith, including (and especially) in obtaining profit. Undoubtedly, both the social function and social responsibility corollaries aim to further the constitution's directives and fundamental objectives and make them become a reality.

The social function of corporate asset property is a legal way to obtain profit, while acknowledging the value of human labor and a dignified life. Therefore, profit shouldn't be seen negatively, even though consumers have now more rigorous demands, the population, or capital itself, has increased; not even though methods of production evolved and there is a significant difference in consumer demands.

Especially since profit has a positive connotation, a study of its legal aspects must be compatible with constitutional and nonconstitutional legislation.

Moreover, it is impossible to analyze the legal aspects of profit in the civil code if not in harmony with the above-mentioned constitutional corollaries. Likewise, understanding its legal nature requires confronting all the different definitions and perspectives on the locution profit. Parenthetically, to study the legal aspects of profit, it is important to clarify that up until a while back, before the current civil code, "thing" and "assets" were used interchangeably,[35] including in the wording of the law.

Assets may be tangible or intangible, as long as they may be owned and have a measurable economic value, composing part of its owner's property.

The civil code states, in articles 93 and 94:

> Article 93: appurtenances are assets that, although not an integral part of the principal, are intended, in a lasting way, for the use, service or betterment of another asset.
>
> Article 94: legal transactions related to the principal thing do not include appurtenances, unless the law, the will of the parties or specific circumstances determines differently.

Although appurtenances are accessory, they are still distinct and autonomous; they are economically subordinated to the main asset, since they facilitate its use or provide a service, but still remain discrete.

As Maria Helena Diniz states:

> Although not explicitly mentioned by law, the accessory logically adheres the principal thing, due to the legal gravity principle, unless otherwise specified (articles 92 and 94 of the civil code; Court of Appeals Journal, vol. 177, page 151.) Therefore, the accessory's characteristics will follow. If the principal thing is movable, so will the accessory be. If the main obligation is void, so is the liquidated-damages clause, because the latter is an accessory. The principle that the accessory must adhere to the principal is applicable to fruits, products, improvements and integral parts; an explicit law is unnecessary,

---

35 Silvio Rodrigues, for instance, asserted that "thing" is the genus and "assets" are the species, since "assets" have an economic value and denote usefulness and rarity.

*excluding appurtenances that, according to article 94 of the civil
code will only adhere to the principal thing if demanded by law
or the will of the parties.*[36]

Vicente Ráo explains:

[. . .] The Latin expression, according to which *accesorium
sequitur principal, accessorium cedit principali* is only applicable to accessories that are part of the principal thing. Appurtenances are things destined and lent to be used, to provide services or organize another thing, in a lasting way. This
principal thing would still be considered, by most, to be complete even if the accessory appurtenances were removed: for
instance, in the case of assets that have been declared immov-
able and accessories to movable assets, such as a jewelry case,
a scabbard, etc. Thus, the Latin expression quoted above is
not fully applicable to this category of accessories; there are
limitation prescribed by law, due to their purpose.[37]

It is undeniable, then, that profit is, legally, an appurte-
nance, which, after all, is an accessory, destined to preserve or
facilitate the use of the principal, while keeping its own individuality and distinction, so it may have an economic measurable
value.

Profit is intrinsically connected to the business activity
whence it came and, once accrued (positive results), might be
used for the following purposes: (i) reinvestment; (ii) distribution among shareholders or stockholders; or (iii) to pursue
the corporate social responsibility corollary or even help with
human rights initiatives by private initiative, which will be explored in the following chapters.

Profit is not, legally, equal to an improvement: even

---

36 DINIZ, M. *Curso de Direito Civil Brasileiro 1. Teoria Geral do Direito Civil.* São Paulo: Saraiva, 2013, pp. 388/389.
37 RÁO, V. *O Direito e a Vida dos Direitos. Op. Cit.*, p. 195.

though both are accessories, an improvement always must adhere to the principal thing, which does not happen to profit.

At any rate, even though the legal aspects of profit have been established and found in the civil code, the liberal ideas of civil law as, exclusively, meant to regulate property law are obsolete; the principle of human dignity must be appreciated and the focus must move from property to the person.

Professor Roberto Senise Lisboa, in his brilliant article "Dignidade e Solidariedade Civil-Constitucional" ["Civil-Constitutional Dignity and Solidarity"] asseverates that:

> [. . .] after overcoming the liberal course that practically turned civil law into a law for owners, human dignity starts being considered a fundamental principle that can be reached through social solidarity. Considering the focus of civil law was shifted to the person and not property, the modernist course was dismissed in favor of a constitutional orientation. Consequently, there must be an inversion of priorities when analyzing the legal institutes included in the constitution of 1988 and even the new civil code, even though originally more preoccupied about establishing rules for property than for people. It is no longer possible to conceive abstractly that property is a human being's legal personality or even, as Bevilácqua proposes, the economic projection of human personality. Human legal personality uses property to subsist, not to be incorporate or be incorporated.

> [. . .] From the moment in which human dignity, and not property, is the focus, the legal system's shifts into its favored stance, protecting and safeguarding human personality rights. The minimum possessions theory, defended with preeminence by Fachin, seeks to provide sustenance to all people and, as strictly personal rights, nourishment, education, housing and clothing, not as political objectives to be attained by politicians within their own discretion and opportunity.

The quantity of assets required to implement the above-mentioned theory is irrelevant.[38]

Ultimately, after analyzing the concept and legal aspects of profit, it must be concluded that profit cannot be seen as a factor of instability in a dynamic economy. On the contrary, profit must be seen as one of the tools to balance social and labor relations in general, as long as it is accrued and allocated in a legal, ethical and fraternal manner.

---

38 LISBOA, R. *Dignidade e Solidariedade Civil-Constitucional.* Revista de Direito Privado, 2010, # 42, p. 34.

CHAPTER II - MAIN ASPECTS OF HUMAN RIGHTS

Effectiveness, efficacy and applicability of human rights in the present day can be observed both in theory and in practice; its corollaries are inserted in almost all countries' constitutions.

There is good reason why the expression "human rights" is used by scientists, jurists, sociologists and philosophers whose area of study is the human being and the rule of law. Indeed, the way the expression human rights is understood is closely connected to rights that shall be considered inalienable, universal and indivisible, and must be treated as a priority in a context of collective rights.

Although the expressions "human rights" and "fundamental rights" are sometimes used interchangeably, they are not the same; neither are "human rights" and "rights of man," the latter being synonymous to natural law.

As Ingo Wolfgang Sarlet states, with propriety, in this regard:

[. . .] This writer believes in the idea that, as long as human rights are not considered to be fundamental rights, which will be defined further on, they shall not be fully efficacious and effective, although they might, in several instances. For now, the meaning of the expression "human rights" (or fundamental human rights) and "fundamental rights" must be addressed and clarified; they are not mutually exclusive or incompatible; their scope is progressively becoming more inter-connected but still separate, each within a different sphere of the legal system; therefore, these distinctions have practical consequences that cannot be ignored. Still on this subject, to reiterate, it is problematic to sustain that human rights and fundamental rights are equivalent (at least in their foundation in a constitutional or international legal framework, since the differences that have been pointed out are evident); unless, of course, if in a certain language, human and fundamental rights are semantically synonymous; if and when this is the case, international allowances can be made.[39]

In this regard, JJ Gomes Canotilho asseverates that:

[. . .] the rights of man are applicable to all human beings, at all historical periods (jusnaturalist-universal dimension); fundamental rights are the rights of man instituted and guar-anteed by the legal system and limited by space and time. Hu-man rights are intrinsic to human nature, which is why they are inviolable, atemporal and universal: fundamental rights, on the other hand, are rights actually into force within a con-crete legal system.[40]

Regardless of criticism on the use of expressions such as "rights of man," "fundamental rights" or even "human rights" to designate only international rights, the concept of human rights will always be, to this writer's understanding, broader and, therefore, more comprehensive than the expressions fun-damental rights or rights of man.

Nonetheless, defining human rights is not an easy task.

---

39 SARLET, I. *A Eficácia dos Direitos Fundamentais — Uma Teoria Geral dos Direitos Fundamentais na Perspectiva Constitucional.* Porto Alegre: Livraria do Advogado, 2009, pp. 29/30.
40 CANOTILHO, J. *Direito Constitucional e Teoria da Constituição.* Coim-bra: Almedina, 1998, p. 369.

On this subject, Joaquim José Barros Dias states that:

> [. . .] any and all precise definitions of human rights will be only vain attempts or sheer pretension. Philosophically and ethically, however, a few important reflections must be made to an overall understanding of the topic. Despite all that has been discussed and written about human rights, it still has not been enough to offer definitive answers to what the rights of man truly are, and even how far they will advance, just as the actions taken to solidify these rights within people's relationships still seem wanting. The existence and preexistence in history of innumerable conflicts in countries' internal affairs and in a supranational level convey clearly that, in effect, human beings themselves have been disregarding universal human values.[41]

Human rights are basic rights and freedoms inherent to all human beings and their concept is connected to the idea of freedom, equality and fraternity. They are, therefore, faculties, freedoms and demands inherent to each person, predicated solely upon their human condition.

So, in this regard, human rights are inalienable, irrevocable, nontransferable and non-renounceable because, originally, the definition of human rights came from natural law philosophy, according to which they were attributed by God.

In fact, human rights cannot be *neutral*, since they take the side of human beings to protect them and advocate for their dignity in all realms.

The first historical phase of human rights arrives with the modern era; it is, quintessentially, a Western culture creation. Chronologically, in 1648, the Peace of Westphalia protected, for the first time, the right to freedom of religion; in 1789, the Declaration of the Rights of Man was a milestone of the French

---

41 DIAS, J. *Direito Civil Constitucional*. São Paulo: Malheiros, 2002, pp. 33/34.

Revolution; and the Virginia Declaration of Rights in 1776 delineated the United States' independence. The second historical phase came in the 19th century, by universalizing human rights, going beyond domestic affairs and dealing with international issues, such as abolition of slavery, which imposed limits to how international states should treat fellow human beings. However, human rights issues only elicited a deeper interest after the events of World War II.

Historically, the expression "human rights" is associated to the Declaration of Independence of the United States from 1776 and the French Declaration of the Rights of Man and of the Citizen from 1789.

However, the philosophical bedrock of early Western civilization was already jusnaturalist thought and understanding of human nature and the inherent human condition; always within a religious viewpoint.

The organization of ancient civilizations was based on religion. Both Greek and Roman civilizations saw the establishment of legal rules as part of their religion; men could even be a part of the creation process, but they did not originate from will alone; rules needed to be accepted and worshiped. In this regard, whether due to religion or philosophy, Greco-Romans already valued human dignity, freedom, equality among men; these beliefs were the root of the declarations of rights that came later.

Undoubtedly, the birth of democracy and the need for minority representation heralded political rights to all free men and a rethinking of social inequality; this resulted from philosophical and religious systems of Greco-Roman society.

On this subject, Alfredo Culleton says:

[…] attributed to stoicism the return of human dignity to the focal point and, at the same time, identified in Christianity one of the factors that consolidated the importance of human rights. Within these circumstances, though, an undeniable characteristic of human rights and its logical placement in the modern age was highlighted: by granting prominence to human beings, a process of social alienation began, elevating individualism to a human behavior pattern within an epistemic nominalist paradigm. From this time forward, a new civilization emerged, consisting of a blend of classic institutions, Christian values and German mores. It was the Middle Ages. According to Comparato (2003, p.44), all through the High Middle Ages, European civilization was dominated by feudalism; it was a time when economic and political power disintegrated. The idea of limiting the power of the governing classes only gained expression from the 11th century forward, with the first declarations against misconducts in power struggles between clergy and nobility: in the Iberian Peninsula, with the Cortes of León of 1188 and in England, with the Magna Carta of 1215. Even though tailored in favor of the higher strata of society, the value of freedom was the first expression of human rights.[42]

Greek philosophy, especially after Socrates, attributed rules of behavior to the human conscience and did not accept the sacrifice of humanity by the government; the concept of dignity now applied to all men, not just those who had citizen status, as it was before.

With the advent of Christianity, government was finally separated from religion, but maintained values such as benevolence and justice among all those who descend from a common father.

In the 13th century, however, due to a vast social chasm, political retrogression opened the door to authoritarian regimes. Only in the 17th century, after most absolutist regimes fell, that part of the current outline of human rights began to be drawn. In England, for instance, the Petition of Right was drafted in 1628 and, in 1679, *Habeas Corpus* originated — a measure

---

42 CULLETON, A. *Curso de Direitos Humanos*. São Leopoldo: Editora Unisinos, 2009, p 31.

to protect personal liberty. In this same stead, the Bill of Rights was drafted in 1689.

Clearly, all these historical factors influenced the Declaration of Independence of the United States of America and the Declaration of Rights of Man and Citizen of 1789. It is undeniable that the movements that would permanently change the scope of human rights originated in Europe, decisively influencing the current outline of human rights.

Similarly, the jusnaturalist influence in the history of human rights is undeniable. The thirteen colonies' independence in North America and the historical period that preceded the American Declaration of Rights were decisive to build the structure of human rights as we know them now. These historical events led to the beginning of the defeat of old regimes, often authoritarian, and rebirth of democratic governments that were concerned about human dignity and fundamental rights.

As Alfredo Culleton states:

[. . .] According to the French, the people were the source of all power and the origin of every law. The North-American viewpoint was different, as they believed power came from the people, but the source of law was the constitution. To the French, the greatest problem was finding a ruler who would substitute the absolutist monarch, for, although people acquiring rights implies limits to power, paradoxically it also demands the existence of a center to said power. This was how, in place of the sovereign ruler, the Third Estate — a heterogeneous group seen with a negative slant, composed by the common people — was granted political sovereignty. From Sieyès pamphlet, in which the equation was solved in abstract, the common people gained a place in the assembly; the assembly, in its impersonal role, then, began to exert political power. The nation existed symbolically but only acted by its representatives, in accordance to article 3 of the Declaration of 1789. "The principle of any sovereignty lies primarily in the nation." Its representative nature was, finally, defined in the

1791 constitution; the people, as the true purpose of nation, reigned symbolically but did not govern.[43]

Social rights were understood as an aspect of citizenship, attributed to members of a specific community. This is why by the end of the 19th century there was a growing interest, within communities, in applying equality in practice, not just theory.

In this context, Mexico's constitution of 1917 elevated labor rights to fundamental rights, along with political rights and individual freedoms. In family law, at the same time, women and men's legal equality was acknowledged, just as children born out of marriage gained the same rights as legitimate children, for example.

From the brief history above, it can be seen that sovereign states began to recognize human rights after the 18th century; however, human rights only became universal in the 20th century, specifically after the UNO's Universal Declaration of Human Rights in 1948 — a document that contains generic rules and pertains to a wealth that belongs to all nations: the human being.

The United Nation's Universal Declaration of Human Rights is composed of 30 articles, divided among general and individual rules. General rules are philosophical and handle inalienable rights, such as human dignity, universal fraternity, freedom and equality among all persons. Individual rules are divided in three classic groups: individual or civil rights, political rights and socioeconomic rights.

The consolidation of human rights is closely connected to its historical and social context and the philosophical leanings of their time. This is not meant to be a full history of human rights; this brief account only intends to demonstrate how human rights evolved and how they were structured after the United Nation's Universal Declaration of Human Rights, which is essential to justify the need of appropriate profit allocation.

---

43 *Op. Cit.*, p. 35.

2.1 - Preliminary Notes on Human Rights

Every person should be granted, from birth, minimal conditions necessary to become a useful member of humanity and reap the benefits that life in society might bring. Therefore, even in different cultures, the stated objective may become viable through similar values.

Affirming equality among people does not mean physically, intellectually or psychologically equal. Each person is an individual, with their own personality, viewpoint and feelings. Likewise, social groups have their own culture, as a result of natural and social conditions.

In fact, all are born equal, with the same rights, but at the same time, all are born free. This freedom is manifested in our intelligence and conscience. It is impossible to force a person to take advantage of all their rights, but freedom, a fundamental human right, must be respected. Exercising rights is a privilege, not a duty. Undeniably, one of the ways to assert equality is to empower all to freely exercise every of their rights and duties.

Dignity is inherent to the human condition, and preserving said dignity is part of human rights. On this subject, the Universal Declaration of Human Rights states on article 1 that "All human beings are born free and equal in dignity and rights." If human rights are respected and solidarity to all is honored within personal relationships, injustices will be minimized and, why not, eliminated; humanity may then live in peace. All must act fraternally towards each other.

In fact, apart from universal declarations, the constitution, fundamental rights and private law are interconnected by a dialectic and dynamic logic of mutual influences, and can be differentiated, in qualitative and quantitative terms, according to the place occupied by constitutional law and its effects on other laws, and the role of private law.

The content of the constitution is constantly being redefined and reconstructed, influencing the drafting and altering of the letter of the law, both in constitutional and nonconstitutional levels.

Therefore, even though there have been changes in the constitution and the law's functions, overall, the constitutionalization of the legal system is a still ongoing process.

2.2 - Human Rights Hierarchy

As we have said, the movement to universalize human rights gained impetus in the 20th century, specifically after the United Nation's Universal Declaration of Human Rights of 1948.

In Brazil, currently, article 5 of the Federative Constitution prescribes that:

> All persons are equal before the law, without any distinction whatsoever, Brazilians and foreigners residing in the country being ensured of inviolability of the right to life, to liberty, to equality, to security and to property, on the following terms:
>
> Paragraph Two — The rights and guarantees proclaimed in this constitution do not exclude others that might originate from its political system and principles or from international treaties of which the Federative Republic of Brazil may be a party.

However, there is dissent regarding the incorporation of human rights international treaties by the constitution. There are two distinct phases, though: before and after Constitutional Amendment 45, which included paragraphs 3 and 4 to article 5 above:

> Paragraph Three: International human rights treaties and conventions that have been approved by both Houses of the National Congress, in two rounds, by three-fifths of the votes will have the same force as a constitutional amendment.
>
> Paragraph Four: Brazil is a state party to the statute of the

International Criminal Court, and accepts its jurisdiction.

There are three positions regarding international treaty rules and constitutional hierarchy. With reference to the incorporation of human right treaties in the Brazilian legal system, Carlos Henrique Bezerra Leite asseverates that:

[...] The Brazilian constitution of 1988, unlike other constitutions, did not establish the procedure to incorporate human rights international treaties into the Brazilian legal system. In consequence, the legal community and some sections of Brazilian society started to pressure Congress to change their position about human rights. Thus, in time, some courts began to mention human right treaties and their principles, valuing them above national laws and, in some cases, the constitution itself. It was not enough, however; the legislative branch had yet to act and give legal support to the issue through law, thus granting legitimacy to court decisions based on international treaties. Therefore, on December 8th, 2004, Constitutional Amendment 45 was approved and, among other issues, added paragraph 3 to article 5 of the constitution, prescribing that: "International human rights treaties and conventions that have been approved by both Houses of the National Congress, in two rounds, by three-fifths of the votes will have the same force as a constitutional amendment." From then on, all regulations protecting human rights that had been incorporated into the Brazilian legal system by approval, in two turns, by at least 3/5 of the votes in each House would be at the same level of a constitutional amendment. It was progress, since this ruling granted status of a constitutional amendment to international laws incorporated into the Brazilian system by the specified procedure.[44]

---

44 LEITE, C. *Direitos Humanos*. Rio de Janeiro: Lumen Juris Editora, 2010, pp. 114/115

And the author proceeds:

[. . .] The Brazilian Supreme Court conferred the status of a regular nonconstitutional law to human rights treaties, setting their importance below constitutional rules. However, in a recent decision about detainment for debt, this highest court determined that the Pact of San José of Costa Rica, ratified in 1992, had constitutional force and, as such, would expand the roster of fundamental rights contained in the Brazilian constitution. Although some of the Supreme Court's decisions have been fostering human rights treaties, that is not to say that all decisions will follow this same understanding; there are still cases in which it was decided that international treaties incorporated into the legal system before Constitutional Amendment 45 should not have prevail over the constitution.[45]

As Vicente Ráo states:

[. . .] The principles of natural law inspire, or should inspire, legal systems, perfecting and conducting the law to recognize fundamental rights that are intrinsic to man's nature; but these principles are not vast enough to include or reach all the content within a legal system's rules, several of which are indifferent or very loosely related to the basic precepts of natural law.[46]

Either way, the sovereignty of human rights, as established by the Federative Constitution is undeniable, and accepting of rules contained in international treaties.

In fact, due to article 5, paragraph 2 of the constitution, human rights international treaties have the same status as a constitutional rule; besides, there is still the supralegal hierarchy of human rights treaties, according to decision 466.343 of

45 *Op. Cit.*, p. 117.
46 RÁO, V. *Op. Cit.*, p. 302.

the Supreme Court. A quote from Justice Gilmar Mendes clarifies the jurisprudence on the issue:

> Considering the supralegal aspect of these international rules, subsequent nonconstitutional legislation that conflicts with those rules will have its efficacy paralyzed. For instance, it is what happened to article 652 of the new civil code (Law 10.406/2002), which repeats, identically, art. 1287 of the 1916 civil code.
>
> Therefore, since Brazil ratified, in 1992, the International Covenant on Civil and Political Rights (article 11) and the American Convention on Human Rights, also known as the Pact of San José of Costa Rica (article 7, 7), there is no legal basis to article 5, item LXVII of the constitution that allows detention for debt.
>
> Either way, the constitutional legislator can still submit the International Covenant on Civil and Political Rights and the American Convention on Human Rights — Pact of San José of Costa Rica to the special approval procedure prescribed on article 5, paragraph 3 of the constitution, in accordance to Constitutional Amendment 45/2004, that will grant them the same status as a constitutional amendment.

The principle of utmost efficacy of constitutional rules also justifies the idea that international human right treaties ratified or accepted by Brazil should have constitutional status, since these, in a fundamental rights context, are essential.

2.3 - Human Rights Dimensions

Based in historical moments, classically, human rights are divided in three dimensions. A fourth and fifth dimension, respectively biolaw and virtual rights, have also been discussed.

The commonly-used term "generation" implies superimposition or substitution; that one generation would have come and substitute the other, which is not the case with human rights, that remain universal, indivisible and interdependent. Human rights are, therefore, cumulative and represent a whole.

In this regard, Carlos Weiss states that:

> [. . .] insisting in the idea of generations not only solidifies the imprecision of the expression, considering the current concept of human rights, but it also might help justify public policies that might not identify the invisibility of human dignity and, therefore, of fundamental rights, usually over the implementation of economic, social and cultural rights or the respect to civil and political rights protected by the above-mentioned international treaties.[47]

Using, therefore, the term "dimension" instead, the historical evolution of human rights is as follows:

— First dimension human rights: individual rights and freedoms (liberty, life, safety) and civil and political rights, rights in face of the collectivity (for instance, nationality, asylum, property);

— Second dimension human rights: social, economic and cultural rights (for example, health, education, safety, work, leisure, public transportation);

— Third dimension human rights: diffuse rights and solidarity rights (such as progress, peace, a balanced ecosystem, cultural and historical heritage, biodiversity).

Along with the three classic dimensions, there is a more recent fourth dimension, that includes technological innovations (for example, genetic engineering and biotechnology) and fifth, that includes the right to access and share information with new technologies (such as the internet). However, this writer believes that the fourth and fifth dimensions are already

---

47 WEIS, C. Direitos Humanos Contemporâneos. Malheiros, 2011, p. 54.

included in the third dimension, since technology and information through new media are nothing more than diffuse or solidarity rights.

The general belief is that human rights have no borders, are perpetual and universal. There are different ways to interpret said rights, however, since each culture has their own view, anchored on their unique cultural, historical and religious background.

The protection of human rights, by its own international nature, involves interventionism, and therefore affects national sovereignty; men now have internationally recognized rights and are, therefore, an international law entity.

Before the Universal Declaration of Human Rights was signed, its draft was sent to several intellectuals and writers from UNESCO's member-states, forming the UNESCO Committee on the Philosophical Principles of the Rights of Man. These collected works reflect both understandings on human rights, some accepting and some arguing against "natural law" as the bedrock of human rights. To the former, human beings possessed certain fundamental and inalienable rights before and above society. To the latter, the historical evolution of society is the basis of said rights, which are variable and subject to changes imposed by the current mores.

Despite this philosophical debate, there was a surprising consensus as to the listing of rights contained in the Declaration. Therefore, the content was agreed upon, but there was considerable dissent as to the origins and/or meaning of said rights.

The Declaration is composed of three groups of individual rights and freedoms, following the classic distinctions, which are: (i) individual or civil rights — these aim to protect individual rights and freedom against a government's abuse of power, including the right to life, liberty, safety and equality before the law; (ii) political rights — these include general rights of the people to take part in the government, universal, free and periodic suffrage; (iii) economic and social rights — lifting to an international realm the right to work, free choice of employment, fair salary and protection against unemployment. The right to culture, arts and free scientific advancement, among others also included in the Declaration, are characterized as third dimension rights.

Considering the historical context in which they were created, especially from the Declaration of the Rights of Man and the Citizen, it can be said that first dimension human rights are based in an ideal of liberty, the second dimension, equality and the third dimension, fraternity Next, we will discuss the main characteristics of each of the three human rights dimensions.

2.3.1 - First Dimension Human Rights

The first dimension of human rights followed the bourgeois revolutions of the 17th and 18th century. They are also called individual, subject or liberty rights and are directed towards the human being, considered as an individual.

The object of these rights is freedom, safety and bodily, psychological and moral integrity rights and, also, the right to participate in the public arena.

In this regard, Carlos Weiss states that:

[. . .] first generation rights are those that originate from rational jusnaturalism, a philosophy that influenced the bourgeois revolutions in the 17th and 18th century; their content focuses on individual freedoms, conceived to benefit an abstract, out of context human being. On the other hand, the second generation comes in a different historical moment, when social movements flourished, announcing the need for state intervention as an agent of transformation of the reality of large groups within society — that comes from an emphasis on collective rights, regarding concrete and established human beings. So much so that no writer can mention the subject without clarifying the meaning of said generations and explaining their historical position in the evolution of human rights. Well, metaphors are used to help understanding a subject, by using single words or expressions as a shortcut to a thought. However, considering an explanation is necessary to make the origin of human rights clear, the expression is evidently useless, for it does reach its stated purpose.[48]

First dimension human rights can, therefore, be demanded immediately from the State; they are considered an entrenched clause. To exemplify, we can mention civil and political rights — rights to life, bodily integrity, liberty, equality before the law, respect of privacy, elect and be elected and have a nationality.

Therefore, it is clear that all first dimension rights are founded on freedom.

2.3.2 - Second Dimension Human Rights

Second dimension human rights impose an obligation to the State; a need to perform social actions in benefit of the individual. Social rights are composed by the government's duty to do, contribute and help.

By fulfilling the social function, including these rights in the legal system originated *social constitutionalism*. These second dimension rights are translated into social inclusion rights and demand public policies to guarantee the effective exercise of material conditions that permit a dignified life.

Economic rights are related to the production, distribution and consumption of wealth, and aim to regulate labor relations, as rights that assure fair and favorable work conditions.

Social rights provide a person a dignified way of life, protecting against hunger and poverty, as well as providing food,

---

48 Weis, C. *Op. Cit.*, pp. 51/52.

clothing, living conditions, health, rest, leisure and education. Rolf Kuntz states that:

> [. . .] The so-called second generation rights condensed a large portion of the social conflict of the past hundred years, since midway through last century. Several people died until social rights became a solid concept, even in third world countries. These rights were never implanted in a complete and unarguable way. However, they did become part of a value system painstakingly constructed. Shaped to regulate class relations under the State's watch, these values are under discussion. Social security reform, reduction of unemployment benefits, "flexibilization" of labor relations became, in a short time, watchwords, even to old school socialists. One might argue that these might protect against unemployment. Employers, however, could just as easily mention new worldwide competitive trends. From their perspective, employment rates are not a condition, but a consequence. How to deal with this issue in the emerging economic order? This is a relevant question when discussing issues related to rights. The ruin of communist states is irrelevant. What matters, indeed, as a challenge to workers, is the new triumph of capitalism, which enters a new phase.[49]

Cultural rights allow a person to enjoy their own community's artistic creativity, benefit from science and advances in technology, and to have their own language and culture.

Therefore, it is clear that all second dimension human rights are founded on equality.

---

49 KUNTZ, R. A redescoberta da igualdade como condição de justiça. In: FARIA, J. *Direitos Humanos, Direitos Sociais e Justiça*. São Paulo: Malheiros, 2010, p. 153.

2.3.3 - *Third Dimension Human Rights*

Third dimension human rights are also called fraternity or solidarity rights and come to existence through the awareness of the world's division into developed and underdeveloped or developing countries.

Minorities being granted real access to acknowledged fundamental rights characterize third dimension human rights; this is the reason why said dimension is defined by solidarity and fraternity, by being a collective right in broad terms, by the environmental function of property and by extensive social inclusiveness.

The international movement for inclusiveness was launched through several declarations. For example, we can mention: (i) the Universal Islamic Declaration of Human Rights,[50] (ii) the Universal Declaration of the Rights of the Peoples; (iii) the American Declaration of the Rights and Duties of Man, and (iv) the Solemn Declaration of Indigenous People, among others.

All these declarations share a common characteristic: they externalize the social exclusion of some minorities and contain rules for the social inclusion of human beings affected by different forms of bigotry.

Thus, we can say that third dimension human rights are characterized by their scope beyond individual interests, by being solidarity rights that are a result of a democratic state and

---

50 It must be said that Islamism does not accept, among other rights, the principle of equality among the faithful and infidels, as well as among men and women, which is, of course, incompatible with the fundamental rights doctrine. Likewise, there is no freedom of belief, since the Islamic faith cannot be abandoned. Women are not granted the freedom to marry men who profess other religions. Political rights are reserved to the Muslim and only the Muslim can be judges. At last, it accepts polygamy. Therefore, there is a distance between the Islamic conception and the ideas contained in the Universal Declaration of 1948 (full document at http://www.un.org/en/documents/udhr/).

leading to the social inclusion of minorities.

The social exclusion issue goes back to ancient history: at that time, foreigners were treated as different citizens and some cultures were considered inferior and, therefore, deserved to be conquered by the Roman Empire, for instance.

Anyway, with globalization — a form of economic, financial and cultural integration among people — and the massification of cultural and consumer patterns came a new kind of imperialism, focused on a social vision of aesthetics and social exclusion.

Third dimension human rights are founded on fraternity (solidarity) and are becoming more relevant in the humanistic capitalist system espoused by the Brazilian constitution.

2.4 - Human Rights and Human Dignity

The Universal Declaration of Human Rights of 1948 reiterated respect for human dignity, protected by article 1, item III of the constitution.

Therefore, we also must provide some background on the concept of human dignity, a major principle, inherent to all men and the guidepost for applying all legal rules.

The word dignity comes from the Latin *dignitate* and is connected to integrity, honor, nobility, respect, decency and self-respect. This term is not solely germane to human beings; it can be applied to certain jobs, institutions and even some attributes of Christianity and aspects of philosophical and political theories.

As Wagner Balera teaches:

[...] Indeed, human dignity can be considered the normative path offered to the community. Said community cannot reject this path without suffering severe consequences. Accepting human dignity means accepting that this existential vector will grant the community all essential means and elements to achieve its ultimate goal. This choice demands that any and all interpretative efforts use this value as a guidepost. Therefore, as an example, freedom of speech, that, all agree, is a fundamental right, must acknowledge human dignity and is restricted by a person's honor and the good name they created for themselves. What was a fundamental right, apparently absolute, may, if improperly used, be cause for punishment.[51]

The word "person" is strictly meant for human beings. The definition comes from a Christian line of thought (that borrows from Greek, Roman and Jewish traditions). The Greek used the word to identify a species; Romans, to designate a legal and formal aspect and Jews, to designate an interlocution between man and God.

In fact, the definition of human dignity is related to the concept of person, in the sense of their status: the status of being human.

Alfredo Culleton asseverates that:

[. . .] modernity itself created a problem to the present day, from controversies over the concept of person, in which the following issue is posed: to be a considered a person, it is enough to be human, that is, to have "human nature," or to be a person one must be fully conscious, capable of speech, thought, etc. These are different concepts, which have implications to the origins or basis of human dignity. In the first case, dignity comes from the mere fact of belonging to the human race (just for being human) and, in the second, as a result of having morally relevant characteristics; using these abilities fully would be an indispensable condition to be human. The first concept is supported by vitalist doctrine; the second, by Neo-Kantian doctrine. Both focus on Boethius' above-mentioned classic definition, but distance themselves

---

51 *Revista do IASP*, # 25, p. 365.

from each other when they assign a different value, in their conception of person, to a current presence or ability to be conscious, have a language, thoughts, feelings, memories and so forth. In Neo-Kantian doctrine, the concepts of person and human being are not the same. Human beings are not valued for themselves, based on who they are; moral value is attributed to their actions (thinking, reasoning, feeling) and to the individual only if they are able to perform said actions.[52]

All these roots of the word person influenced the creation of the expression human dignity. The term human dignity is undoubtedly connected to the meaning attributed to the word person, originally used to recognize a value, representing a moral principle based on the purpose of human existence and related to the nature of the species and its manifestations of rationality, freedom and self-purpose, in which a human being is constantly developing and searching the fulfillment of self.

Historically, human dignity was closely connected to a person's social place in society. The concept of dignity as we know it today began to solidify after World War II; thus, a long time after the Napoleon Code of 1807 and the Brazilian Civil Code of 1916.

Nowadays, the idea of dignity is connected to the appropriate attitude towards human beings. It is necessary, therefore, to understand the limitations of the word person — an individual that exists in itself, not as a genus or species, but as a human, who has a specific nature, and is part of a rational and social existence.

Consequently, human dignity demands that a human being is seen as a person, an individual; not necessarily connected to naturalism or subjectivism, but equipped with sufficient understanding to create an argument.

---

52 CULLETON, A. *Op. Cit.*, p. 62.

2.4.1 - Brief History of Human Dignity

The author does not intend to fully cover the subject of the historical roots of the human dignity principle; just to contribute to the understanding of how historical events influenced the definition of human dignity, the basis of article 1 of the constitution of 1988 and, consequently, in acquiring private autonomy, conserving legal transactions and finding a more appropriate application to profits accrued by companies.

Human dignity, according to article 1 of the Brazilian Federative Constitution, defines the contemporary law's constitutional and democratic state.

However, history, from ancient Eastern times to contemporary days, has not always recognized the primacy of the human being. From slavery, common in Eastern, classical and European civilizations, to the Inquisition's persecution, social discrimination was notorious and peacefully accepted by philosophers of that time.

Actually, in the ancient world, dignity was related to honor; because the concept of dignity was closely connected to the person:

> Augustine retrieves the term person (*persona*), brought by Tertullian (155-220 A.D.) to the Western world to distinguish members of the Trinity. The term person brings a great advantage. It does not identify a species, but something singular and undue. [...] the name of [...] person is not used as the name of man, common to all men. It is used only to specify an actual man, such as Abraham, Isaac or Jacob. Or any person one at whom one can point. [...] According to Boethius (480-524), Thomas Aquinas defines person as follows: Person means [...] one who subsists within a rational nature.[53]

---

53 ALMEIDA FILHO, A. *Dignidade da Pessoa Humana — Fundamentos e Critérios Interpretativos.* São Paulo: Malheiros, 2010, pp. 42/43.

Aristotle (384-322 B. C.) and Saint Augustine (354-430) dedicated part of their studies to the distinction between things, animals and human beings. Saint Thomas Aquinas, several years later, associated the concept of dignity to the fact that human beings were created in the image and likeness of God, connecting the principle of human dignity to the biblical superiority of man, while also affirming man's capacity for self-determination, that comes from their own will.

Francisco de Vitória, amid the jusnaturalist movement in the 17th and 18th centuries, approached the issue of human dignity by criticizing the enslavement and exploitation of native people by Spaniards; he claimed natives were, in principle, free and equal and should be respected as subjects of rights.

Additionally, Pufendorf postulated that a Monarch should respect human dignity, since human beings are free to choose and act according to their own judgment, based on their social nature.

However, Immanuel Kant (1724-1804), through his criticism and analysis about the possibilities of knowledge offered one of the most decisive contributions to the definition of human dignity.

In this regard, Ingo Wolfgang Sarlet explains that:

[. . .] in a particularly significant way — Immanuel Kant's way, whose conception of dignity comes from human beings' ethical autonomy, considering it (the autonomy) the cornerstone of man's dignity, and also sustaining that a human being (the individual) cannot be treated — not even by themselves — as an object. It is with Kant, in a way, that the process of secularization of dignity is completed. Once and for all, dignity abandoned its sacral vestments, although one cannot dismiss the deep influence (although withdrawn from theological justification) of Christian thought, especially those thoughts developed by Boethius and Saint Thomas Aquinas (notably regarding the idea of a person as an individual substance, with a rational nature, and the relation between freedom and dignity) on Kantian theory. Constructing his concept from the rational nature of the human being, Kant explains that the autonomy of will, understood as the ability to act with self-determination and in obedience of certain laws, is an attribute exclusive to human beings and the basis of the dignity of human nature. Based on this premise, Kant sustains that "Man and, generally speaking, all rational beings, exist as an end in themselves and not just as a means for the arbitrary use of this or that will." On the contrary, in all their actions, both directed to themselves, and to other rational beings, they must always be considered simultaneously as an end [. . .]. Therefore, the value of any object we may acquire through our actions is always conditional. Beings whose existence depends not really on our will but on our nature, if irrational, will only have relative value, as means to an end; that is why they are called things. On the other hand, rational beings are called persons, because their nature sets them apart as beings with an end in themselves; something that cannot be used as a mere means to an end and, as a consequence, limits all judgment (and is an object of respect) Still according to Kant, in affirming the peculiar and irreplaceable quality of a human being "in the realm of ends, all have a price or a dignity. When something has a price, one can replace them with something equivalent; but when something is above any price and, therefore, has no equivalent, then they have dignity [. . .]. This assessment shows, thus, how dignity is the value of such a disposition; it is infinitely above any price. Dignity could never be calculated or compared to anything that has a price without injuring its sanctity."[54]

Likewise, Hegel contended that the concept of dignity is linked to ethics. To him, a human being is not born with dignity, but gains it by becoming a citizen; unlike Kant, Hegel detaches a

---

54 SARLET, I. *Dignidade da Pessoa Humana e Direitos Fundamentais na Constituição de 1988*. Porto Alegre: Livraria do Advogado, 2009, pp. 35/36.

person's condition and their dignity from rationality.

In this regard, Eduardo C. B. Bittar asseverates that:

> [. . .] ethics for human beings comes directly from the principle of human dignity. This principle, effectively, can be compared to a common shelter to all generations of human rights, from first to third. Justice cannot be understood in itself, without the human dignity principle, just as power cannot be exercised in spite of human dignity. Assuredly, all other principles and values that guide the creation of national and international laws bow before this common identity, this minimum that belongs to all peoples. The 1948 Declaration itself grants that superior position, in face of all other principles and values. This principle, as a motivating reference of human rights culture is not only fundamental; it has universal value. However, despite its universality, its structure is not the result of a reasonable deduction, but of a historical construct; as such, the use of its meaning must be broadened to various historical contexts, and to reality and language games [. . .] Dignity only exists, therefore, when human condition itself is understood, perceived and respected in its various dimensions, which imposes, necessarily, the expansion of an ethical conscience as a daily practice of respect towards human being. It is an ideal and, as any ideal, it has an anticipated goal to reach; it is not, however, an Utopian ideal, because it depends closely on human beings themselves and can be elevated to a value that should be pursued and desired, simply because (paraphrasing Nietzsche), it is "human, all too human."[55]

Dignity can be seen as a behavior regulator, because a bearer of dignity must be treated in a certain way. Dignity is the binding expression of an identity; it means seeing said identity as valuable and, therefore, as a behavior regulator. Monarchs

---

55 BITTAR, C. *Direito Civil Constitucional* São Paulo: Revista dos Tribunais, 2003.

and presidents are names given to people, identities closed related to values. Thus, all that they meet must observe strict behavior patterns. The identity of monarchs, presidents and other authorities so demands.

Granting value to identity is not a subjective and arbitrary process; after all, in a broad way, all value whoever has an identity (kings, authorities). Thus, dignity is a positive value and the goal of an identity. Change in the behavior pattern will happen by recognizing the value of someone else's identity. By recognizing an identity, one automatically recognizes dignity, that is, they are inseparable concepts.

For this reason, human dignity demands that all human beings be recognized as a person (identity). To say a certain behavior injures human dignity is saying a human being has not been considered a person (identity).

Predicative or scientific knowledge can be considered synonymous, as a pattern in contemporary society. Predicative knowledge means to "know that" something is the way it is; that is to say, a dogma, a being) cannot be understood by a different definition of human being as a natural creature (rational and social animal). For that reason, they might be the object of scientific — predicative — knowledge. According to scientific knowledge, human beings can be understood only through their recognition as a person; in other words, "I know that" a human being is a person.

Recognition is different from predicative knowledge; the latter happens in the phenomenon horizon, of what appears to me and is controllable by setting criteria. However, when considering a person, there are no criteria. One cannot establish criteria for this; after all, every human being is a person.

However, Western history has used a standard to define those who are more or less human: rationality. The naturalist conception defines human beings as rational and social animals. So, by decreasing some humans' rationality, they could be compared to animals that, being "less human," would have to submit to beings of reason, that is, to the fully human.

The definition of person does not allow this conception. Persons are not contained in a universe from which certain cases, within certain criteria, could be expunged, as would happen in a scientific setting. A person is existence; existence cannot be defined or expunged.

Accordingly, it is said that a person is a mystery, not a problem, because the latter might be solved by science, with all its criteria and hypotheses. A mystery, however, is not exhaustible; it is what forces reason to acknowledge its limits. Recognizing a human being as person, epistemologically, means considering them as a mystery that transcends representations and definitions.

Using any criteria to define a person, aside from belonging to the human race, will inexorably be meant to exclude some and elevate other, which will always end in exclusion, oppression and annihilation.

After the war, establishing human dignity in the constitution happened as a reaction to the conscious violation that was planned and implemented by totalitarian states because they believe the human being is a problem to be solved by a definition, by establishing criteria; those who do not fit in, then, should be eliminated.

A person's dignity can never be deemed unimportant, nor can it be marketed; a value (price) will always be set against a standard (gold, salt, money). The problem is that a standard, though, is by its nature defined by someone else. Human dignity demands that human beings are seen as a whole, which means their identity as a person is not relative and does not depend on external factors. Recognition of this identity does not depend on opinion or any sort of interference. For every human being, it is a privilege to recognize themselves and others as a person, at any moment, in any place and under any circumstances.

Recognizing another being as a person is a starting point to practical, moral, legal or political reasoning, even though human dignity's definition cannot be explained by theories focused on interpreting and applying laws; only by a theory of recognition.

The Declaration of Rights of Man and of the Citizen, of August 26th, 1789, is an important milestone in the history of the human dignity principle in modern times. Article 6 states that: "All citizens being equal in its eyes are equally admissible to all public dignities, offices, and employments, according to their ability, and with no other distinction than that of their virtues and talents."

The human dignity principle can be found, also, in Pope Leo XIII's encyclical *Rerum Novarum*, about workers conditions. The document mentions human dignity in a religious context, as a way to value social conditions of human labor, even in a liberal state. The encyclical *Rerum Novarum* stated that "The following duties bind the wealthy owner and the employer: not to look upon their work people as their bondsmen, but to respect in every man his dignity as a person ennobled by Christian character."

Another important historical moment for the development of the human dignity principle was the text approved in 1946, at the 29th Session of the International Labor Conference in Montreal, that stated what follows: "All human beings, irrespective of race, creed or sex, have the right to pursue both their material well-being and their spiritual development in conditions of freedom and dignity, of economic security and equal opportunity."

However, it is important to note that human dignity does not only happen when it is recognized by a legal system; it preexists any form of legislation. It is undeniable, though, that the law has an essential role in furthering and protecting human dignity.

In this regard, Ingo Sarlet asseverates that:

[. . .] one cannot forget that dignity — at least according to what seems to be the majority's opinion — does not depend on factual circumstances, since it is inherent to any and all human beings, considering that, in principle, everyone — even the worst of criminals — is equal in dignity, in the sense of being recognized as a person — even if they do not behave in an equally dignified way in their relationships with other or even themselves. Therefore, even if one might understand human dignity — as José Afonso da Silva reminds us — as a way of behavior (which can be dignified or not), still, exactly because it is — in this sense — an intrinsic attribute of all human beings (but not necessarily inherent to their nature, as if it were a physical characteristic!) and expresses their absolute value, which is every person's dignity, even those who commit the most undignified and infamous actions cannot be disregarded. This is what can be understood from article 1 of UNO's Universal Declaration (1948), according to which "All human beings are born free and equal in dignity and rights. They are endowed with reason and conscience and should act towards one another in a spirit of brotherhood." This belief, in a way, revitalized and gave universal appeal — after the terrible brutality into which humankind sank into in the first half of this century — to the main premises of Kantian doctrine.[56]

2.4.2 - Human Dignity and the Brazilian Federative Constitution of 1988

In Brazilian law, the principle of human dignity is the true basis to the implementation of Democratic State ideals, in accordance to article 1, III of the constitution.[57] Notably, the subject was elevated to a principle; it is not included in the

---

56 SARLET, I. *Dignidade da Pessoa Humana e Direitos Fundamentais na Constituição de 1988. Op. Cit.*, p. 49.

57 "The Federative Republic of Brazil, formed by the indissoluble union of the states and municipalities and of the Federal District, is a legal democratic state and is founded on: I - sovereignty; II - citizenship; III - the dignity of the human person; IV - the social values of labor and of the free enterprise; V - political pluralism. Sole paragraph - All power emanates from the people, who exercise it by means of elected representatives or directly, as provided by this constitution."

list of fundamental rights and guarantees.

Fundamental rights are based on human dignity; autonomous fundamental rights can be deduced. It is impossible to recognize the existence of a fundamental right to dignity, even though they are closely connected. Because dignity is an intrinsic human attribute, the legal system cannot assign it to anyone. However, the Supreme Court considers that, while it is impossible to remove the dignity of any human being, in some cases, a person's protection, which exists due to the principle of human dignity, can be violated.

As a fundamental principle, stated in article 1, item III of the Federative Constitution, its formal and material constitutionality declares human dignity a rule within the legal framework, fully effective and bearing a fundamental legal value; it is an essential source of the contemporary legal system, held up as a higher hierarchy constitutional principle.

The legal system is built on principles, rules and values; the efficacy of human dignity is fully recognized in a national, constitutional level, which raises it to a fundamental principle, gaining even wider efficacy and effectiveness.

Dignity is listed as a fundamental principle within constitutional rules to improve its existing factual and legal possibilities. The content of the dignity rule is based on its position as a principle, even when other principles might also apply.

The current principle, established in our constitution, is absolute, meaning it will always prevail over other principles. There is no argument in a conflict with other principles. Interpretation must always answer to the content of dignity, revealing a structural difference regarding fundamental rights rules.

Considering the binding nature of human dignity, from which springs its efficacy and applicability, its connection to fundamental rules and guarantees gains a special position; however, its nature is absolutely compatible with applicability and efficacy in the legal rule sphere, whether in an objective or subjective perspective.

This principle can be analyzed from several angles. Even

though legal transactions, typically, belong in the private law sphere, a constitutionally focused analysis is pertinent; specifically, within the subject of human dignity, regarding the efficacy of fundamental rights in civil law.

In fact, the scope of the constitution's applicability and consequent interpretation — relating to nonconstitutional matters — is always very relevant, considering that, unquestionably, constitutional rules are the linchpins of the system. This is how the freedom, safety, equality, social justice and dignity ideals become the main feature, when interpreting and applying principles that guide legal transactions.

Indeed, as was mentioned in our brief history, the text approved in 1946 at the 29th Session of the International Labor Conference in Montreal stated, "all human beings, irrespective of race, creed or sex, have the right to pursue both their material well-being and their spiritual development in conditions of freedom and dignity, of economic security and equal opportunity;"

Protecting legal transactions not only protects their reliability, but also aims to maintain economic security, material well-being, balance between the parties and, consequently, human dignity. Incidentally, violations to fundamental rights within private relationships are not unusual.

Human dignity is the bedrock of the existence of the republic itself, not to mention of the rule of law; it is the main principle of the legal framework, whether in the public or private sphere. Human society is based on this principle, which assists relations between people.

As Antonio Junqueira de Azevedo states:

[. . .] Life, generically speaking, represents the value of all that exists in nature. This value exists in itself and does not depend on man. From the first living being to current times, there has been a continuous vital flux; all living beings have their own spark of life, but each individual spark comes from a fire that, since the beginning, burns on Earth and, in this fire, each spark is part of a whole. Life in general is the basis of environmental law and animal rights. However, ontologically, human life represents its excellent part. This is why human life — universally and in each of its sparks — deserves more attention from jurists. From the point of view that interests us, that is, of each human, life is a condition of existence. The legal principle of dignity, as the bedrock of the Republic, must have, as a presupposition, human's life intangibility. Without life, there is no person; without a person, there is no dignity.[58]

The current Federative Constitution of Brazil prescribes in its first article that the basis of the democratic state lays in a dignified human existence. Indeed, the constitution's preamble asserts the existence of a democratic state of law, and also expresses the importance of principles such as well-being, development and justice, among others.

Undoubtedly, the need for health and education to assure a dignified existence is evident, but that is not all. Other fundamental guarantees, such as the free exercise of religious, political and cultural convictions, are equally important.

In fact, the inviolability of the rights to life, freedom, equality, safety and property — as prescribed by article 5 of the constitution — is related to each society's economic order. It must be stated that the right to life, political and religious freedom and even freedom of locomotion cannot be compared to the macro functions of the economic order and the allocation of accrued profits.

2.5 - Human Rights and their Constitutional Efficacy

The social value of labor is a basic postulate of human

---

58 AZEVEDO, A. *Estudos e Pareceres de Direito Privado.* São Paulo: Saraiva, 2004, p. 14.

dignity, and a corollary of citizenship itself. Social labor rights are intended for other types of workers, even if they do not benefit from a typical labor relation (employees), such as service providers, temporary worker and public servants, for instance.

The 1988 Brazilian constitution altered the ideology of previous constitutions that, by their traditionally individualistic nature, excluded social rights from the list of human rights; the new order inserted human rights among other fundamental rights and guarantees; this is where the expression "fundamental constitutional rights" comes from.

The current constitution is compatible with the International Covenant on Economic, Social and Cultural Rights, adopted by General Assembly, resolution 2200A (XXI) of 1966; it was ratified by Brazil in 1992.

This covenant considers social, cultural and economic rights as inherent to the actual fulfillment of human dignity and asserts that human beings gain freedom and are freed from poverty when conditions are given for the exercise of economic, social and cultural rights, as well as civil and political rights.

The Brazilian constitution is a social state constitution, in which problems regarding power relations and exercise of rights are examined and solved based on the principles and objectives stated in Title I.

Therefore, to be fully effective and affect other laws within the legal system, rules defining human rights must be drafted by the competent institution and follow all legal prescriptions to their creation, edition and publication, thusly obeying all requirements so they can come into force.

The difference between civil, political, economical, social and cultural rights is in their field of efficacy, since they all come into force according to the law. In this regard, international treaties have to not only demonstrate the rights a person has, but also the inherent state obligations. The government must always keep expanding the implementation of social, economic and cultural rights, up to their greatest extent, with no retrogression, so as to maintain the full efficacy of the above-mentioned rules. The government has the power to follow these rules without using force or appealing to international organizations.

There has been a change in perspective that creates specific demands, with new beneficiaries, such as legislation about children and teenagers, the elderly and people with special needs, among others. In this regard, there is a conflict between two lines of thought: one, asserting the government's power must be as limited as possible; the other, contending the scope of government's intervention should be broad, as a way to decrease inequality between people and social groups.

Either way, it can be said that civil and political rights are valid in practice because they are a part of the legal system; therefore, they are efficacious even when the government is omissive, unlike rules pertaining social rights, which depend on action from the state in a complex and coordinated procedure.

The Brazilian program for the eradication of poverty and marginalization and reduction of social inequality demonstrates the need for economic, social and cultural law rules; the government cannot act discretionarily in these cases. The intensity and manner in which public entities carry out their duties regarding these rights is a different matter altogether from the choice they have in complying with social demands. The fact that several services exist to help marginalized and/or excluded social groups is proof positive of the effect of economic, social and cultural laws, within a minimum of efficacy and effectiveness of the law.

Therefore, it is impossible to compare the efficacy of civil and political rights with the efficacy of economic, social and cultural rights, in a constitutional context, since their objectives are specific. Economic, social and cultural rights depend on public policy and cannot be taken away, considering the breadth of civil and political laws.

Concern for the environment, for instance, even in face of private enterprise's need to obtain profit and positive results, sprang from the degradation of life conditions and the ability to calculate how this decline would progress; that led to the realization of the importance of preserving ecosystems, to maintain a dignified existence for all.

There are several studies from the United Nations Organization that seek to set at least a few immediate duties and prioritize helping historically neglected social groups, considering obligations the state accepted before international organizations. Thus, the concern about rights of children, women, the elderly and special needs people, among others, is clear.

A distinction has been noted, in current times, between economic, social and cultural rights that are immediately applicable and those that are granted gradually. This way, it is easier to identify the government's duties in a more effective way and make their fulfillment simpler. Several efforts are being made to provide better access to these rights, aiming to improve the precision and clarity of international texts, to extract collective, diffuse and individual subjective rights, which results in an attempt to better evaluate how well a government is faring in the performance of its duties.

In certain cases, gradually granted economic, social and cultural rights, as well as civil and political rights, do not need nonconstitutional legislation to be effective and, therefore, can be enjoyed immediately. Some, however, do need specific legislation to be effective. For example, the rights to form a union or to freely pursue employment are a classic example of immediate enjoyment rights; impeding the exercise of said rights is a violation to the abstract conception of a human being.

Yet some other civil and political rights need specific legislation to gain full efficacy. That was the case of criminalization of torture, which became a law only in 1997.

Furthermore, liberal human rights depend on executive branch actions to gain full efficacy, such as the right to a fair hearing; said right might be affected if someone does not have legal representation, provided by the government when necessary, whether paid by the defendant or not.

Overall, as for the issue regarding allocation of profit accrued by a company and private enterprise, no specific legislation is needed, since the general principles and rules that guide the Brazilian legal system are already enough to solve the matter.

2.6 - Human Rights Efficacy

Globalization, a process that has been intensified in the last decades of the 20th century, has historical roots in Western society's ethnocentrism, in the context of colonial and post-colonial domination. The process of colonization undeniably wrought several injustices; globalization insists in preserving some of those.

It is the world's inescapable destiny, an inexorable process.

In this regard, Alan Greenspan realistically states:

[. . .] Individual economies grow and prosper as their inhabitants learn to specialize and engage in the division of labor. So it is on a global scale. Globalization — the deepening of specialization and the extension of the division of labor beyond national borders — is patently a key to understanding much of our recent economic history. A growing capacity to conduct transactions and take risks throughout the world is creating a truly global economy. Production has become more and more international. Much of what is assembled in final salable form in one country increasingly consists of components from many continents. Being able to seek out the most competitive sources of labor and material inputs worldwide rather than just nationwide not only reduces costs and price inflation but also raises the ratio of the value of outputs to inputs — the broadest measure of productivity and a useful proxy for standards of living. On average, standards of living have risen markedly. Hundreds of millions of people in developing countries have been elevated from subsistence poverty. Other hundreds of millions are now experiencing a level of affluence that people born in developed nations have experienced all their lives.

On the other hand, increased concentrations of income that have emerged under globalization have rekindled the battle between the cultures of the welfare state and of capitalism — a battle some thought had ended once and for all with the disgrace of central planning. Hovering over us as well is the prospect of terrorism that would threaten the rule of law and hence prosperity. A worldwide discussion is under way on the future of globalization and capitalism and its resolution will define the world marketplace and the way we live for decades to come.59

The globalization phenomenon brings in itself a contradiction, since it exhibits a common present, but a different past. As Melissa Folmann asseverates, in this context:

> [. . .] From this brief retrospective analysis of the human rights internationalization movement, it can be seen that the discussion about which rules should be universalized for all humanity, as well as their relative or absolute nature, has been developing all along, in every step of the way. This discussion, that used to be polarized mostly within the communism-capitalism ideological axis, today is being held in several axes, such as north-south, developed-underdeveloped countries or west-east. However, in an era of globalization, attempts to compartmentalize the conversation do not make much sense, as the speed and expansion of people's means of communication and transportation convey that distinct cultural expressions do not necessarily come from different geographical locations.[60]

---

59 GREENSPAN, A. *The Age of Turbulence: Adventures in a New World.*
http://www.panzertruppen.org/ebooks/27.pdf pp.364/365.
60 FOLMANN, M. *Direitos Humanos - os 60 anos de Declaração Universal da ONU.* Curitiba: Juruá, 2008, p. 338.

In politics, globalization is defined by the interdependence of various states, which lost their autonomy and sovereignty in benefit of political and economical interests of new international actors, such as the United Nations, WTO and transnational companies. This opened the path to an attempt to westernize the world.

In this scenario, a hierarchy has been noticed, among citizens that have access to certain rights, according to their social class. Thus, multiple levels of citizenship have been created and, as such, vulnerable populations that are treated as second-class citizens, like ethnic minorities and native communities, deserve protection.

An effective (from the Latin *effectivus*, from *efficere*) rule must be observed by both jurists and the public for whom the law is intended — by the jurist, in all its interpretative possibilities; by the public, in its applicability sphere.

Effectiveness cannot be confused with efficacy (from the Latin *efficacia*, from *efficax*). Efficacy means that a rule serves its purpose, solving the issue for which it was created to address. Efficacy is the possibility of any rule having an effect, while an effective rule is a rule that has legal consequences in practice. Likewise, effectiveness does not equal lawfulness. A lawful rule was created in the way it is supposed to, according to the legal system, by the competent government branch.

Effectiveness means rules are into force and being followed; it transforms rules into instruments for the promotion and distribution of justice and, therefore, the distribution of juridical safety.

Protecting human rights in practice, even locally, depends on their global effectiveness. One cannot mention human rights, whether nationally or internationally, without acknowledging the United Nations' 1948 Universal Declaration of Human Rights, which contains thirty articles, divided into general rules and three groups of individual rights of philosophical, legal, political and guiding nature, such as universal fraternity, freedom and equality among men.

Before said declaration, there were already laws and international organizations that acted in defense of human rights, but in still an incipient form. The 1864 Convention of Geneva, for example, drafted the first international document with humanitarian law rules — which are also human rights, although in this case, related to war laws and aimed to regulate international armed conflicts, to preserve fundamental rights of the affected population.

In 1920, after World War I, the League of Nations was created to prevent new conflicts and set economic-military sanctions; the league was dissolved in April 1946, when the United Nations Organization was created.

The International Labor Organization, also created after the war, seeks to improve labor conditions throughout the world; it is responsible, in consequence, for several relevant social advancements.

The Universal Declaration of Human Rights, adopted and proclaimed by the United Nations General Assembly on December 10th, 1948 and successive international treaties are not theoretical only; its signers must endeavor to universalize the rights within.

The International Bill of Rights contains documents that form a general system and a special system as part of a global human rights protection system, which works alongside regional systems and acts as a subsidiary and supplementary law. Both are meant to build and guarantee additional protection to human rights when national instruments fail.

The International Covenant on Civil and Political Rights was adopted in 1966, and came into force only in 1976, once all ratifications or accessions were signed. This covenant protects new rights, such as children's rights, rights to a name, nationality and cultural and religious identity, among others. Besides these rights, the covenant prescribes that the States parties must assure to all individuals under their jurisdiction the protected rights, except under exceptional circumstances, such as a state of emergency, or when said limitations are necessary for national security reasons or maintenance of order. The innovation laid in the monitoring system: when a state ratified the covenant, they agreed to send periodic reports describing administrative, legislative and judiciary measures to assure recognized rights were effective and on the progress made in the enjoyment of those rights.

Through the pact, a state can report another state's violations by written communication. The committee will only act, however, if both states have accepted the competence of the committee to process and settle such disputes.

The First Optional Protocol to the International Covenant on Civil and Political Rights was adopted on March 26th, 1976, establishing a mechanism to send individual complaints to the UN Human Rights Committee for analysis. With this step, the International Bill of Rights gave full procedural capacity to individuals in the international realm.

Still on the subject of human rights effectiveness, whether through said written communication or not, Ingo Sarlet states that:

> [. . .] Although the terms ("human rights" and "fundamental rights") are commonly used interchangeably, the usual, and correct, explanation for their differences is that "fundamental rights" refers to those rights that are recognized by and part of the constitutional legal system of a certain state; "human rights," on the other hand, are associated with international law documents, which recognize human beings in themselves, a position that does not depend on being a part of a certain constitutional order; it is universally valid for all people, at all times, and has categorical supranational (international) distinction. "Human rights" also cannot be compared to "natural rights," by the fact itself that the former have been recognized by international law rules, according to Bobbio's lucid teachings; this recognition reveals, in an unassailable way, the historical and relative dimension of human rights, that have thus — at least in part (even to those who defend the

jusnaturalist theory) — detached themselves from the concept of natural law.[61]

It is believed that international law is moving towards making abuse to said rights actionable by individuals, thus creating obligations for international states to create concrete measures that help implement these rights, such as development programs for education and nourishment, for example. However, currently existing mechanisms are limited, considering the worldwide demand.

At last, measures still have to be taken by international states, so obtention and allocation of profit are in consonance with third dimension international human rights corollaries, for example. That is because the constitutional and nonconstitutional rules herein mentioned, such as social function, for instance, are exclusively national laws.

2.7 - Human Rights in Current Times

Contemporary society seeks social and cultural unity, and the 1948 Universal Declaration of Human Rights reflects this reality. Evidently, there is still a lot to be done, but the current globalization movement not only grants visibility to the subject of human rights, but also highlights our differences and points out another fundamental characteristic: the cultural and multicultural issues.

Culture is a dynamic phenomenon. The relation between different cultures destroys, builds, changes and recreates other cultures or parts of them, not only economically, but also socially, strongly influencing habits and viewpoints around the world.

The first analysis focuses on general aspects of globalization and human rights, emphasizing cultural and political

---

61 SARLET, I. *A Eficácia dos Direitos Fundamentais - Uma Teoria Geral dos Direitos Fundamentais na Perspectiva Constitucional. Op. Cit.*, pp. 34/35

fragmentation and the historical imposition of Western ethno-centrism.

The second step considers human rights from the perspectives of plurality, universality and relativism and demonstrates the need to build a multicultural conception of human rights, based on dialogue between cultures and aiming for an emancipatory multiculturalism.

At last, the third approach intends to establish intercultural conversation and find, through dialogue, a new meaning for human rights regarding isolated native communities, observing and recognizing distinctions and the right to keep said differences.

The subject of human rights must be approached in a pluralistic, universal and relative way. Pluralism conforms to multiculturalism, as it allows the coexistence of several different perceptions on a same issue, generating dialogue between diverse cultures to reach a pacific coexistence, with positive results for all.

Multiculturalism can be relativist or universalist. To universalists, human rights arise from dignity, which is a value intrinsic to human nature. Universality is synonymous to equal dignity for all men, no matter in which geographic space they are. The relativist viewpoint, however, does not establish minimum criteria for dialogue between cultures, since all is accepted and correct. In other words, everything is considered to be culturally relevant and, therefore, each culture and society should establish their own values, habits and social mores.

Relativist theory lost importance, seeing that through universalist multiculturalism it is possible to maintain the general applicability of the 1948 Declaration for all, in any place and at any time. After all, as long as human rights are not understood as universal, they will still function as a "globalized localism."

The 1948 Declaration exclusively undertakes themes and values that are essentially Western; therefore, human rights fall into this globalized localism. Some pro-human rights manifestos have an emancipatory facet and are, explicitly or implicitly, anti-capitalist, anti-hegemonic or non-Western, establishing therefore intercultural dialogue on the subject. In this context, native communities, for instance, should have guarantees in defense of their culture and sustainability within democratic institutions. The name "isolated peoples" refers to certain groups that have little to no contact with the society in their country. It is a unique situation, only found in South America.

Considering cultural and ethnic aspects of isolated natives and Brazil's current legislation, it is understood that natives have the right to remain isolated and must be protected by the government. The organization responsible for the preservation of isolated peoples is the Isolated Indians General Coordination Team (CGII — Coordenação Geral dos Índios Isolados), a branch of Brazil's National Indian Foundation (FUNAI — Fundação Nacional do Índio) According to FUNAI, isolated natives are groups that have no permanent relations with the rest of the country's population. In 2000, FUNAI established eight guidelines for the preservation of these communities; the main point is that contact is not mandatory. In 2005, FUNAI held, in Belém, the First International Symposium on Isolated Indigenous Peoples. During this conference, the International Alliance for the Protection of Isolated Indigenous People was created, calling to action the government of countries in which said people, either isolated or still in the first stages of contact, live (countries in the Amazon region and the Gran Chaco), to provide protection not only to the natives themselves, but also their habitat and, especially, their right to isolation. Internationally, the protection of the isolated peoples comes from covenants, treaties and declarations, such as Convention 169 of the ILO, which holds very advanced views, although it doesn't mention native peoples specifically. Said Convention is applicable not only by analogy, but also by including isolated peoples in the situations therein described; article 14 mentions nomadic peoples and shifting cultivators, which perfectly applies to isolated peoples.

Globalization or worldwide integration is an uncontrollable process that excludes non-Western cultures; these cultures, however, are emerging from the bonds of single (Western) thought and moving forward to life in a multicultural society, organized around emancipation and communication movements.

Multicultural communication or dialogue allow the emancipation of personal and collective life and attribute new meaning to human rights. Consequently, a theory of translation becomes necessary; one that makes different battles mutually intelligible and allows the collective agents to dialogue on the oppression they resist and aspirations that empower them.

In this context, profit can and should be applied and allocated considering the fraternity principle and herein mentioned human rights.

In this regard, Vicenzo Buonuomo states that:

> [. . .] As a value, fraternity is also an answer to the universality crisis that involves the dimension and meaning of human rights. Indeed, considering that every person belongs to the human family brings us to an essential thought: are rights universal, or is the human being? Human dignity becomes real in an individual dimension and in the collective, fraternal one; it does not change geographic coordinates or historical facts, but maintains its cohesive nature and value, as a constitutive element of fundamental rights. Essentially, the value of fraternity in international human rights law has a substantial root on the common conscience of humankind. It is an inspiration and orientation for international rules drafted in consonance with the Universal Declaration and its expression. According to this perspective, and reading the Universal Declaration with special attention to article 29, it is possible to find a real, although certainly not exhaustive indication of the effects of fraternity. These rules follow its fruition in an individual dimension and the effective exercise of human rights in a communitarian dimension: "Everyone has duties to the

community in which alone the free and full development of his personality is possible." There is no doubt that this orientation rests on a cohesive view of the human being's dimension, aware of their right to live with dignity and fully accomplish their own aspirations without isolation, but in a necessary and complementary relationship with others — a reciprocity that begins in their living environment and spreads until it reaches all the human family.[62]

Therefore, it is fundamental to see fraternization of profit as a way of making human rights concrete, in their universality and in a modern and safe manner.

---

62 BUONUOMO, V. Em busca da fraternidade no Direito da comunidade internacional. In: CASO, G. et al, orgs. *Direito & Fraternidade: ensaios, prática forense.* São Paulo: LTr, 2008.

CHAPTER III - PROFIT AND THE EFFECTIVENESS OF HUMAN RIGHTS

The capitalist economic system that dominated society after the Cold War created a competitive economic environment of capital accumulation and solely concerned with positive financial returns (profit), setting money, for capitalists, as a value above everything and everyone.

In this regard, Paul-Eugène Charbonneau says, "the supreme law of profit (therefore, of money) that dominates capitalist thought confirms, incidentally, the system's materialistic nature. Where profit is sovereign, money is God. With such a divinity, there could be no other religion but materialism.[63]

In fact, in a market that becomes more competitive every day, people are looking for any way to make profit, whether through a productive process or service provision. For the capitalist system and its market economy, productive activities and economic cycles have no other purpose but to obtain profit, which not always focuses on the community's well-being and sustainability.

In the incessant search to accrue and increase profits, capitalists ask, adopting the premises of Adam Smith and David Ricardo's theories, for the end of state interventionism, free enterprise, the end of protectionism and monopolies and they also

---

63 CHARBONNEAU, P. *Entre Capitalismo e Socialismo: a Empresa Humana. Op. Cit.*, p. 56.

assign responsibility for social exclusion to workers in capitalist production themselves, and not to society or production units.

However, from a legal standpoint, profit obtained through degradation of the environment, using child labor, false advertising, bad labor conditions, exploitation or segregation of human beings or, well, in practices that negate human rights and collective interests we mentioned on the previous chapter, is no longer tolerated.

Indeed, allowing profit from commercial activity as a negative liberty, without any control or balance is a way to prevent human rights from being effective. The concept of profit is also related to sustainability, since it is no longer possible to imagine the idea of profit as a company's sole purpose; the ways in which it is obtained must also be taken in consideration.

This concept of sustainability requires a new business management model, one that weighs both positive and negative externalities of the productive activity or service provision such as, for instance, the socioeconomic development of a certain region, improvement in the local community's quality of life, control of greenhouse gas emissions; in short, it must take in consideration how a business will impact its environment. In this regard, some economy sectors have more issues than others: for example, paper and cellulose, mining and steel, energy generation, oil and gas, and transportation.

Furthermore, it is not a matter of neglecting profit or even compromising financial results, but of taking responsibility on how these profits are generated and the impact it will have on their collaborators, the local community and even, why not, society as a whole, indirectly.

There are several examples of profit accrued in a sustainable way, aimed towards the community's well-being and respecting all dimensions of human rights. As Andrew W. Savitz explains, in this regard:

> [...] those exploring social entrepreneurship point to specific organizations that have made a positive difference by deploy-

ing for-profit techniques on behalf of social goals — organizations like the Grameen Bank of Bangladesh, whose founder, Muhammad Yunus, launched the microlending movement. By providing loans in tiny amounts (the equivalent of $5 or $100) for start-up capital to poor men and women in rural Bangladesh, the Grameen Bank has helped launch tens of thousands of small businesses and lifted many villages out of poverty. [. . .] An ambitious example is the Safe Water Drinking Alliance, which describes itself as "a strategic public-private collaboration" whose goal is to help households in some of the world's poorest countries obtain a regular supply of safe drinking water. Most residents of the developed world take clean drinking water for granted, but an estimated 1.1 billion people around the world have contaminated water supplies, and the related diarrheal diseases result in the needless death through dehydration of some two million children annually.[64]

Indeed, a theory on profit should do more than just provide a definition; profit must be systematically described as a subject connected to its allocation. In this regard, Paul-Eugène Charbonneau asseverates that:

> [. . .] although profit is legitimate when accrued in fair proportion, it can never be considered a company's main reason to exist. In point of fact, in this issue, just as in the ones before, neo-capitalism is an heir to liberal viewpoints and Adam Smith. It is true that this outlook has been, up to this day and age, tempered by the fact that rights have been given back to the common good and profit was made to fit into said good's demands. But, once limits are set, profit is always king. Profit is the ultimate reason for investments, distributed

---

64 SAVITZ, A. *The Triple Bottom Line: How Today's Best-Run Companies Are Achieving Economic, Social, and Environmental Success— and How You Can Too.* http://pro-ex.org/books/archive/files/b76eaa14ccc6578769babbe61aea-ca39.pdf pp. 246/247.

less to cover needs and conveniences, and more in view of expected benefits, from which arise a consumer, luxury and profit economy. Starting always from the supposition that a company needs profit to survive, it can be concluded, by sophistic reasoning, that its reason to exist — its purpose, therefore — is profit. However, need and purpose are two essentially distinct concepts; profit cannot be recognized as a company's purpose, although it is necessary, for that would mean accepting money rules over man. Maximum profit is still the rule, although it should minimum profit, as we will see further along, so purchasing power is at a maximum. To neo-capitalists, profit is economy's goal; according to humanist thought, it is only the motor. As Villain states: "On the day the profit becomes, instead, the supreme goal of businesspeople and the ultimate purpose of their activities, we shall say the purpose hierarchy is upended and that economy is no longer in service of man." Today, as it was yesterday, money is the measure. In a neo-capitalist context, we must still recognize, along with Leclercq, that "one of the aspects of current day demoralization is the invasion of the spirit of profit, that seeps through all professions and puts a spotlight on professions that aim profit.[65]

Therefore, a legal interpretation and analysis of profit is necessary, to make it compatible with all dimensions of human rights: from the start of the economic flux to its final activity, weighing how profit was gained and its final allocation.

Profit, thus, will also have an important task that will benefit all: as an instrument for human rights effectiveness, every time it improves people's quality of life and helps preserve the environment and support sustainability.

Profit will then be compatible with all dimensions of human rights and, even more, will be an instrument for the effectiveness of these rights through cooperation from those who

---

65 CHARBONNEAU, P. *Op. Cit.*, p. 82.

hold the power to change or, at least, to influence the factors of production: the government and productive units, especially and including those who pursue a business activity.

3.1 - The Role of the Government in Helping Profit Guarantee Human Rights Effectiveness.

The government, in obedience to its legally imposed obligations, must provide legitimate and democratic protection to citizens and foreigners, resident in the country or not, to ensure their rights. For this reason, it aims to pursue and assure the exercise of social and individual rights, as well as freedom, safety, well-being, development, equality and justice, considered to be the supreme values of a nation founded on social harmony.

However, since the end of the 20th century, the government has distanced itself from monopolistic and protectionist attitudes, abstaining from interfering in the economy and transferring activities that are constitutionally meant to be state-run to private legal entities, albeit in exchange for economic interests.

In any case, the government's role is essential to make all dimensions of human rights effective through profit, since the government can and must intervene in economic activity, by setting a checks and balances system on the capitalist viewpoint, that shows no concern about society and people, and is solely interested in profit.

In this chapter, the author defends that the government has an essential role because, in a democratic state such as Brazil, it can adopt effective political and economical measures to ensure that companies and capitalists, when obtaining and allocating profit, submit to legally supported state control.

The historical evolution of government's intervention in economic activity through legal and political measures shows the government definitely can and must intervene in profit gained by capitalists, and make them rethink how profit is obtained and allocated — respecting the supremacy of human rights in all its dimensions.

The age of decline began in the 1930s, going all through the 1940s and reaching its pinnacle in the 1950s and 1960s. During the 1970s, there was a new reduction on the growth rate, along with the growing instability of macroeconomies. The 1980s reflected a progressive inability to both rationally plan state intervention in the social change process, and to produce answers both effective and systematically consistent within a scattered and contradictory bevy of tensions, conflicts and demands — a portrait of four decades of government interventionism decline.

The 1990s were a historical time during which two economic eras crossed over: the post-war, characterized by state planning through governmental intervention, conceptual and pragmatic innovations in production and distribution market regulations, the use of the law as an instrument for control, management and direction, among others; and the globalized economy era, defined by a return of private capital accumulation flow, unregulated markets, financialization of capital, extinction of public monopolies, privatization of public companies, among others. Dependence on the geometric growth of innovation rates is one of the most important characteristics of the new era.

During the ascension, the government's main objective was the integration of macroeconomic policies for the expansion of capitalism, investing against conventional thinking. Keynes maintained that, in a capitalist economy, there was no need to have previous savings to make investments, since they depend on the profit expectations of businesspeople and the financial managers' disposition.

The Keynesian state did not only reestablish the balance in bilateral resource transfers, eliminating factors that had been causing crises in capitalism, but also helped make private accumulation viable and fulfilled the legitimizing role of granting the industrial society an established identity which, legally, led to standardizing labor relations and politically, guided governmental action to identify points of tension.

The government turned out to be incapable of handling not only new problems created by transformations in the international economic order, but also older problems, changed from their general patterns within macroeconomic policies, which led to the reformulation and reinterpretation of economic, administrative and labor laws, resulting in a decline of the economic system and proving a lack of political, administrative, operational and organizational efficacy of the Keynesian system.

The costs generated by the governability crisis grow faster than the means to finance them and, once effected, they become social rights that cannot be suppressed without great tension. The government is, then, forced to transfer political system surpluses, reducing the public and private investment capacity in the same system.

After the crises of the 1960s and 1970s, governability began to be seen as a condition for reform, and reform, as a more adequate strategy for restoration. Currently, with the 2008 international economic crisis and the domino effect in several financial institutions as an example, it is clear that the market and the economy cannot be set totally free; they need government intervention, which refutes Adam Smith's theory.

Keynesian theory was a guideline during the recovery period of the world crisis, since worldwide economies believed the state and its respective power could give incentives to internal economy by fostering consumption, internal investments and creating an infrastructure that supported internal economy and made people's lives better.

In this regard, Moisés Marques, economy professor at the Fundação Escola de Sociologia e Política of São Paulo says, "even so, Keynesian theory is not omnipotent." The government cannot rescue the market alone all the time. The market must support itself. Therefore, the best policy is to regularize and monitor free enterprise.[66]

---

66 According to Marcia Rodrigues. *A História do Pensamento Econômico - Os Grandes Teóricos e seus Pensamentos*. São Paulo: Discovery, s/d, p. 11.

Consequently, the government must rely on the legal system to assure the control of private activities is effective. To accomplish that end, the government must intervene whenever necessary, creating rules for economic relations so there is a real balance between economic activity and people, as well as making sure economy is in service of man, and not the other way around. It is unacceptable, for instance, that slave labor still exists in any economy segment in the 21st century.

Therefore, the law is the first working instrument the government has to control and intervene in the economy, directing the way capitalists obtain and allocate profit, especially so they adopt the implementation of human rights as an indissoluble objective, along with the goal of their economic activities, that is, so profit has a dependency relationship with all dimensions of human rights.

In the context of the legal system, the efficacy of a certain rule is defined as the power to generate concrete legal effects to regulate situations, relationships and behaviors specified in codes and laws. In another, more sociologically sensitive line of thought, rules and laws are efficacious when they find in the reality they regulate the necessary social, economic, political, cultural and even anthropological conditions.

Aware that its codes and laws needed this support, the regulatory government adopted a subtle strategy of distancing itself from its rules, to the point that, several times, it became an accomplice to behaviors and decisions that violated said rules by action or omission. In relation to the informal perspective, the government began to edit, in an asynchronous way and in logical-formal, material and temporal terms, successive behavioral, organizational and programmatic rules. As happens with economic inflation, though, the unbridled and disorderly production of laws compresses the horizons of decisions, aggravates conflicts, cripples rational thought and disseminates generalized insecurity in the sociopolitical life and the business world.

Legal inflation is the progressive devaluation of the legal

system, which obstructs the law from performing its regulating and controlling basic duties through rules, laws and codes. Legal inflation also includes the outbreak in the number of lawsuits and the already mentioned problem of excessive use of the courts to solve political issue, which is a highly dysfunctional process in the change and evolution of the law.

In the specific context of a nation, its legal institutions were reduced, in terms of the number of rules and regulations, to make the judiciary system faster and more flexible. The government kept creating legislation, including in economic, financial, monetary, tributary, social security, labor, civil and business matters.

In a world economy context, financial and business transnational organizations, acting on the premise that decisions based on the successive stages of the productive activity should not be taken separately, but simultaneously, expanded the production of their own rules, so that organizing systems and methods, production manuals, disciplinary regulations, codes of conduct and contracts were standardized in a global scale.

Important aspects of said structural changes are the multiplying and interweaving of four types of rules: technical rules, rules created by transnational corporations and rules and procedures created by multilateral organizations.

Another tendency has been viewing through the angle of legal pluralism the chains of rules of worldwide economy, transnational legal forms and the intersection of rules created by financial and business corporations themselves with the legal system of each nation. International law and legal pluralism were never treated as a priority, considering the dogmatic emphasis given to the categories: international law, due to its low power of coercion, lack of hierarchic differentiation of rules and debates on its viability or the possibility of a supranational formal sovereign power; legal pluralism, due to its corrosive potential or for being dysfunctional in the dogmatic field, since it reveals the heterogeneity of the law in each state and the existence of several legal systems in a same geopolitical space. The increased value of international law rests in the fact that, due to the acclaimed weakness of its organized coercion power, its definitions evolved.

The main rule of analytical focus to the identification, in all its structural complexity, of the profile of legal institutions created with the globalized economy is from the capitalist society as a political formation constituted by several means of producing power, articulated in specific ways, based on a pluralist, informed and legitimized approach.

In a capitalist society, the nature of power and character are not attributes of any specific social, institutions, resulting from its distinct possibilities of articulation; continuously interacting, these spaces tend to create complex, dynamic and new relations among themselves, resulting in a combination of several concepts of legality and different generations of rules. The fragmentation in these multiple chains and legal microsystems created from these interactions and crisscrossing, however, is far from chaotic; although structurally autonomous, these spaces are reciprocally influenced in their relations.

In the post-war economic era, the legal system of the interventionist state, with its regulatory instruments, consisted in a central law that had effective conditions to influence and condition the right of production and what was produced in the market space, due to the fact that companies depended on tax barriers, commercial protectionism, incentives and credit offered by industrial development and growth programs, and also on the expansion of consumer laws.

Competitiveness, productivity and integration in the economic sphere, associated to fragmentation and marginalization on the social sphere designate, on one side, the functional differentiation of society and, on another, a growing structural unemployment, followed by the degradation of living conditions for those who were expelled from the formal labor market.

It seems that social law lacks an essential condition for its implementation, which is an economy under the regulatory eye of a strong state, whether facing different local political organizations or any specific social group within its territory. This law was created when stratified social bonds were broken by bourgeois innovation, ending power fragmentation or dispersion in feuds, duchies, baronies, principalities and the church, and the suppression of local religious or birth differences.

Among possible answers to the continuity of social law in the contemporary agenda is the use of the idea of social law as a transformative project with an utopian side, in the sense of what path can be taken; this path has been formulated and developed in an attempt to build impossible worlds, not necessarily including the historical process.

Yet another difficult issue is how far can reach reflexive law jurists contemplation on institutional, organizational and legal changes in contemporary government, especially those originated from attempts to face legislative inflation, juridification and a systemic governability crisis. By limiting its objectives to the control and harmonization of different negotiation procedures in decentralized levels, in the context of productive chains, reflexive law faces the challenge of affirming its systemic identity.

On one side, institutions show that political-institutional models are exhausted since the second post-war era, in the form of Keynesian states and highly interventionist and regulatory legal instruments; on the other, several dilemmas and conundrums are being created and expanding, in a changing world scenario full of uncertainty.

Initiatives for regionalization, as a strategy specially conceived to make obtaining better conditions of participation in world exchanges more viable included, in the first place, the concentration of European integration experiences, beginning between 1950 and 1951 — with the creation of the International Authority for the Ruhr and the European Coal and Steel Community, that instituted the supranationality principle, combining international law and internal public law rules — and turned effective by the Maastricht Treaty since 1992.

The second initiative was the creation, also in 1992, of The North-American Free Trade Agreement (NAFTA), between Canada, USA and Mexico, a common area for free trade of goods and services.

The third initiative is represented by the formation, after decades of intense competition and reciprocal mistrust, of a very dynamic area of economic cooperation for the Americas, Southeast Asian nations and Oceania's APEC — Asia Pacific Economic Cooperation — which now includes 21 countries.

The fourth initiative came from efforts to eliminate trade barriers, by adopting a common external tariff, formulating a conjoint commercial policy to third parties, raising the volume of regional commerce and deepening the respective economies of the countries in the southern cone of Latin America — MERCOSUL

At the same time, that globalization reveals facets that are too original and complex to allow a precise evaluation, legal institutions that follow the economic globalization will be affected by inevitable course changes.

Based in these ideas, it is clear that, in Brazil, the government's legislative direction to intervene in the economy and in the ways to obtain and allocate profit comes from the economic constitution, especially the main rule of the economic order, stated on article 170 of the constitution. The Federative Republic of Brazil's goals are prescribed on article 3, and the prevalence of human rights, on article 4, II of the constitution.

We maintain, therefore, that the government must intervene in the way profit is obtained and allocated, overseeing the process so human rights are respected by the company, and checking if said company observes, as a premise for obtaining profit, the economic foundations of the constitutional order (valuing human labor and free enterprise, for instance) and the objectives of the social order (ensuring a dignified existence in accordance to social justice's dictates). This, because we understand that violating the communitarian principle prescribed in the constitution when obtaining and allocating profit is more than enough reason for the state to intervene in the economic order, generating practical results in the implementation of human rights in all its dimensions.

In this regard, Andre Ramos Tavares asserts that:

> Social justice, in short, should be adopted as one of the communitarian principles of the 1988 constitution that interfere in the economic order, aiming to implement living conditions in a dignified and satisfactory level to all, with the intrinsic social aspect of justice.67

Concluding, the government must always intervene and keep economic activity in check whenever human rights are violated while obtaining and allocating profit, using the governmental power granted by the legal system into force, especially economic-constitutional rules.

3.2 - The Social Function of Private Enterprises and Human Rights

The concept of social function as a state power that is, dually, also a duty, appeared first in the German Weimar constitution in 1919, moving past the purely individualistic concept of property. In this context, a right's *social function* is connected to societal interests. However, the term social function is vague, imprecise.

As Fabio Konder Comparato states:

> [. . .] If we look closer at this abstract concept of function, in its multiple iterations, we'll see the objective pursued by the agent is always someone else's interest, not of who holds the

---

67 TAVARES, A. *Direito Constitucional Econômico*. São Paulo: Editora Método, p. 129.

power. Activity development is, therefore, a duty; specifically, power-duty; not in a negative sense, as respecting certain established limits to perform an activity, but in positive way, of something that must be done or accomplished.[68]

The concept of social function is in the Federative Constitution, in its articles 5, XXIII and 170, III; it is closely connected to the satisfaction of a need.

In this regard, Guilherme Calmon Nogueira da Gama asseverates that:

> [. . .] The meaning of the expression social function must correspond to the human being, not only *uti singulus* or *uti civis*, but also, *uti socius*. In this context, the social function doctrine emerges as a philosophical matrix, able to restrict individualism present in the main legal institutes, protect collective interests and grant material equality to all.
> [...]
> The idea of social function as an instrument comes from the expression's etymology. In Latin, the word *functio* comes from the verb *fungor* (*functus sum, fungi*), that means to accomplish something, perform a duty or a task; that is, to reach a result.[69]

Corporate social function, although it originated from the social function of private property, is an entirely different issue. Although social function is part of the structure of property, the independent nature of the company's social function must be highlighted; undeniably, the principle of corporate social function and the principle of private property social function are autonomous, especially considering a company is a legal entity and its activity must be performed observing the social function.

---

68 COMPARATO, F. *Estado, Empresa e Função Social*. São Paulo: Revista dos Tribunais, 1996, n° 732, p. 41.
69 GAMA, G. *Função Social no Direito Civil*. São Paulo: Atlas, 2007, pp. 3/4.

In this regard, social function took an important role in the alteration of the Brazilian political and economic scenario, because it is a practice that aims to benefit society by searching ways to perform measures that compensate the impact caused by constant socioeconomic transformations from corporate activity and capitalism.

A company's social function becomes a reality if corporate activity embraces solidarity, promotes social justice, free enterprise, the pursuit of full employment, reduction of social inequality, the social value of labor and human dignity, and follows environmental guidelines; that is, if it obeys all constitutional and nonconstitutional principles that govern economic activity.

The new civil code, attuned to social needs, was structured with rules of an ethical, social and operable nature, setting general clauses and imposing correlated duties such as cooperation, information, probity, correction and collaboration in private relationships, clearly establishing the corporate social function in the legal system.

As Professor Fábio Konder Comparato teaches, "the social function of legal institutes is a constitutional tendency; corporations must be included, as an operator in a socially socialized market."[70]

In this regard, Statement 53 of the Federal Judicial Council states that:

> Article 966 — although not explicitly mentioned, the social function principle must be considered when interpreting corporate laws.

In fact, the 2002 civil code (Law 10.406/2002) strengthened the corporate social function concept, which had already

---

70 COMPARATO, F. Função Social da Propriedade dos Bens de Produção. In: *Revista de Direito Mercantil, Industrial, Econômico e Financeiro*, ano 25, n.º 63, São Paulo, 1986, p. 76.

been professed by the constitution since 1988 and, in a subtler way, by Brazil's Corporation Law. The new civil code, as the constitution before it, instituted general clauses with generic and abstract content, but meant as a guideline, with power to give coded rules more mobility and mitigate rules that are too rigid.

In this context, profit must not be the only goal; the consequences of the manager's actions on society must also be examined, not only by using private assets in synchrony with society, but also bringing social achievement to the businessperson and all who helped attain the objective.

A company must also hire fairly, obeying contractual justice. It must to search solutions for the effects of its legal transactions, uniting ethical rules and principles and searching for a balance between a free market and the social good. Also, the company must fulfill its economic and social function, obeying constitutional precepts and acting ethically in the resulting relationships, because a community and society's development depend on a strong economy, and corporations are some of the main agents of production and circulation of goods and services. The goal of a company is to circulate wealth of a specific community; by obtaining profit, they might help improve people's quality of life.

3.2.1 - Social Function and the Implementation of First Dimension Human Rights

As stated above, freedom, security, psychological, moral and bodily integrity are protected by first dimension human rights, which also guarantee the right to be a part of public life.

By fulfilling its social function, a company brings economic development compatible with first dimension human rights, respecting human freedom, safety and integrity. When an economic private agent or private productive unity correctly allocates its profits to make human rights effective, the human law of the productive unit itself is fully realized.

Ultimately, when the law not only permits, but safe-guards, the right of the economic agent to choose how to allocate profit (for instance, for a cultural development social project), it is guaranteeing the right of freedom towards profit; that is, protecting the first dimension human right of freedom to own property and engage in free enterprise.

Corporate profit can bring human rights to reality when obtained and destined considering human well-being and sustainability. In this context, profit obtained from child labor, slave labor or under hazardous conditions (dangerous, unsound or under moral harassment), that is, from exploring and segregating human beings, is no longer tolerated.

On the contrary, obtaining profit through factors of production — human labor and natural resources — can grant effectiveness to rights to freedom, equality and safety, respecting human integrity and dignity. A human being out of work or in a hazardous work environment has their dignity stolen, which leads to social exclusion and separation from constitutionally protected social justice, as well as their own position as an agent of the economic cycle.

On the other hand, when obtained responsibly, profit strengthens the production factors, generating more dignity to people and protecting the environment.

The solution to any conflict on the different interests of corporate activity must be guided by the constitution's article 170, which makes clear that obtaining profit while respecting the social function and appropriately allocating the results serves freedom, equality, private property and citizenship human rights.

3.2.2 - Social Function and the Implementation of Second Dimension Human Rights

Obeying the corporate social function when allocating profit is also instrumental to the implementation of second dimension human rights, as it fosters the achievement and growth of human rights.

Second dimension human rights are rights to labor, health and education, among others; the government is responsible for granting said rights to those entitled to receive them. These rights came into the legal system by the liberal French constitutions of 1791 and 1793, and the population — the main interested party in the implementation of said rights —, which became necessary due to problems resulting from the industrial revolution and the living conditions of workers, amplified by the Human Rights Declaration of 1948.

Profit, when originated from a corporate activity connected to its social obligations, and destined for investments in social programs, in culture, education, leisure, health and environment conservation, fully provides second dimension human rights. It has nothing to do, however, with transferring government duties to private enterprise; it is just a way companies contribute to the achievement and implementation of these rights and participate in these social accomplishments, since profit can also promote economic development and make human rights a concrete reality.

3.2.3 - Social Function and the Implementation of Third Dimension Human Rights

The social function of the company, at last, also makes third dimension rights effective, as it brings the spirit of solidarity and fraternity, and respect to broad collective rights.

Third dimension human rights are identified by including diffuse rights and by not having specific beneficiaries. The receivers of said rights are social groups, and their protection is transferred to the whole collectivity. These rights are not only ethical recommendations the government must follow, but laws regulating human rights that, forcibly, authorities must protect.

In this context, while obtaining profit, a business cannot

degrade the environment (article 170, VI of the constitution), and must respect consumer rights (article 170, V of the constitution), in attention to third dimension human rights.

It is noteworthy to mention that fulfilling human rights in any of the described dimensions is not a corporate activity obligation, nor its social function; that is, it is not exclusively a corporate duty. The government is also responsible for protecting those rights in the very performance of its duties, as said in the previous chapter.

It cannot be said, either, that appropriate profit allocation is a matter of benevolence or liberality of a private productive unit; it is actually a legal duty towards human rights effectiveness in all its dimensions, aiming to improve the community's living conditions and conserve the environment, based on corporate social function. It is the government's duty to establish rules and public policies on profit that can, concurrently, be also an incentive for both public and private production units to allocate part or all of their profits to implement all dimensions of human rights.

It must be noted, incidentally, that the preamble to the Universal Declaration of Human Rights states "every organ of society," which includes private corporations and governments (and its state enterprises) must respect human rights.

In this same regard, Decree 7.037 of 12/21/2009, which approved the National Human Rights Program — PNDH-3 — "proposes instruments for the advancement and reinforcement of public policy proposals aiming to reduce social inequality through income redistribution, incentives to the solidarity economy and cooperatives, the expansion of agrarian reform, fostering aquaculture, fishing and extractive activities and promotion of sustainable tourism."

In this context, state enterprises, as productive units, must also choose to allocate profits for the common good. However, the obligation to distribute profit in a community cannot be attributed solely to the government and public enterprises, considering that, in practice, human rights implementation is not prioritized over profit in state enterprises. In a recent example, the Chamber of Deputies voted against the government and destined 75% of oil royalties to fund education and 25%, to health. The government intended to spend 100% in education. While the government intended to allocate 50% of the revenue of the Social Fund to education, the Chamber and Senate decided to allocate 50% of the full amount accrued by the Fund, not just the revenue.

Therefore, it becomes clear that the correct allocation of profits to implement human rights is a legal duty, not a liberality, considering that in the capitalist system adopted in Brazil, there is a risk that other interests might prevail over human rights, when considering profit allocation.

This is why we sustain that companies, as all actors of the economic cycle, have to support human rights in all its dimensions through profit allocation, in view of the common good and human development, by offering practical results that meet the needs of human beings, such as culture, employability, health and medication, among others.

Therefore, the government has an important role as inspector of the implementation of human rights and also must propose public policies for the reduction of social inequality, through income distribution actions and incentives to solidarity economy. At this point, it must be concluded the appropriate destination of profit, in view of the common good, is an example of real income distribution and solidarity economy, implementing human rights in all its dimensions, which makes it a legal duty.

At last, *the social function of a corporation cannot be mistaken for a company's social responsibility*. After all, social responsibility is voluntary; a choice from whomever runs a business. The corporate social function, on the other hand, is mandatory due to a constitutional command and is, therefore, an obligation. The social function of the company will be accomplished if the production goods have a purpose compatible with the common good, by producing and distributing these goods to the community, circulating wealth and generating wealth; it is a true general clause.

Furthermore, observing the company's social function is closely connected to its corporate purpose, while fulfilling a social responsibility may go beyond that said purpose. Indeed, social responsibility is not a legal duty; an opposing view — that such social actions are mandatory — implies, inevitably, in a violation of the legality principle, according to which a private person cannot be not *"be obliged to do or refrain from doing something except by virtue of law."*

At any rate, whether it is mandatory or not, it is important to delve further into social responsibility as a way to ensure the effectiveness of human rights.

3.3 - Corporate Social Responsibility and Human Rights

Social and environmental imbalances around the world convinced large corporate conglomerates, which usually have relevant economic and political power, to take social responsibility on the degradation of the environment, abusive pricing practices and even the quality of life of their direct and indirect collaborators, as well as other consumers of their goods and services.

This social responsibility, initially taken only by large corporations, became part of the life of small and medium enterprises as well, in proportion to the size of their business, of course. A company's usefulness to society began to be questioned and, consequently, not only its way of obtaining profit, but also the proper allocation of said profit.

The evolution of the concept of sustainability in the past years is undeniable. In fact, the more its implications on business are explored, the more the productive process is changed to, for instance, reduce residue generation, pollution and the impact on the extraction of natural resources, among others.

Along with the evolution of the concept of sustainability, the idea of how profit is traditionally seen has also changed. Obtaining profit just for itself, without measuring consequences such as its sustainability impact, can no longer be accepted.

Observing sustainability practices does not mean neglecting profit or financial results, but obtaining them in a more rational and safe way, respecting the common good. In this regard, profit is a reward for acting in view of the common good.

It must be remembered that in pre-historic groups, the basic rules were the protection of life, solidarity and sharing with all, since communities were small, compared to modern times. Originally, in their midst, peaceful cooperation was the goal, not competition. Obtaining fraternal profit is a form of peaceful cooperation, unlike competition that destroys the resources that keep a community alive.

With the socioeconomic differentiation caused by the new international labor division and by the flexible specialization paradigm of post-Fordist production, which generated heterogeneous structures that cross over and interweave through the diversity of interests from different places, regions, countries and continents, current society became a conflicting plurality of multiple groups, organisms and communities, all with specific interests, language patterns and rational calculations for their actions, such as commercial and investment banks, pension funds, insurance companies, corporate conglomerates, unions, chambers of commerce and other representative institutions.

In this international context, some societies have deep roots in their history and others are in a constant innovation, transformation and generalization process of the patterns of production, consumption and labor. Expansion and multiplication of these groups, organizations and communities fragment political life even more, change the profile of institutional regulations, modify social integration practices and procedures and condition the direction of society's evolution.

This not a new phenomenon; it was first detected, in

reach and implications, by Max Weber's writings, that show how modern society subjects individuals to a daily grind with no place for spontaneity, leading to a path of individualism without soul, to alienation, technification, juridification and bureaucratization of social life. Among several consequences, one of the most important is that people are no longer identified solely by their relationships with other human beings; now, they are considered to be part of a group and of their community. Likewise, family life is increasingly being led in a corporate setting, due to, among other reasons, globalization and new management styles, rationalization and performance adopted by companies that do not necessarily result in free time, in which there are concrete possibilities of leisure and expansion of people's intellectual and spiritual abilities.

On the other hand, considering large corporations have several productive units that cannot function on their own, connected by horizontal and vertical relationships to an industrial matrix, these procedures paved the road to more instances of people working from home, which transformed the domestic sphere into a large contingent of families in a real work space. Family, social, political and cultural life start being led, essentially, under the shelter of complex organizations; the more these organizations expand their self-control techniques based on functional hierarchies in the interconnection between planning and execution, the more an emphasis on personal performance is substituted by inspiring team work efficiency, using material goods and combining symbols, values and rules, transforming its members into organizational people, who are capable of adapting, tolerant of frustrations, and highly loyal to the organization.

Consequently, some values, goals and procedures become harder to achieve, if they do not disappear completely, since these organizations are too complex to guarantee their integrity through common beliefs and a civic-moral bedrock. In this society, citizens are no longer capable of making deals; they simply accept and follow, without criticism, the directives imposed by organizations to which they are connected and inserted, its main characteristic being the triple capacity for strategic, associative and creative action in face of the growing complexity of the environment.

The government shows its eminent traits when it cannot manage to promote macroeconomic coordination without the consent and collaboration of these complex organizations. Unlike the classic liberal state, with its political-institutional structure set on centrality and exclusivity of legislative production and the division of powers, this state takes on a more reduced, condensed and compact organizational dimension, and starts being guided and conditioned by the market.

Legal institutions that appeared during the transnationalization of the input, finance, production and consumption markets dynamic are still being configured and developed; this interweaving could be made viable with a peculiar kind of rule, either procedural or juridical, whose role would be supporting interaction and ensuring the balance of the different organizations within. On the other hand, in practical terms, this rule would be able to make different complex organizations take in consideration, in their decision-making process, antagonistic and conflicting demands of their environment, field or sphere of action, aiming to neutralize the natural propensity of said organizations, especially those working in strategic sectors of the economy.

Considering it increases the complexity of these characteristics, no system, be it productive, financial, educational or cultural, has the means to aspire to actually conduct society; this an attribution of the political system, that autonomously fulfills its objective and, at the same time, is connected to all by an interdependent relation that does not allow the prevalence of any given system.

Formed by organizational and directive distribution of competences rules and, over all, by procedural and juridical rules, reflexive law must conserve self-regulation procedures in each specific area of society and ensure the integration of its partial system differentiation, not interfering with the autonomy in the mechanisms of each particular system and trying to balance different pressures from external systems.

These particular systems are, therefore, companies that pursue an economic activity in the economic market system, and must integrate with external factors, adapting their internal conduct in a way that is compatible with the common good, from which a social responsibility, for all and with all of mankind, emerges. The subject of corporate social responsibility came into the public eye in the mid 1950s, specifically in the United States, through Howard Bowen's work, Social Responsibilities of the Businessman, which was translated into several languages.

Concluding, the practices and behaviors of for-profit companies must not result in the violation of human rights. To achieve that end, corporations must participate actively, extensively and responsibly in society and the environment, showing concern not only with their profit, but also to those who submit to their corporate practices and depend on them for survival. Socially responsible practices joined with profit obtention are the aspired result, not only in the long term, but also short and medium term, so business can be sustainable. It is, therefore, economic and financial development tethered to social responsibility, in a way that generates profit: fraternal profit, or profit that respects all dimensions of human rights.

In this regard, Paulo Rogério dos Santos Lima teaches that:

[. . .] In this environment of discussion and reflection, ADCE-Brazil drafted ten points it believes can unite business-people around the idea of a solidary and active corporation. It is relevant to mention these goals, as they were the first step towards dialogue in Brazil.

1- We accept the existence or transcendent value of social and corporate ethics, to which we submit our motivations, interests, activities and rationality of our decisions.

2- We are convinced that a corporation, apart from its economic function in the production of goods and services, has a social function materialized through the promotion of its workers and the community into which it must be integrated. In performing this function, we find the noblest incentive to self-fulfillment.

3- We believe a corporation performs a service to the community and must be open to all who desire to lend their abilities and savings to a social and creative purpose, because we consider the purely individualistic conception of corporation obsolete and anachronistic.

4- We view profit as an indicator of a technical, economical and financially healthy corporation, justly remunerated for its effort, creativity and risks taken. We reject, thus, the idea of profit as the only reason for entrepreneurial activity.

5- We view the demands made on corporations in name of the common good, usually by tax legislation and social law, as an ethical compromise.

6- We share the conviction that our entrepreneurial activity must contribute to Brazil's growing technological, economic and financial independence.

7- We consider that all who work with us are collaborators, at any level of the corporate structure. We respect the essential human dignity of all, with no discrimination, and want to motivate them to join responsibly in our goal towards the common good, awakening potential and bringing them to participate progressively more in the company's routine.

8- We consider that constantly elevating productivity levels, along with the parallel growth of all salaried workers as an imperative measure of social justice, is an important goal for Brazilian corporations.

9- We commit to grant conditions for labor, professional qualification, personal and family safety to all our collaborators, so life in the corporation can be an element of complete fulfillment for all human beings.

10- We are open to dialogue with all who share our ideals and concerns, to contribute with the constant advancement and improvement of our economic, legal and social institutions, so Brazil may go through fair, complete, harmonious and fast growth (Opinion ADCE - Brazil, 1984)[71]

A corporation's conduct has been historically linked to its economic function, with the objective of accumulating capital, also through profit. Thus, through profit accumulation, it was possible to distribute dividends among members or stockholders or reinvest in the business. However, competition for more and better profit must be handled with peaceful cooperation and not competition that causes the destruction of the natural resources that are necessary for the survival of the species.

In this context, the definition of social responsibility includes all of the corporation's ethical, social and environmental commitments to achieve their contractual and/or statutory purpose.

As Paulo Rogério dos Santos Lima asseverates:

[. . .] values related to ethics, social aspects and the environment, among others, must walk alongside to build a sustainable environment for society and the corporation itself. Therefore, economic values or indicators cannot be the only component of the relationship between a corporation and its various publics. Otherwise, the company will always be immersed in a system restricted to their economic function's purpose, which does not represent a real and open system of an institution that is part of society. [72]

The definition of corporate social responsibility was revealed during the World Business Council for Sustainable Development that happened in 1998, in the Netherlands: "Corporate Social Responsibility is the continuing commitment by business to contribute to economic development while improv-

---

71 LIMA, P. *Responsabilidade Social - A experiência do selo Empresa Cidadã na cidade de São Paulo.* São Paulo: Editora PUC-SP, 2005, 31/32.
72 *Op. Cit.* p. 38.

ing the quality of life of the workforce and their families as well as of the community and society at large." The Ethos Institute, a non-governmental organization also created in 1998 to help explain and consolidate the definition of social responsibility, improved said definition, stating as follows:

> [. . .] it revolves around the constant commitment of businesspeople to ethics and economic development that also improves the lives of their employees and their families, as well as that of the local community and society as a whole, aiming for justice and sustainability.[73]

Notably, a corporation's role in society is no longer exclusively economic; it also has a social aspect; the one who accrues profit from any corporate activity can no longer separate economic and social interests.

Social responsibility is characterized by internal and external factors. Internal ones are related to human capital in the productive process or service provision; external are related to a concern with the environment or public health, for instance.

As Paulo Rogério dos Santos Lima asserts:

> [. . .] Corporate organization is involved with what can be conventionally called internal social responsibility (isr), that is, the obligation to care for the full development of its employees, especially regarding quality of life. Alencastro (1997), with some propriety, succinctly explains the main mechanisms of the internal side of corporate social responsibility. According to him, most organizations of any size may develop mechanisms to improve their employees' satisfaction. These mechanisms may be services, installations, activities and opportunities, such as: personal and professional counseling; career and occupation development (preparation for the labor market; cultural and recreational activities; non-work-related education; childcare; infirmaries, special leave to handle family and/

---

73 Source: http://www.ethos.org.br/docs/institucional.

or community responsibilities; retirement plans; security out side work; flexible hours; professional relocation and placement; retirement benefits, including healthcare; drug and alcohol rehabilitation programs; transportation; meals and prevention of work-related injuries and illnesses).[74]

Those are typical internal factors, indeed. Social responsibility's external factors, however, focus on investments on social or environmental programs, among others. It is not charity, but a commitment to the corporate organization's very existence. Ethical-corporate commitment is immersed in these factors, which embody a moral way of gaining profit, no matter its allocation. Social responsibility (internal and external factors), relevant during the process of obtaining profit, cannot be mistaken for the appropriate and socially responsible allocation of said profit, which is within the company's social function.

All changes in the Brazilian government generated a division in three social sectors: (i) the first sector is the state, the government and public purpose; (ii) the second sector, private; and (iii) the third sector is represented by civil society organizations that attend to social demands.

Companies in the private sector (second sector) can and must have profit as their main objective, or lose the purpose of their very existence. Profit, however, cannot only be distributed among members or stockholders or reinvested, but can also be spent on activities that might help improve people's quality of life.

In this regard, Cristiani de Oliveira Silva Duarte states that:

[...] In a globalized world in which information is progressively faster and more accessible and businesses are always in view of markets and international capital, ethical behavior is becoming a matter of survival. The greatest investors have re-

---

74 LIMA, P. *Op. Cit.*, pp. 52/53.

jected being a part of companies with a history of disregard to human rights and the environment. On the other hand, companies that have a good or great track record and allocate part of their profits to activities that help improve their employee's and the community's quality of life have seen an increase in investments. [. . .] It can be concluded, therefore, it is irrelevant to discuss if this new surge in ethical practices and corporate social responsibility exposes a new mentality, the latest fad or even a sales strategy; the point is: a company that chooses this new strategy of positive restructuring will have an extra asset to maintain itself in a globalized and highly competitive market.[75]

Profit is still an important aspect of the company's activity, but its application must promote equity and social justice. This goal can be reached through an appropriate allocation of profit, by improving the quality of life of its collaborators and, consequently, of their families. The improvement in the quality of life of the local community and society as a whole are indirect, but important, consequences.

3.3.1 - From Ethics to Profit

Ethics are a significant issue related to social responsibility as a contributing factor to obtain, then allocate profit. To act ethically is to do good, combat weakness and cultivate virtues. The word comes from the Greek *ethos*, which means way of being, character.

Ethics describe a science of customs and intends to regulate the way human beings should live and be, translating a conscious and intuitive process that guides the choice between a vice or a virtue, good or evil, fair or unfair. Ethical practices

---

75 DUARTE, C. *Responsabilidade Social Empresarial: dimensões históricas e conceituais*. São Paulo: Editora Fundação Peirópolis, p. 31.

in corporate activity require disposition, political will and appropriate competences to make corporate actions concrete and objective, minimizing resistances and incomprehension.

Taking an ethical stand will build the reputation of a company and its brand; the brand's value is linked to the company's image. The example must be set in all fields in which they act, with no exception. Both the companies and, individually, the people that are part of it, must establish and follow behavior and attitude directives and parameters as a reference.

Corporate activity must abide by a body of values that guide a delimitation of the directives that must become habits and customs. Corporate ethics practices guide priorities while working towards the organization's objectives.

Even if a company does not have a formal ethics code, it still must have a body of principles and rules that guide its daily practices. Ethics must be upheld in relations with clients, suppliers, competitors, employees, and the government: that is, in all spheres, so profit is gained in the broadest context of productivity and social responsibility.

The first steps are: abandon the concept of profit at any price and the use of morally and legally baseless explanations for common unethical practices. To justify ethics in corporate activity, Newton de Lucca explains that:

> [. . .] how and when can we find, then, the philosophical justification for corporate ethics? It could be said, in a simple attempt to provide an answer, that corporate activity is, evidently, a profession. As it had been said, it is the economic activity organized for the production and circulation of goods and services. It is, therefore, a profession and, as such, needs its own body of ethical rules, just like judges, attorney, district attorneys, doctors and other professions have.
>
> The absolute importance of professional ethics is well known; it is a group of rules of conduct to which those who practice a certain activity should submit (or, at the very least, consider themselves under its purview). These behavior rules

— called deontological by many — distinguish themselves from general moral rules, because there the ethical standards must be higher for a company's activity than for ordinary pursuits, although in some circumstances, depending on the nature of the professional activity, these standards might even be lower.[76]

Ethics are concerned with universal value judgments, related to free people's activities; this is why it matters in the context of a study about obtaining profit while acting with social responsibility. Ethical responsibility is about the use of activities and policies that obey certain behavior rules, patterns and expectations consistent with collective and diffuse public interests — values that should fulfill appropriate social expectations and affect profit obtention and even the credibility of an organization.

In this regard, Paulo Rogério dos Santos Lima states that:

> [. . .] Economic agents' social actions cannot be based solely on citizenship actions and commitment to social projects plans and programs. Conducting business ethically is also part of a corporation's social responsibility. Being ethical is respecting the rights of all that interacts with the organization and, of course, of all of those with whom it has no connection. Being ethical is respecting existing moral patterns in the society of which the organization is a part. Being ethical is performing an economic function without illicit artifice to gain any sort of advantage. Being ethical is respecting the environment and protecting life, as we shall see later.[77]

But it is not just about influencing the local community or being seen with good eyes by society. Corporate organizations

---

76 LUCCA, N. *Da Ética Geral à Ética Empresarial*. São Paulo: Quartier Latin Editora, 2009, p. 341.
77 LIMA, P. *Op. Cit.*, p. 81.

must think about social responsibility. This writer believes that social responsibility is not only a businessperson's commitment to an ethical behavior pattern that contributes to economic development, a strategy to improve the quality of life of employees, their families and all society. Although social responsibility is, by nature, voluntary, that is, it comes from a businessperson's discretional act, it is still essential to implement human rights; the fruition of all its dimensions should be mandatory to all, whether it is a legal duty or not.

3.4 - Taxing Profit to Achieve Human Rights Effectiveness

One of the first experiences in Brazil on taxing profit occurred in 1944, when a tax on extraordinary profit was instituted, aiming to force companies to create a statutory reserve to change industrial equipment or regulate their stock, as well as neutralize inflation through reduction of people's purchasing power. Another goal was taxing war profits so part of them was used to benefit the community.

Government action on each of the economy sectors is also an important factor on obtaining and allocating profit. As an organized economic activity, corporations are subject to changes in financial, tax and political policies, as determined by the government.

In fact, the amount of taxes paid by a corporation is directly related to its profits and non-operating income and to concessions granted by the government when calculating the taxable amount and the applicable rate.

As José Luiz de Almeida Nogueira Porto states:

[...] Actions developed by the government in each of these sectors spurred certain movements of the time, that reflect in the company's profit, forcing them to continuously readjust to new conditions. A) Companies are directly affected the most by financial policies. Taxes elevate expenses and costs. Public loans generate a vaster search for available financial capital; it must be noted that the government offers indirect benefits to those who take their bonds, that corporations cannot offer, such as tax exemptions, tax relief and even interest payment in foreign currency which, in Brazil, is forbidden to private enterprises. When all these incentives are insufficient, the government appeals to compulsory loans and the companies themselves are compelled to subscribe said loans, when they are the government's competitors in the financial capital market. [. . .] Specific tributes, exemptions or reductions for certain activities might also hinder or encourage capital, labor and initiative embezzlement, from one sector to another or one place to another. Relatively moderate taxes on agricultural activities in Brazil intend to compensate for the fact that agriculture is less profitable. Tax exemptions for certain industries or activities are measures also commonly taken in several Brazilian towns, to attract companies to their territory. Fiscal policies are never neutral and taxes are, frequently, an instrument for government intervention, which can generate changes in the nation's economic structure, considered beneficial by the general public.[78]

Likewise, if there is internal currency depreciation that does not follow international depreciation, national production will suffer against foreign competition, which affects profit obtention directly. The government might still, according to global needs, encourage expansion in certain areas of the economy, by lowering or raising taxes.

Therefore, taxes are the cornerstone of actions taken to improve quality of life, as the government invests more in health, education, leisure and housing; that is, in all collective needs.

---

78 PORTO, P. *Op. Cit.*, pp. 185/188.

Thus, legislation that taxes profit, or not, as, for instance, income tax regulations and profit and result share programs are instruments to help implement human rights in all its dimensions.

Indeed, when obtention or allocation of profit are taxed or even when obtention is not, human rights are also implemented in all its dimensions, since profit aids economic development.

When profit, appropriately taxed or not, considers social well-being and the environment, it fulfills its social function and also the corporate social function which, as explained earlier, cannot be mistaken for social responsibility. When new taxes are created, generally, on environment exploration, for capital and profit remittance to a foreign country or on great wealth, the collectivity and the environment benefit. On the other hand, overtaxing accrued profits might prevent the company from reinvesting in the business (and from accruing profit), or even allocating it properly.

Therefore, taxing profits is a way to implement human rights in all its dimensions and it is an instrument in service of economic balance, social well-being and conservation of the environment.

3.5 - Sharing Profit through Corporate Activity and Employment

One of the ways of fraternally sharing accrued profit is through employees' participation in a company's results. The right to profit is primary and connected to the position of member, stockholder or owner of a corporation. This participation is an incentive for the improvement of economic organizations, making them better equipped to face competition.

The 1946 constitution of Brazil prescribed mandatory and direct participation of employees in the company's profits, but the rule was not immediately applicable. Participation in profits depended on a nonconstitutional law to be effective, and said law never came into force. Unlike the 1946 constitution, the 1967 and 1969 constitutions do not mention direct and mandatory participation: in the two latter, the economic-productivist conception, typical of capitalism, was adopted.

The 1988 constitution includes, among the rights of urban and rural workers, profit or result sharing, apart from remuneration and participation on the company's management. The Constitutional Plenary Session granted participation in company's management, exceptionally. The constitution can only bestow said participation as an exception, not a rule.

Recently, participation in profits was prescribed by provisional presidential decrees, although this is a discernibly inappropriate mechanism to regulate the issue. There is a nonconstitutional law about profit sharing: article 35 of Law 2004 of October 3rd, 1953, that grants the right to Petróleo Brasileiro S.A. (Petrobras) employees. Also, Provisional Presidential Decree 955/95 prescribes that profit sharing is not a substitute for or complement to any employee's remuneration, nor can it be used to calculate employment or social security charges, as it is not a habitual portion of the salary.

The regulation is flexible; unlike in older projects, there are not many conditional demands to the profit share programs. The legislator set guidelines, but left the content of the program to be established through collective negotiation between the company and a committee chosen by its employees. Considering the flexibility of Provisional Presidential Decree 955/95, any of the profit sharing criteria can be adopted by an agreement between the company and the representative committee. Profit participation will be decided by a committee that represents employees in general; to share specific results, though, the committee will be composed only by those with a direct interest in the production of the sector that set said goal.

Participation in results occurs when a specific operation fulfills its productivity quota, achieves product quality or a previously set goal. Participation can be related to productivity; employees will, then, gain some sort of benefit when they produce more than predicted, or also can be related to quality, in which case benefits will be granted when the product achieves a previously set quality standard; it can also be given when goals are reached and surpassed.

The first characteristic of results or incentives (elsewhere, a supplementary salary that aims to improve productivity) participation is complementarity, because it is never the only type of remuneration received; it must always be added to a salary.

The second characteristic is related to the workers' productivity, in quantity or quality. The first is a production incentive (collective) and, the second, a performance incentive (individual); employees that display assiduity, budget consciousness and other qualities may also receive an incentive.

All benefits, given when present the above-mentioned characteristics, are not part of the salary; they are participation programs, as incentives to goal achievement and productivity. These benefits may come in the form of goods, not necessarily money. The Brazilian Consolidation of Labor Laws expressly stated that participation does not need to be paid in cash; it can also be paid in goods. Programs for participation in results cannot be subjective; incentives must be conditioned to objective circumstances.

Profit sharing programs became an instrument for integration between capital and labor, as an incentive to productivity. Profit sharing is a social solution that connects the worker to the company's development; it does not, however, eliminate class warfare. The fact that employees have no control over business management or balance sheets shows, clearly, that participation cannot solve social issues on its own.

Profit sharing is an instrument for the conversion of an employee into a partner interested in the success of the company, not an antagonist. If profit sharing comes with participation in management, it will be a way of including the employee in the company's development. Considering profits are a gain, benefit or acquisition obtained through a certain activity and that depends of previously set goals that might be reached, it is important to highlight positive results and give the employees an opportunity to reap pecuniary benefits, also previously agreed upon.

Employees do not own the company's profit, since they are not the ones who assume the risk of corporate activity, which might yield positive or negative results. They will only share in positive results and have, thus, secondary participation rights. Employees will not suffer losses, as they are not associated with their employer. Only the company assumes the risks inherent to economic activity and, consequently, there shall be no sharing of negative results.

Few countries establish that employees must share in the company's profit. As an example, Bolivia, Chile, Ecuador, Mexico, Peru and Venezuela can be mentioned. In these instances, nonconstitutional legislation prescribes that, in case the employer obtains profit by the end of a certain fiscal year, a portion of it must be shared with the employees. In other countries, if there is profit sharing, it is based on collective bargaining agreements or by a decision from the board of directors.

Professor Sérgio Pinto Martins did extensive comparative law research on the subject, and teaches that:

> [. . .] In Germany, collective agreements establish periodic profit sharing, as there is no law on the subject. The Incentive to Build Employee's Wealth Law (*Drittes Gesetzes zur Förderung der Vermögensbildung der Arbeitnehmer*) from 1975, altered in 8/16/77 establishes in article 7 to 11 just one form of participation in results (*Ergebnisbeteiligung*), as long as there are material savings, waste reduction, better time management and better work methods. [. . .] Argentina. Article 14 "bis" of the Argentinian constitution prescribes, as a right, "participation in the profits of enterprises, with control of production and collaboration in the management." Decree 390/76, which regulates Law 21.297,

establishes that profit sharing is a type of remuneration (article 104); it is a complementary or supplementary salary, an addition, as a result of labor, but it cannot be the only form of employment remuneration. [. . .] Austria. Austrian law prescribes different types of remuneration, including profit sharing (*Gewinnbeteiligung*). However, in this country there is a reward (*Tantieme*) to members of the executive boards and high-level executives (*leitende Angestellte*). Profit can be shared among all the company's employees, or just part of them. [. . .] Belgium. Belgium does not exactly have a system of participation in profits, because the National Social Security Institute demands a contribution of part of the distributed amount. However, they have a system of participation on the capital through stock options. The stock acquired by an employee can only be negotiated after five years [. . .] Bolivia. A law of 11/21/24, part of the 1942 Labor Law, establishes that employers must pay their employees an annual incentive (*prima anual*), as long as the company has turned a profit at the end of the fiscal year, corresponding to a fraction of the salary of manual and non-manual laborers, never less than a full month's salary. (Article 57 of the 1942 law). [. . .] Costa Rica. Article 164 of the Labor Code of 1943 expressly prescribes that profit participation is a form of salary. [. . .] Ecuador. The percentage employers receive on the profits is 7% of the net profit (Decree of 12/2/48). It is owed to all employees, from manual laborers to executives in higher positions, in proportion to their salary. The employee, however, will receive only 5% of their share; the rest is deposited in their name in a fund that finances social assistance programs that benefit the employees. [. . .] Spain. The Spanish constitution of 12/9/31 prescribed, in article 46, "the participation of workers in management, administration and the benefits of businesses." Currently, Montoya Melgar (1978, 335) believes that profit sharing is part of the salary, since it is only a portion or all the payment received from the employer to the employee. [. . .] Chile. Article 55 of Decree 2.200 of

5/1/78 establishes that for-profit companies that obtain profit must pay bonuses to their employees, consisting in no less than 30% of said profits or surplus. The participation will be distributed proportionally to time of service, in each annual period. [. . .] Colombia. Article 127 of the Substantive Labor Code defines salary and includes profit participation as one of its types (*participación de utilidades*). Article 28 elucidates that the worker will receive a share of the profits, but does not assume the risks or losses inherent to corporate activity. The year-end bonus, that is based in profit sharing, is mandatory *prima anual ou prima de servícios*) [. . .] Japan. In Japan, there is a biannual bonus linked to the company's profitability. This bonus equals about 20 to 25% of each employee's total salary. [. . .] Mexico. Profit is calculated from taxable income, according to internal revenue legislation. Profit participation is divided in two: half, in equal shares among workers, according to the number of days each worked during the year. The other half is distributed in proportion to salaries, minus eventual supplements. [. . .] Panama. The 1946 constitution does not establish profit sharing, but it states that the law can prescribe said benefit, according to the country's economic health. Article 13 of Law 8, of 4/30/81 states that participation in profit established by law or [. . .] Peru. The current constitution of 1979, states in article 56 that the government recognizes the right of workers to participate in the company's management. Thirty percent of the profit accrued by the end of the fiscal year must be distributed among employees. Profit is shared according to the company's activity: (a) 4% in mining, (b) 8% in fishing, (c) 10% in the telecommunication industry. All employees receive in proportion to the time they have been providing their services in each fiscal year. [. . .] Portugal. Article 262 of the Labor Code states that "participation in the company's profit is not considered part of the salary, as long as the employee's contract guarantees certain, variable or [. . .] Switzerland. Article 322, item 1 of the Obligations Code states that if a worker is entitled to participate in the profits, the amount will be calculated based on the result of the fiscal year. Several times, workers receive, along with their salary, additional remuneration, which is called result or production gratuity. The amount paid, based on the total of the result of the business is called participation on the results of the enterprise. [. . .] Turkey. Article 323 of the Obligations Code prescribes that, if it is stipulated that part of the profits must be added to salaries, the employer must provide employees with information on the gains or losses and allow them to examine the company's books. The supplement is considered to be part of the salary, but cannot be the employee's only remuneration. [. . .] Uruguay. Uruguayan legislation does not mention participation in profits. However, it is understood that the payment is a matter of the employer's liberality and will be due once a year. This remuneration cannot substitute the employee's salary. If it is paid habitually, it will become part of the salary. [. . .] Venezuela Article 87 of the 1961 constitution mentions profit participation, which must be in established by law. The 1975 *Ley del Trabajo* states, in article 82, that every company must distribute to the employees 10% of the net profits, subtracting from the gross profit the company's general expenses, interest from capital, which is limited to 6% per year and 10% destined to the reserve fund.[79]

There are several ways in which a company's collaborators can participate in the profits: (i) partially, if only some of the employees are entitled to it; (ii) fully, if all employees are entitled to receive the benefit, regardless of having achieved the company's goals; (iii) individually or collectively, when participation is directed to one person or group with specific characteristics; (iv) current or deferred, when the profit participation is set for the future; (v) immediate or monthly, depending on how results are calculated.

---

79 MARTINS, S. *Participação dos Empregados nos Lucros das Empresas. Op. Cit.*, pp. 11/23.

Either way, to distribute profits, that is, to share profits with employees, the company's results have to be positive. In this regard, profit distribution among employees cannot be mistaken for annual bonuses or gratuities not linked to accrued profit. Likewise, participation in social profits is not the same as a salary bonus. Indeed, some countries establish the payment of an extra bonus, but it has a different legal nature.

Still on this subject, participating in profits is not the same as participating in management, nor is it equal to gratuities, premiums, commissions, tips, piece rates and productivity incentives. Although all forms of remuneration are paid to workers, their origins and motivation come from the existence of frequency in the payment or not, which is completely different from other institutes, as the name of each forms of payment clearly states. Universal treaties and declarations (such as, for instance, The Universal Declaration of Rights of Man) do not establish rules for the employee's participation in social profits.

The first document that mentioned employee profit sharing was a Napoleonic decree from October 1812, which regulated the participation of Comédie Française actors in the profits of the Théâtre Français.

In Brazil, since the 1946 constitution, there have been several attempts to turn employee profit sharing into a law.[80] However, the implications are not only on labor law but, to say the least, also in corporate, civil and tax law.

Some companies pay annually their employees for participation in the social profits, which makes said payment habitual. In this case, the Superior Courts have understood that it constitutes habitual remuneration, whether by a percentage or

80 Several bills have been proposed, such as: 2.403/76, by Antunes de Oliveira; 4.397/77, by Octávio Ceccato; 5.606/78, by José Zavaglia; 332/79, by Humberto Lucena; 410/79, by Getúlio Dias; 86/79, by Jorge Arbage; 1.195/79, by Celso Peçanha; 1.209/79, by Antônio Zacharias; 1.399/79, by Freitas Diniz; 1.400/79, by João Faustino; 1.840/79, by Moacir Lopes; 4.480/81, by Benedito Marcílio; 5.232/85; by Raul Bernardo; 8.411/86, by Floriceno Paixão; 1.090/88, de Francisco Amaral.

any other improper gratuity method, which is why Precedent 251 of the Superior Labor Court states that "participation in a company's profit, when paid habitually, is to be considered as part of the salary, for all legal effects."

It must be noted that, if a company accrues profit in several consecutive fiscal years and pays the employees, whether based on a percentage or not, said payment is part of the salary, for all legal effects. Article 7, item XI of the constitution states that "participation in the profits or results, independent of wages, and, exceptionally, participation in the management of the company, defined by law." As has been stated, the words profit and results are not synonymous; they have absolutely distinct connotations, which is why the legislator chose to add "or results."

As to the possibility of immediate applicability of item XI, Sergio Pinto Martins says that:

> [...] There are three theories about the immediate applicability of art 7, item XI of the constitution: The first theory states that the part that mentions the independence of wages is immediately applicable, and would not need a supplementary law. The second theory complements the first and asserts that only participation on management needs a specific law, but not participation on profit or results. The third claims there is a need for a specific law to make item XI immediately applicable. [...] This writer understands, however, that all of article 7, item XI of the constitution does need to be regulated by nonconstitutional law, not just part of it. Therefore, if a company had shared profits with its employees before the regulating law, the old Precedent 251 of the Superior Labor Court applies: if the participation in a company's profit is paid habitually, it will be considered as part of the salary, for all legal effects, including the calculations for the Guarantee Fund for Length of Service (FGTS) and social security contributions. If understood otherwise and there were no need for a regulatory law, it could pave the way for fraud, because the em-

ployer could create fake payments, labeled as profit participation, just so they would not be included in the salary, so taxes over the extra amount would not have to be paid. Article 28, paragraph 9, item j of Law 8.212/91 (Social Security Funding Law) gave the correct interpretation to the issue, saying that social security contribution will be taken from profit sharing amounts only when a specific law comes into force. It is an authentic interpretation, by a legislator, of the constitutional rule in article 7, item XI. [81]

Law 10.101, of December 19, 2000, states in article 1 that: "this law regulates workers' participation in the company's profits or results as instrument for the integration of capital and labor and inducement for productivity, as stated by article 7, item XI of the constitution."
And continues, in article 2:

[. . .] Participation in profits or results must be negotiated between the company and its employees, through the procedure described next, chosen by the parties through mutual agreement: I - a committee, chosen by the parties, including a representative nominated by the category's union; II - collective labor agreement. Paragraph 1 - the documents resulting from the negotiation must include clear and objective rules, setting substantive rights to participation and adjective rules, including mechanisms for obtaining information to monitor compliance to the agreement, frequency of distribution, effective dates and agreement revision dates. The following criteria and conditions, among others, may be considered: I - productivity, quality or profitability indexes; II - previously agreed goals, results and due dates programs."

The Brazilian's legislator concern with productivity, quality or profitability indexes and goals, and programs for results

---

81 MARTINS, S. *Op. Cit.*, pp. 79/83.

and due dates must be emphasized. Specifically, because participation payment for employees is connected to profit obtention, regardless of how habitual it is.

Tax incentives on workers' participation on social results, even if habitual, will be, undoubtedly, one of the ways of fraternizing the company's results and, therefore, an effective way to deal positively with profit obtention or positive social results, in all its forms.

If a company is healthy, that is, their costs of production of goods and services are balanced, obtaining profit not only can, but must be habitual, just as employee participation, even if it is not part of their salaries.

There are several advantages in distributing profit to a certain company's collaborators, including making labor laws more flexible and granting higher efficiency to the company's organized activity. However, the greatest advantage in fraternally sharing profit is that it might help social responsibility develop.

Sérgio Pinto Martins lists some advantages to employee participation in social profits:

> [...] These are the advantages to profit participation: introducing a system that makes labor rights more flexible; higher efficiency for the company or its recovery and better capacity for growth; better integration of worker in the company, with a consequent increase in productivity; incentives to productivity and job stability; for companies that want to pay said participation there would no longer be FGTS and social security taxation, neither would the participation be part of the salary, as it is unlinked to remuneration; a way to introduce variable or flexible salaries, that would also involve the worker's performance to achieve the company's objectives; participation in profit creates a favorable psychological environment, with harmony between capital and labor; development of management improvement ideas to adapt to competition existent in a globalized economy; incentives to production that create a climate of reciprocity between employee and employer, which

can only bring benefits and gain to the company. It would generate lower taxes to the company, as they would be able to pay an employee a fixed, lower salary and a variable, possibly higher salary. That would mean a reduction in the company's fixed costs and a decrease in the price of its final product; the remuneration aspect could guarantee jobs, more hiring, a decrease in unemployment, and maybe even lower inflation; it could also be a way to ensure the company's survival.[82]

Therefore, it is undeniable that one of the ways of fraternally sharing profit accrued by a company is through employee participation in its product. It is a form of treating profit positively and, thus, an incentive to obtaining it fraternally.

However, employee participation cannot be used as a way to make them bear the risks inherent to the business, nor is it meant to compensate for low salaries; its objective is to allocate a company's positive results in a more effective way, encouraging a repeated pattern of positive results and an expanded fraternity chain.

3.6 - Interruption of Corporate Activity and of Profit Sharing as a Human Rights Violation

Corporate activity and respective profits depend, of course, on the existence of the company and the conservation of its economic activity; there is also a social interest in the existence of said activity, which generates jobs and income.

Indeed, a company in operation generates countless direct and indirect jobs, stimulating the economy and improving the quality of life of a specific group of people and those who depend on the company for their survival (not only employees, but also service providers and suppliers). Therefore, abruptly interrupting corporate activity, whether by the company's bank-

---

82 *Op. Cit.*, pp. 109/110.

ruptcy or other reasons, will cause the loss of several jobs and fewer taxes will be collected, among other consequences.

It is not without reason, then, that the Reorganization Law of Brazil states clearly that its main purpose is to keep the company in activity, as expressly established by article 47 of Law 11.101/05: "the process of reorganization aims to help the debtor overcome its economic-financial crisis and protect its production, employees' jobs and creditors' interests, promoting, thus, the company's preservation, its social function and its incentives to economic activity."

Indeed, interruption of corporate activity has several negative consequences, not only to the members and stockholders, but also to direct and indirect collaborators. Depending on company's importance in a certain region, its bankruptcy or even the interruption of its activities can affect the economy of a community or even of the whole area.

Preservation and continuity of the company, therefore, are relevant to human rights and, as such, should be a concern to all, from the businessperson to the government and all people. On the other hand, it is undeniable that, the larger the corporate activity risk, the higher is the probability of gaining profit in a large scale.

In this regard, Alan Greenspan states that:

[...] The greater the economic freedom, the greater the scope for business risk and its reward, profit and thus the greater the inclination to take risk. Societies that comprise risk takers form governments whose rules foster economically productive risk taking: property rights, open trade, and open opportunities. They have laws that offer few regulatory benefits that government officials can sell or exchange for cash or political favors. The index measures a country's degree of conscious effort to restrict competitive markets. The rankings are thus not necessarily a measure of economic "success," as each nation, over the long run through its policies and laws, chooses the degree of economic freedom it wants.

[...]
Thus, we are left with a critical question: granted that open competitive markets foster economic growth, is there an optimum trade-off between economic performance and the competitive stress it imposes on the one hand, and the civility that, for example, the continental Europeans and many others espouse? Many Europeans contemptuously brand America's economic regime "cowboy capitalism." Highly competitive free markets are viewed as obsessively materialistic and largely lacking in meaningful cultural values.[83]

Chances must be taken in corporate activity responsibly and not in an unrestrained manner, as to not risk the loss of several jobs and the nonpayment of corporate taxes, among other consequences. Therefore, it must be concluded that interrupting a company's activities and profit gain is a way to violate the human rights of the people who depend on it.

In this regard, in case the corporate activity respects all dimensions of human rights, the company's actions must count as a reason to preserve its existence by, for instance, deferring the reorganization, so profit can be accrued responsibly and respecting the premises herein mentioned.

There are several examples of companies that paralyzed their activities and precipitated a domino effect in the economy of a certain area, by not only harming their employees, who sometimes cannot even receive their labor rights, but also suppliers and transporters that make a living from the local economy, even inducing them to migrate. Accordingly, a for-profit company that protects all dimensions of human rights must be preserved.

Thus, it must be noted that human rights effectiveness through profit obtention happens in several levels, from measures taken to gain said profit, to the allocation of the positive results.

---

83 GREENSPAN, A. *The Age of Turbulence. Op. Cit.*, pp. 276/277.

CHAPTER IV - PROFIT AND CAPITALISM

4.1 - Capitalism and Profit Allocation

Free initiative and private property are capitalism's pillars for the obtention of profit, a procedure allowed by the system. However, it is unacceptable that capital should only be transformed into more capital, without considering human beings and improving their quality of life.

Following this line of thought, we have seen that profit, when effectively obtained and/or allocated, is an instrument for the implementation of human rights in all its dimensions. When discussing human rights, it is especially difficult to forget the constitutional focus on humanist capitalism; that is, of the capitalist-humanistic regime adopted by the Brazilian constitution.

Therefore, another facet of profit as an instrument for the implementation of human rights emerges: the appropriate obtention and allocation of profit makes equality, freedom and fraternity effective, as well, all due to human rights in the capitalist system, seen from a humanistic angle.

Although capitalism founded economic liberalism and brought development, it has not shown itself to be a perfect system; it is liable to collapse and cannot solve the main problems that affect human beings on the planet. Especially during the 1920s, market activities could not avoid a crisis that seemed chronic and lowered employment levels, generating a lack of job positions. However, even with the possible crises, the capitalist production system still dominated most of the countries on the planet, in several historical and social formations, going through transformations whenever necessary to obtain a higher profit margin.

The market economy that took over the world was not enough, in itself, to balance economic relations, nor to bring only benefits to humankind; government intervention in the economic order became progressively more necessary to prevent world crises from causing destructive effects to human beings. From the 20th century on, the government began to inject capital into the economy through expenditures, in prevention against private investment crises.

With time and as a consequence, capitalism developed into a system under state-controlled finances, labor and prices, while the government became the biggest buyer in the market, from armaments, ammunition and provisions for the army, to essential supplies for the general population. This scenario, seen in World War II, was much wider in scope than during World War I.

The years following the end of World War II were a starting point for the unique path the capitalist system took. Suffering from the consequences of war, several countries rebuilt their productive base using the financing and expansion plans from the military economy. This economy era was even called "the thirty glorious years" of capitalism, as economic growth was strong and continuous in several parts of the world.

These days, the so-called economic globalization allegedly brought more economic development, without, however, setting human well-being and dignity as its goal and privileging only one way of increasing profit by opening markets worldwide and setting prices, also in a global scale.

In this regard, Alan Greenspan states that:

> [...] The problem is that the dynamic that defines capitalism, that of unforgiving market competition, clashes with the human desire for stability and certainty. Even more important, a large segment of society feels a growing sense of injustice

about the allocation of capitalism's rewards. Competition, capitalism's greatest force, creates anxiety in all of us. One major source of it is the chronic fear of job loss. Another, more deeply felt angst stems from competition's perpetual disturbance of the status quo and style of living, good or bad, from which most people derive comfort.

[...]

I never thought kindly of rival firms seeking to lure clients from Townsend-Greenspan. But to compete, I had to improve. I had to offer a better service. I had to become more productive. In the end, of course, I was better off for it. So were my clients, and I suspect so were my competitors as well. Down deep that is probably the message of capitalism: "creative destruction" — the scrapping of old technologies and old ways of doing things for the new — is the only way to increase productivity and therefore the only way to raise average living standards on a sustained basis. Finding gold or other natural wealth, history tells us, does not do that.

There is no denying capitalism's record. Market economies have succeeded over the centuries by thoroughly weeding out the inefficient and poorly equipped, and by granting rewards to those who anticipate consumer demand and meet it with the most efficient use of labor and capital resources.[84]

Globalization is nothing more than an attempt to set prices all over the world, in search of higher profit margins, by creating an international market. Thomas Jefferson's famous words bear repeating: "The selfish spirit of commerce knows no country, and feels no passion or principle but that of gain."

Therefore, only by appropriately allocating profit for the good of humankind and within multidimensional human rights parameters, can capitalism be humanized and fraternal, albeit globalized. Capitalism demands some conditions to get established and prosper; the government, which might be hostile or agreeable, according to its powers of resistance, draws these conditions.

---

84 GREENSPAN, A. *Op. Cit.*, pp. 268/269.

The future of capitalism truly materialized in the field of social hierarchies, among them military, religious and political. Western societies all have one point in common: lower classes, or the non-dominant bourgeoisie, through time (sometimes, centuries), maintain a parasitic relationship with the dominant classes, living next to them, profiting from their mistakes and taking advantage of their consumption habits, indolence and improvidence. Even with new generations always willing to emerge, the process is endless.

This is why it is essential that capitalism harmonize private initiative and property with all dimensions of human rights, including in the obtention and allocation of profit.

4.2 - Capitalism in Brazil and Profit

The owners of the means of production organized Brazil's mercantile production; back then, workers were slaves or serfs. Up to the beginning of the 20th century, market economy was marked by the need for subsistence, since people's lives, in general, depended on domestic economy; often, even clothing was produced at their homes.

The period when the crisis in colonial economy started was, also, the moment when the mercantile economy in the country emerged, based on coffee plantations and slave labor. In this regard, it can be said that both slavery and mercantile production, which was no longer colonial, gained new strength. This revitalization affected the whole country's economy.

The implementation of the slave industry had little chance of success after the coffee oligarchy-slavery economy crisis occurred. Another factor was that local economy began to suffer intensely from foreign influence; for instance, Brazil was forbidden from making cloth in 1785, which benefited Portuguese commercial capitals that imported British fabrics to the country.

In this context, the effects of the industrial revolution

reach Brazil and change the past concept of profit. Profit used to be understood as the business owner's revenue for running a business, minus expenses. However, we do not believe this is the correct way to define profit. Profit is not revenue, much less to the owner of the business. Quite contrary; profit comes from improving the production technique of a good or service, and must benefit all who contributed to the company's purpose, including stockholders or members. Therefore, although not all will become members or stockholders of a corporation, it is possible to adequately and effectively allocate profit, so the community can benefit, albeit indirectly and not in the same proportion as stockholders or members.

It was not what happened in Brazil at the time.

On the other hand, this writer believes the issue of obtention or not of profit should be unlinked to the existence of social classes, because if profit obtention comes in fraternal way to benefit a community (albeit indirectly and in different proportions), the existence of social classes will make no difference, then. In this regard, Alan Greenspan's assessment of how a local culture can influence wealth accumulation and distribution among all social classes is especially pertinent:

> [...] Positive attitudes toward business success, for example, a deeply cultural response, have in the course of generations been an important springboard to material well-being. Clearly, a society with such attitudes will give enterprises far greater freedom to compete than a society that perceives competitive business as unethical or unsettling. In my experience, even many of those who acknowledge the advantages to material well-being of competitive capitalism are conflicted for two somewhat related reasons. First, competition and risk taking cause stress, which most people wish to avoid; second, many feel deep-seated ambivalence toward the accumulation of wealth.
> [...]
> The purpose of the welfare state is to lessen that income and

wealth concentration, which it does largely through legislation that, via regulation, constrains risk taking and, via taxation, reduces the pecuniary rewards that may result from taking risks.[85]

The idea that the dominant classes are entitled to accrue more profit than others must be substituted by the concept of possibly benefiting the collectivity, regardless of their social class.

Obtaining profit just for profit is not what the 21st century solidly established as a social factor. There are several examples of socially responsible companies, who obtain profit that benefits not only their organized corporate activity, but also the collectivity, that can also benefit from capital reinvestment that makes the company self-sustainable or from social capitalization — a kind of social security in times of crises, to avoid the need for layoffs when the company is not turning a profit, for instance. There is, yet, the possibility to accrue profit through speculation, but it is not consistent with the company's social function or social responsibility.

At any rate, profit is essential to maintain a healthy company; a private entity's survival is closely connected to its ability to turn a profit. If this ability disappears, the company might not be capable of fulfilling its corporate purpose. In a capitalist system, without profit, workers lose their jobs, cities decline, rural areas decay and no further development happens.

In a socialist system, for instance, the absence of profit affects free initiative and innovation, which implies stagnation and a substantial technological slowdown. However, profit must be obtained responsibly and without misuse. Profit is misused when it exceeds the governmental rule established by previous law. It is important, for this reason, to observe what nonconstitutional legislation states about profit accrual and analyze if it is compatible with the multidimensional incidence of human rights.

---

85 *Op. Cit.* p. 272.

In Brazil's case, profit comes from economic activity within a capitalist system, but it is a humanized capitalist system, in which the economic order's main rule is stated in article 170 of the constitution, in harmony with principles expressed in articles 1 and 3.

4.3 - Humanistic Capitalism and Profit

If the legal structure of capitalism in Brazil is correctly analyzed, it becomes clear that the constitutional dictates on the economic system are not compatible with liberal capitalism, nor is the system adopted the capitalism that guides economic globalization; it is humanistic capitalism, one that recognizes the supremacy of human rights over the national legal order, under a humanistic perspective of economic law.

This is the theoretical bedrock of humanistic capitalism, which is based on legal-humanistic philosophy and believes that strengthening the structures of freedom, equality and fraternity is a support for capitalism in humankind's benefit. The Universal Fraternity Law is a legal theory applied to capitalism; its main tenets are love thy neighbor, represented by the love of Jesus Christ as a symbol of Christian humanity and "we are brothers, connected to everything and everyone," as says Ricardo Sayeg.[86]

In the Universal Declaration of the Rights of Man is the synthesis of this legal line of thought and of the legal analysis through which its principles protect human dignity, a constitutional principle currently prescribed in article 1, III of the constitution.

Traditional capitalism, founded on a free market economy, mas not enough to make peoples' lives better. Neoliberalism, in particular, brought back Adam Smith and David Ri-

---

86 SAYEG, R.; BALERA, W. *Humanistic Capitalism*. Petrópolis: KBR, 2011, p. 21.

cardo's theories, based on individualism, lack of fraternity and economic efficiency thinking. Humanistic philosophy, however, accepts the Universal Fraternity Law and transports it to economic law, contending capitalism and its problems deserve being solved by fraternity.

Indeed, humanistic philosophy applied to economic law reconciles negative freedoms with responsibility to others; that is, it applies fraternity to juridical and economic relations as a legal, not just moral, obligation for those who perform economic activities to always balance individual interests with the common good.

Consequently, to fraternize the allocation of profit against social exclusion, humanistic philosophy applied to economic law and capitalism is an answer, especially in its position that fraternity is a legal obligation for all (government, civil society and all men)

In fact, from a wholly humanistic perspective of law, based on fraternity and Christian thinking, the humanistic doctrine reaffirms respect for human rights in all its dimensions and applies them to the law, integrating them with economic law all of the 1988 Federative Constitution of Brazil's principles, which are based in a capitalist-humanistic view.[87]

Ergo, the importance of respecting human dignity, well-being for all and the need to minimize inequalities by applying all dimensions of human rights in practice.

Indeed, although capitalism won global economy, we know that the greatest problems of humankind, such as hunger, poverty and epidemics, have not been overcome; one thing

---

87 According to Sayeg, "Such is the Humanistic philosophy of the Economic Law. Simply put, it is about bringing the Law of Universal Fraternity into the Economic Law. This is what we propose here, for it would certainly constitute a new theoretical framework according to which we would analyze Capitalism from a judicial standpoint, whose objective within the economic field is to find solutions through fraternity and, while taking into consideration the three subjective dimensions of Human Rights, the dialectic tension between liberty and equality." *Op. Cit*, 25/26.

is certain, though: adopting this economic regime contributed to the development of man and can serve as an instrument to improve humankind. To achieve this purpose in this theoretical and philosophical context, the constitutional legal instrument that can be applied to capitalism is legal fraternity, applicable to profit as a supreme constitutional value.

The preamble of the constitution states that:

[. . .] We, the representatives of the Brazilian People, convened in the National Constituent Assembly to institute a democratic state for the purpose of ensuring the exercise of social and individual rights, liberty, security, well-being, development, equality and justice as supreme values of a *fraternal*, pluralist and unprejudiced society, founded on social harmony and committed, in the internal and international orders, to the peaceful settlement of disputes, promulgate, under the protection of God, this Constitution of the Federative Republic of Brazil. (Italics by the author).

Fraternal societies and their respective fraternalism are nothing more than the Universal Law of Fraternity implemented in legal relations, so human rights are applicable in all its dimensions, that is, in the "spirit of brotherhood," as stated in article 1 of the Universal Declaration of the Rights of Man. This is legal humanism, which, if applied to capitalism, will consolidate the issue in practice, as states Ricardo Sayeg: "Thus, as far as a Capitalism based on liberty is concerned, the Human Rights mission becomes clear: To reflect its multidimensional nature, from a consolidation perspective, in order to have it recognized and added to equality and fraternity."[88]

A natural duty of fraternity is embedded in capitalism, then, demanded of all human beings, in benefit of all human beings.[89]

---

88 SAYEG, R.; BALERA, W. *Op. Cit.*, p. 34.
89 According to Sayeg, "By implication, Man, Mankind, and the Planet must

In the economic sphere, the integration between the capitalist system adopted by the Federative Constitution and fraternity is prescribed in the guiding rule of economic law set in article 170 of the constitution. Indeed, it is to be concluded in light of the Universal Fraternity Law that the objectives of the economic order, especially the guarante of a dignified existence, in accordance to the precepts of social justice, are themes associated with solidarity and fraternity, according to the guiding rule of the economic order in the constitution, simultaneously materializing, in practice, human rights of first, second and third dimensions.

In conclusion, fraternity must be seen as legal obligation for economic activities, not solely a moral virtue. And when considering profit, if part of it is destined to the excluded and the planet, automatically all dimensions of human rights will materialize.

Profit, when appropriately allocated, grant dignity to human beings that live in a humanized capitalist system and respect the pertinent human rights. In other words, sharing profits fraternally, therefore, is a consequence of humanistic and three-dimensional economic law, which puts capital in service of man and not the other way around.

It is in human dignity and the spirit of brotherhood, constitutional principles that guide all economic activity, that lie the boundaries to forbid the pursuit of profit just for itself; it is a checks and balances system to guarantee that profit will work in service of all dimensions of human rights and is compatible to the humanistic capitalism of the constitution.

be fraternally protected, thus the realization of Human Rights in all their dimensions within Capitalism arises of a natural duty to Fraternity, as the subjective natural right that benefits the destitute, in special, and is demanded not only of the State, but also horizontally of civil society and every Men to encompass all private individual relations." *Op. Cit*, p. 237.

4.4 - Human Dignity and Fraternity through Profit

Human dignity is a person's attribute and exists solely because the person exists; it demands respect, not only from the government, but also from society, to guarantee a healthy existence, in the broadest possible way.

In this regard, Ingo Sarlet asseverates:

> [. . .] human dignity is the intrinsic and distinctive quality recognized in all human beings that make them deserve the same respect and consideration from the government and the community, enclosing a system of fundamental rights and duties that protect the person against any and all degrading and inhuman treatment and guarantee all basic existential conditions for a healthy life, also providing and promoting their active and co-responsible participation in their own destinies and life in communion with all other human beings.[90]

From the above quote, a clear concern emerges: the recognition of rights constitutionally guaranteed, not only by the government, but also society, as a characteristic of an inalienable human right and relevant fact to be considered in legal transactions, although those are typically a private law matter.

In this regard, it is possible to extract a stimulating function, not only in obtaining profit to promote a business, but also open new companies, without harming the human dignity principle; on the contrary, by respecting its dictates and peculiarities as a constitutional principle.

Finding a unanimous, concise and universally valid definition for human dignity is a huge challenge. Reason must be used, and its relationship with the human condition itself, since the complex system of the legal-constitutional order demands protection and acknowledgment.

---

90 SARLET, I. *Dignidade da Pessoa Humana e Direitos Fundamentais na Constituição de 1988. Op. Cit.,* p. 67.

Carlos Ayres Britto asserts that:

> [. . .] all the historical and formal proclamations stating human beings have an "innate" dignity is the law itself recognizing that humanity lives in each of us and is the logical bedrock or legitimating document of said dignity; to the law there is no other role, but to acknowledge it. Not to grant dignity, because it has always existed in all of us.
>
> In other words, the humanity in us all is what grants exceptional dignity. Dignity recognized by law as a factor of legitimacy within itself and a cornerstone of government and society.[91]

However, human dignity cannot be the reason for extremist and unfounded actions by those who allegedly defend fundamental rights. Some believe that understanding and applying these rights is like "a dam preventing the free flow of fundamentalism," working as a lasting barrier against those who violate human rights.

According to this line of thought, civilization and humanization of economic globalization will result in the reduction or even neutralization of evils that cause human rights violations; these ideals could be presented worldwide if there was a globalization of the legal system, with human dignity as a starting point.

It can be said that members of the communitarian and legal orders that do not respect the quality, values, duties and rights attributed to human beings do not respect their own humanity, nation and their own beating heart and do not deserve reciprocal respect and care. The commitment level of each member of the world's society is directly connected to the success in respecting the human rights function in the above-mentioned legal globalization.

---

91 BRITTO, C. *O Humanismo como Categoria Constitucional*. Belo Horizonte: Editora Forum, 2010, pp. 25/26.

Just as we noticed this close connection between the function of human rights and every person's commitment, there is another connection between the most varied conceptions of human dignity, from several religions and beliefs; there is even a "civil religion" that reins in evident extremism, but not as a result of moral, ethical, religious or political extremism.

Ergo, believing that profit may be obtained or allocated while violating human rights is the same as considering human beings less important than profit, which contradicts the whole humanistic economic and fraternal system established in the constitution.

4.5 - Fraternity in the Obtention and Allocation of Profit.

Based on these theoretical landmarks of humanistic capitalism, the best solution to make profit compatible with the humanistic capitalist system is through fraternity and solidarity when obtaining and allocating profit.

4.5.1 - Fraternity in All its Meanings

Fraternity is the acknowledgment of the essential rights of human beings (creatures of God), extending said knowledge to other people. The ethics of fraternity are the study and practice of human beings' essential rights, which have humanitarianism and good as a goal.

The Fraternity Law is the Law of God that unites us and makes no distinction of race, social class, culture or belief, among others. The more people evolve, the more they understand the fraternity law and their perception of universal fraternity deepens.

Fraternity is giving unto others what we would like to

have and eliminating economic and social inequalities. According to the Gospel, those who do not embrace fraternity and do not treat others as brothers will be treated the same way, whether in actions or thoughts, since we can often repudiate events.

Agnes Bernhard defines fraternity like so:

> [. . .] according to general opinion, the concept of fraternity is connected to the freedom and equality principles, which are protected by the constitution of all modern governments. The concept of fraternity assumes that all men have the right to individual freedom and equality, and establishes a mutually interdependent relation with these principles. The roots of these three concepts are in human dignity. The attained objective of protecting human rights as a legal guarantee to each individual should work — according to the definition of fraternity — as a minimal assurance to each individual, at each time and place, including social rights. From the concept of fraternity, one can reflect in a completely new way — considering the connection to the principles of freedom and equality — on the bedrock of fundamental rights and rights in general. Those fundamental rights, when analyzed from the viewpoint of fraternity, embrace their meaning, not as a good attributed to an individual, but as an ability to create order among individuals and groups. Freedom, property or equality are relevant rights only if they organize relations among men and are defined in this plural context. Some authors criticize the exclusively individualistic nature of human rights. Others call fundamental rights "relational rights." René-Jean Dupuy noted that, gradually, we realize we all belong to a same human family and that the legal protection of human rights is not limited only to our own rights, but of others, as well. Cohen-Jonathan claims a broader view of man is necessary; one that considers any offense to one as an offense to all. This concept of fraternity also includes solidarity and equity.[92]

---

92 In: CASO, G. *Direito & Fraternidade: ensaios, prática forense. Op. Cit.*,

In this regard, Fausto Goria asserts that:

> [. . .] this fraternity may consist, for example, of listening to the opposing party to understand all their demands — in a private law context — whether in pre-contractual negotiations or while the contract is being fulfilled or in general, in a relationship (for instance, in labor relations, work by the job and even in matrimonial crises), or in a lawsuit. Several times, this attitude induced the opposing party to act in the same way, to mutual advantage. Considering a legal or public organization, if a public servant acts in a fraternal way, they will be able to use their powers to meet demands, even if minimal or contingencies, of interested parties.[93]

In this context, profit will be considered positive when obtained and allocated in a good way, as it will be another instrument for the common good, decreasing social and economic inequalities.

4.5.2 - Fraternity or Solidarity Principle

The French Revolution equality and freedom ideals, achieved by the revolutionaries, may be seen in several modern rights, such as universal suffrage, a constitutional order, the end of privileges to clergy and nobility and less state interference in private relations. However, the French did not value one of their revolution's ideals, fraternity. In their 1791 constitution, fraternity is mentioned, but merely as a civil virtue, not a principle. In 1848, when drafting a new constitution, fraternity was officially declared as part of the wider scope of their concept of solidarity.

In the Universal Declaration of Human Rights of 1948, fraternity is set as an essential human rights principle,

---

pp. 61/62.
93 *Op. Cit.*: pp. 28/29.

a guide to economic and social rights.

From the 18th century on, fraternity became one of the main issues defended by revolutionaries that intended to end the *Ancien Régime*. However, only in the 20th century did fraternity start being practiced.

In Brazil, we can see the application of this principle in the implementation of minority quotas in public universities and tax exemption for the poor, as established by the constitution. It is possible to verify the application of the fraternity (solidarity) principle also in the protection of the environment, which becomes a human right and, consequently, a duty for the government and the whole society.

In May 2008, the Supreme Court of Brazil acknowledged once more the fraternity principle and, in view of well-being in a fraternal society, allowed research with embryonic stem cells to find cures for diseases.

As states Carlos Aurélio Mota de Souza:

[...] the fraternity principle takes center stage, for a fraternal society is, before all, solidary. Fraternity is a social organization principle that permits differences among fellow creatures and guarantees the freedom to act in the economic sphere, within a global vision of society. Solidarity is necessary in the dynamics of productive activity, as in the social responsibility actions taken by corporations. Economic relations are human and communitarian facts with an ethical dimension, that happen during the productive process, not later.[94]

On the other hand, regarding profit and its fraternization, there are several examples throughout history about its *stimulating function*, such as the discovery of new usable raw materials, invention of new machines, improvement of labor techniques and maintenance of scientific research areas, among others. The profit expectancy is, without a doubt, an incentive

---

94 *Revista do IASP*, n° 25, p. 103.

for progress of the means of production and implementation of new techniques in providing services.

It is also possible to see in profit an *orienting function*, which analyzes the saturation or dissatisfaction of markets. If a market is saturated or dissatisfied, it is possible to direct production to a new path. On the other hand, the orienting function of profit also can evaluate possible deficiencies in the market and, likewise, direct production.

As has been stated in this chapter, profit has a fiscal function, as the government gets some of its necessary resources from private enterprise profit, through taxation. Profit also has a capitalization function, through which part of it is retained and reinvested in the business, as self-financing.

In this regard, José Luiz de Almeida Nogueira Porto asseverates that

> [...] the fact that profit is the main source of new investments does not mean it is always a convenient solution. In point of fact, investments cause a momentary substitution of the search for consumer goods for the search for capital assets, which only after a certain time brings again the search for consumer goods. [...] Only in case of underinvestment, in which savings are higher than investment opportunities, can retaining company profits be really pernicious.[95]

And:

> [...] Profit, when obtained, is not yet capitalized for the most part, and the businessperson does not even have a slight illusion that they will decide how it will be allocated. Because in a company there are no succeeding stagnant transactions that generate a measurable and palpable profit, but a continuous flow of interdependent and inseparable transactions, whose individual results are frequently ignored. Business de-

---

95 PORTO, J. *Contribuição para a Teoria do Lucro. Op. Cit.,* p. 222.

velopment forces a continuous reinvestment of profit, including implicit interest. This reinvestment does not happen only
when they are calculated in a balance sheet, but the moment
they are gained.[96]

Obviously, these are not the only functions profit currently has but are, of course, a reason that explains the importance of fraternal profit.

One of the main problems of modern society is to make
profit also serve the collective interest; the results of progress
will be distributed among citizens, whether by decreasing work
hours, increasing buying power, or promoting sustainability for
the planet.

In this regard, concrete and responsible allocation of
profit through corporate activity can help better wealth distribution, improving quality of life in the work environment and
the distribution of tax burdens, for instance. This signifies the
possibility of fraternizing profit, which is, basically, reverting
part of it to guarantee first, second and third dimension human
rights, according to the corporate object and the amplitude of
the corporate activity.

---

96 *Op. Cit.*, p. 227.

Chapter V - Profit and Respect for Human Beings

Brazil adopted the economic system of capitalism, expressly prescribed in the constitution in articles 1 and 170, in which respect for human dignity and the value of labor are beliefs that stand above mere accumulation of capital. However, adopting a capitalist regime is not enough to solve social issues, since economic freedom, individualism and personal interests held above the collective good are part of the problem.

Economic efficiency, positive results and profit often answer to merely speculative aspects of capitalism and offer no solidarity to fellow men, especially the socially excluded or do not show any concern about sustainability.

Indeed, profit is intrinsically connected to the corporate activity whence it came and, once earned (positive result), may be allocated thusly: (i) investment in the corporate activity whence it originated; (ii) distribution among members or stockholders: or, yet (iii) materialization of the corollaries of corporate social function and human rights through private enterprise.

It is certain that profit cannot be an end into itself, or nothing will be shared with the community, social exclusion will increase and the planet will not be protected.

Neo-liberalism and globalization of the economy made developing countries poorer, increased social inequalities and decreased human dignity, for the sole purpose of gaining profit.

Globalization, at first, brought terrible consequences, as it had no concern for planetary sustainability, no respect for minorities, and did not contribute at all with the well-being of humankind.

Fundamentalist liberal capitalism increases inequality among human beings and separates the socially excluded from their dignity. The solution to diminish the tension between freedom and equality and for capitalism to advance in a fair and empathetic manner is found by applying human rights to the capitalist system embraced by the constitution; in short, by humanizing economic relations.

In this context, economic activities developed in the capitalist system by private enterprises (market economy) cannot forget constitutional objectives, especially that of building a just and empathetic society, according to its article 3, I. Since the 1988 constitution, social justice began to interfere in economic activity and related legal relations; there is now an inherent commitment to live in an interdependent relation, think of everyone and ourselves, and act with solidarity so everyone can experience their intrinsic dignity in life and help advance sustainable principles.

Therefore, better wealth distribution is essential to better quality of life and to provide a dignified existence to all human beings, covering at least their basic needs. The main rule of the economic order (article 170 of the constitution), not coincidentally, mentions a dignified existence and social justice, expressly stating principles such as the value of human labor, free enterprise and the objectives of the constitutional order — a dignified existence, according to the dictates of social justice.

The constitutional purposes of economic activity are, apparently, incompatible with profit gained through the capitalist system. As José Afonso da Silva states:

> [. . .] In a system that embraces the essentially individualist market economy, in which accumulating and concentrating capital are the goal, founded on the power of private owner-

ship of the means and production and its respective profits, there will always be vast differences between social classes, and wealth distribution, a demand of social justice, shall never happen. Social justice is achieved through equitable distribution of wealth, allowing each to employ the necessary material resources for a dignified life, which does not occur if the market is allowed to function by its own laws.[97]

Generating wealth through economic activity cannot have the accumulation of wealth to produce positive or negative results as its sole purpose; profit must be an instrument in behalf of human rights.

Also, corporate activity, as an economic organization, transcends the businessperson. Profit is a fruit of capital and must be reverted not only to those who perform economic corporate activities, but also to every person's benefit, in a fraternal way, to decrease inequality and achieve social justice.

To attain this purpose, profit adjustment to the humanistic capitalist system adopted in Brazil is directly connected to how it is acquired and allocated. Allocating profit correctly is merely using the financial results in concrete actions that benefit human rights, such as social projects, purchase of essential goods necessary to a healthy quality of life (food, medication) to distribute among the destitute, investment in programs that promote culture, sports, social inclusion and environment rebuilding, among others.

However, to make human rights work in concrete situation, there must be practical results; mere intentions or decisions to revert profit to the community are not enough. Actions must be taken immediately when profit is gained.

On this subject, to balance and restrain solely speculative interests of the market economy, legal systems that adopt the Universal Law of Fraternity manage, by implementing hu-

---

97 SILVA, José Afonso da. *Curso de Direito Constitucional Positivo*. 16ª Ed. São Paulo: Malheiros, 1999, p. 763.

man rights, to offset the capitalist regime with human dignity, so capital is in service of man and not the other way around. In the legal sphere, profit is permissible and juridical. It is a consequence of property and free enterprise, but must also revert to benefit the community, so all dimensions of human rights may be applied in practice.

The way the expression "human rights" is understood is connected to rights that are considered inalienable and universal; they must be treated as a priority in a context of collective rights.

Competitiveness, productivity and integration in the economic sphere, and fragmentation and marginalization in the social sphere demonstrate the functional differentiation of society on one side and, on the other, a growing structural unemployment, along with the degradation of the quality of life of those who were expelled from the formal labor market.

5.1. - Unlawful Use of Child and Slave Labor and the Government's Role

In this book, the author has several times mentioned that using slave labor in any segment of the economy is unacceptable, and much more so at the present time.

Profit obtained by polluting the environment, using child or slave labor and false advertising is not acceptable, as aren't any practices that violate collective or diffuse interests, especially those that hurt human dignity and contribute to the draining of planetary resources, which would take us back to a fundamentalist capitalist regime, in which accumulating profit is a *raison d'être*.

The reality of current slave labor is different from the slavery existent until the 19th century in Brazil, which was legal and accepted by society. Currently, slave and child labor have specific characteristics, such as baiting, and are perpetrated by those who will benefit from an eventual final positive result — profit.

Considering that this type of labor is absolutely illegal, workers are usually lured by false promises and are led into debt, which will is then used as a hook to keep them working in a condition similar to slavery — this debt includes, for instance, transportation to the workplace and purchase of food, hygiene products and medication, which can only be bought from the employer at higher prices than can be found in other establishments. If they move to a foreign country, their documents and passports can be withheld to prevent them from escaping in the future.

Usually, these workers do not have access to dignified nourishment, housing or healthcare; they suffer from imprisonment, physical violence and environmental damage, as do the victims of child labor; of course, several labor laws are also broken. Slave labor feeds on two elements: the vulnerability and economic frailty of the victims, allied to their exploiter's expectation of impunity.

In Brazilian law, the 1988 constitution protects the free practice of any work, trade or profession, as long as the worker possesses the necessary professional qualification established by law (article 5, item XIII) and, in article 6, establishes that work is a social right. Article 49 of the Brazilian Penal Code, altered by Law 10.803, of December 11, 2003, deals with crimes against personal freedom and prescribes that:

> Article 149. Reducing someone to a slave-like condition, whether by subjecting them to forced labor or exhausting hours, or by subjecting them to degrading working conditions, or by restricting, by any means, their movement on account of a debt contracted with the employer or supervisor.
>
> Penalty - two to eight years in prison and a fine proportional to the violence committed.
>
> Paragraph 1 - Those who commit the following acts are subject to the same penalties established above:

I– curtails the worker's use of any mode of transportation to keep them in the workplace;

II - keeps ostensible guard on the workplace or confiscates the worker's personal documents or objects to keep them in the workplace.

Paragraph 2 - the penalty is increased by a half if the crime is committed:

I - against a child or adolescent;

II - due to prejudice against race, color, ethnicity, religion or origin.

Internationally, the Convention 29 of the International Labor Organization (ILO), approved in Brazil by Legislative Decree 24, of May 29th, 1956 and promulgated by Decree 41.721, of June 25, 1957, defines forced (or compulsory) labor as "all work or service which is exacted from any person under the menace of any penalty and for which the said person has not offered himself voluntarily."[98]

In this aspect, the government plays a very important role. As an example, there is the National Commission for the Eradication of Slave Labor — CONATRAE, a collegiate organ connected to the President of the Republic's Special Human Rights Office, created in August 2003 to monitor the execution of the National Plan for the Eradication of Slave Labor. The plan contains 76 measures that must be performed by the executive, legislative and judiciary branches, the public prosecutor's office, private sector entities and international organizations.

Among CONATRAE's duties are to: (i) ensure the actions prescribed in the National Plan for the Eradication of Slave Labor are being performed, proposing any necessary adaptations; (ii) follow the processing of bills related to the combat and eradication of slave labor in the National Congress and propose normative acts necessary to implement the plan; (iii) follow and

---

98 On this subject, see the summary of decision in Inq. 3412/AL - ALAGOAS, JUSTICE MARCO AURÉLIO, Electronic Official Journal of Courts 222 OF 09-11-2012 published on 11-12-2012.

evaluate technical cooperation projects established between the Brazilian government and international organizations; (iv) propose studies and research and encourage campaigns for the eradication of slave labor.

To this purpose, Decree 5.017 of March 12, 2004 was passed, enacting the Protocol to Prevent, Suppress and Punish Trafficking in Persons, Especially Women and Children within The United Nations Convention against Transnational Organized Crime, aiming to prevent and combat this crime; protect and aid victims of traffic, fully respecting their human rights; and promote cooperation among the states parties to achieve its goals.

The state of São Paulo edited Law 14.946/2013[99] that prescribes the revocation of taxpayer registration for the Tax on the Circulation of Merchandise and Interstate and Inter-municipal Transportation Services and Communications — ICMS — of any company that directly or indirectly uses slave labor, or similar.

This law prescribes sanctions in addition to those already established in federal rules in cases of slave or child labor, such as: (i) a ten year ban from working on the same field, even in a different establishment; (ii) a ten year ban from registering a new business in the same field; (iii) loss of the right to receive credits from the state treasury, as instituted by the Incentive to Fiscal Citizenship Program of the State of São Paulo, established by Law 12.685, of August 28, 2007 (iv) cancellation of already calculated or liberated credits from the Incentive to Fiscal Citizenship Program of the State of São Paulo.

Another example worth mentioning is the State Commission for the Eradication of Slave Labor in Rio Grande do Sul — COETRAE-RS — organized in five groups to promote general actions to challenge and repress; reinsert and prevent; inform and empower, and specific actions to repress economically and to analyze and collaborate with the State Plan for the

---

99 According to Ordinance CAT 19 of 2/22/2013.

Eradication of Slave Labor in Rio Grande do Sul.

Also, the Integrated Action Movement is also noteworthy — a project aiming to reinsert former slave workers into the labor force, released during a public hearing of the Senate's Permanent Sub-commission for the National and International Trafficking in Persons and Combat of Slave Labor. The project was proposed by SINAIT — National Union of Labor Auditors — with technical support from the International Labor Organization — ILO — and intends to insert workers emerging from conditions analogous to slavery in vocational classes and the labor market.

The concept of profit must also be connected to sustainability, as it is no longer possible to imagine profit as the only purpose of a company; the means to achieve their end must also be considered. On the other hand, especially considering the government's role in making sure profit will guarantee human rights effectiveness, the concept of sustainability related to corporate activity and profit gain demands a new business model, one that deals with positive and negative consequences of productive activities or service provision, such as the socio-economic development of a certain region, improvement in the local community's quality of life and greenhouse gas emissions; in short, the impact of the business on its surroundings.

It is noteworthy that companies cannot neglect profit, nor even compromise their financial results; however, they must take responsibility on the way profit is generated and its impact on society, including on their own collaborators, the local community and, why not, on the whole society, albeit indirectly.

Socially responsible practices, paired with profit gain, are the desired result to achieve economic and financial development, linked to social responsibility to achieve a specific type of profit: fraternal profit. Profit obtention must be understood as one of the ways to produce wealth for society, in a sustainable and fraternal way.

Eventual local or world economy imbalances, just as the peculiarities of the factors of production — among which, for instance, labor and search for raw materials — are elements that will determine if there will be profit, whether negative or positive, in the short or long term. Overcoming these challenges is essential to maintain a healthy corporate activity. A company's usefulness to society will be questioned as, consequently, will its way of producing and allocating profit effectively to implement human rights.

The evolution of the concept of sustainability in the past years has been undeniable. In fact, the more its implications in the corporate field are examined, the more productive processes are changed, in an attempt to, for example, reduce residue, environmental pollution and the impact of extraction of natural resources, among others.

Obtaining profit for itself, without measuring the consequences, such as its impact on sustainability, is no longer accepted. Sustainability does not mean neglecting profit obtention or financial results, but obtaining them in a rational and safe way that respects the common good. Accordingly, profit is a reward for the common good; serving the corporate social function includes all ethical, social and environmental commitments made to develop their corporate and/or statutory purpose.

Private sector companies can and should have profit as their main goal; otherwise, they might lose their purpose and have their negative freedoms be violated. However, profit must be apportioned to activities that improve human quality of life.

Profit obtention cannot be seen as just a perquisite in corporate activity; it is a goal. After all, negative results — losses — can cause terrible damage to the company. However, profit cannot be obtained at any price; this would be equivalent to a human rights violation and, furthermore, it would disobey the company's corporate social function.

Respecting negative freedoms — property and free enterprise — might help human rights materialize, if a fraternal view of positive results in corporate activity (obtention of profit) is taken and profit is used to reduce income inequality and help sustain the planet. To achieve this end, it is imperative to improve the quality of life of their collaborators and, consequently, of their families. Advancing the local community and society's quality of life as a whole is an indirect consequence but, certainly, it will be felt.

The constitutional focus on fraternal profit embraces social justice and a dignified existence, considering they are constitutional objectives economic activity must achieve, materializing simultaneously human rights of first, second and third dimensions.

Thus, fraternal profit is gained through corporate and economic activity that respects human rights, from obtention to its appropriate allocation, taking in consideration excluded human beings and planetary sustainability, and aiming to reduce social inequality and maintain a sustainable environment.

BIBLIOGRAPHY

ADEODATO, João Maurício. *Uma Teoria Retórica da Norma Jurídica e do Direito Subjetivo.* São Paulo: Noeses, 2012.

AGUILLAR, Fernando Herren. *Direito Econômico.* São Paulo: Atlas, 2006.

ALEXY, Robert. *Teoria dos Direitos Fundamentais.* São Paulo: Malheiros, 2008.

ALMEIDA FILHO, Agassiz. *Dignidade da Pessoa Humana. Fundamentos e Critérios Interpretativos.* São Paulo: Malheiros, 2010.

ALMEIDA, Amador Paes. *Direito de Empresa no Código Civil.* São Paulo: Saraiva, 2008.

ALTHUSSER, Louis. *Polémica sobre Marxismo y Humanismo.* México: Siglo Veintiuno, 1978.

ANTUNES, Henrique Sousa. *Da Inclusão do Lucro Ilícito e de Efeitos Punitivos entre as Consequências da Responsabilidade Civil Extracontratual: a sua Legitimação pelo Dano.* Coimbra: Coimbra, 2011.

ARENDT, Hanna. *A Promessa da Política.* Rio de Janeiro: Difel, 2005.

ARON, Raymond. *O Marxismo de Marx.* Trad. Jorge Bastos. São Paulo: ARX, 2008.

ATIENZA, Manuel. *Marx y Los Derechos Humanos.* Lima: Palestra, 2008.

ÁVILA, Humberto. *Teoria dos Princípios. Da Definição à Aplicação dos Princípios Jurídicos*. São Paulo: Malheiros, 2004.

AZEVEDO, Antônio J. *Estudos e Pareceres de Direito Privado*. São Paulo: Saraiva, 2004.

BAKAN, Joel. *A Corporação. A Busca Patológica por Lucro e Poder*. São Paulo: Novo Conceito, 2008.

BALERA, Wagner. *Direito Internacional dos Refugiados nos 25 Anos da Declaração de Cartagena*. São Paulo: Editora Plêiade, 2009.

BASTOS, Celso Ribeiro. *Curso de Direito Constitucional*. São Paulo: Saraiva, 1998.

BENATO, João Vitorino Azolin. *ABC do Cooperativismo*. São Paulo: Cenacope, 2007.

BICUDO, Hélio. *Direitos Humanos e sua Proteção*. São Paulo: FTD, 1997.

BIGO, Pierre. *Marxismo e Humanismo. Introdução à Obra Econômica de Karl Marx*. São Paulo: Editora Herder, 1966.

BITENCOURT NETO, Eurico. *O Direito ao Mínimo para uma Existência Digna*. Porto Alegre: Livraria do Advogado, 2010.

BITTAR, Carlos Alberto. *Direito Civil Constitucional*. São Paulo: Revista dos Tribunais, 2003.

BOBBIO, Norberto. *Teoria do Ordenamento Jurídico*. Brasília: Editora Polis, 1990.

BONAVIDES, Paulo. *Curso de Direito Constitucional*. São Paulo: Malheiros, 1997.

BRAUDEL, Fernand. *A Dinâmica do Capitalismo*. Lisboa: Teorema, 1985.

BRITTO, Carlos Ayres. *O Humanismo como Categoria Constitucional*. Belo Horizonte: Editora Forum, 2010.

BULHÕES, Octávio Gouvea de. *Dois Conceitos de Lucro.* Rio de Janeiro: Apec, 1969.

CANO, Wilson. *Introdução à Economia.* São Paulo: Editora UNESP, 2006.

CANOTILHO, José Joaquim Gomes. *Direito Constitucional e Teoria da Constituição.* Coimbra: Almedina, 1998.

CANOTILHO, José Joaquim Gomes. *Estudos sobre Direitos Fundamentais.* Coimbra: Coimbra, 2008.

CARVALHOSA, Modesto. Direito Econômico. In: *Obras Completas.* São Paulo: Editora Revista dos Tribunais, 2013.

CASO, Giovanni. *Direito & Fraternidade.* São Paulo: Editora Ltr, 2008.

CHARBONNEAU, Paul-Eugène. *Entre Capitalismo e Socialismo: a Empresa Humana.* São Paulo: Pioneira, 1983.

CHOMSKY, Noam. *O Lucro ou as Pessoas.* Rio de Janeiro: Bertrand Brasil, 2010.

COBBAN, Alfred. *A Interpretação Social da Revolução Francesa.* Rio de Janeiro: Jorge Zahar Editor, 1987.

COMPARATO, Fabio Konder. *A afirmação histórica dos Direitos Humanos.* São Paulo: Saraiva, 2010.

_____. *Estado, Empresa e Função Social.* São Paulo: Revista dos Tribunais, 1996.

CULLETON, Alfredo. *Curso de Direitos Humanos.* São Leopoldo: Editora Unisinos, 2009.

DIAS, Joaquim José de Barros. *Direito Civil Constitucional.* São Paulo: Malheiros, 2002.

DINIZ, Maria Helena. *Curso de Direito Civil Brasileiro. Teoria Geral do Direito Civil.* Vol.1. São Paulo: Saraiva, 2013.

_____. *Curso de Direito Civil Brasileiro. Direito de Empresa.* São Paulo: Saraiva, 2009.

DUARTE FILHO, Paulo Cesar Teixeira. *A Bitributação Econômica do Lucro Empresarial*. Porto Alegre: Sergio Antonio Fabris Editor, 2011.

DUARTE, Cristiani de Oliveira Silva. *Responsabilidade Social Empresarial: dimensões históricas e conceituais*. São Paulo: Editora Fundação Peirópolis Ltda., 2005.

ENGISCH, Karl. *Introdução ao Pensamento Jurídico*. Lisboa: Fundação Calouste Gulbenkian, 2001.

FACHIN, Luiz Edson. *Estatuto Jurídico do Patrimônio Mínimo*. Rio de Janeiro: Renovar, 2006.

FARIA, José Eduardo. *Direitos Humanos, Direitos Sociais e Justiça*. São Paulo: Malheiros, 2010.

_____. *O Direito na Economia Globalizada*. São Paulo: Malheiros, 2004.

FARJAT, Gerard. *A Noção de Direito Econômico*. Belo Horizonte: Movimento Editorial Faculdade de Direito da UFMG, 1996.

FAYT, Carlos S. *Los Derechos Humanos y El Poder Mediático, Político y Económico. Su Mundialización en el Siglo XXI*. Buenos Aires: La Ley, 2001.

FERRAZ JUNIOR, Tércio Sampaio. *Constituição de 1988: Legitimidade, Vigência e Eficácia, Supremacia*. São Paulo: Atlas, 1989.

_____. *Introdução ao Estudo do Direito: Técnica, Decisão, Dominação*. São Paulo: Atlas, 2007.

_____. *Poder Econômico. Direito, Pobreza, Violência, Corrupção*. São Paulo: Editora Manole, 2009.

_____. *Teoria da Norma Jurídica*. Rio de Janeiro: Forense, 2006.

FOLMANN, Melissa. *Direitos Humanos. Os 60 Anos da Declaração Universal da ONU*. Curitiba: Juruá, 2008.

FONSECA, João Bosco Leopoldino da. *Direito Econômico*. Rio de Janeiro: Forense, 2010.

FOUCAULT, Michel. *A Verdade e as Formas Jurídicas*. Rio de Janeiro: Nau Editora, 2005.

FREDERICO, Celso. *Marx no Século XXI*. São Paulo: Cortez, 2008.

FROMM, Erich. *Conceito Marxista do Homem*. Rio de Janeiro: Zahar Editores, 1983.

GAMA, Guilherme Calmon Nogueira da. *Função Social no Direito Civil*. São Paulo: Atlas, 2007.

GILISSEN, John. *Introdução Histórica ao Direito*. Lisboa: Fundação Calouste Gulbenkian, 2008.

GOMES, Fátima. *O Direito aos Lucros e o Dever de Participar nas Perdas nas Sociedades Anónimas*. Coimbra: Almedina, 2011.

GRASSI, Ernesto. *Humanismo y Marxismo*. Madrid: Biblioteca Hispânica de Filosofia, 1977.

GRAU, Eros Roberto. *A Ordem Econômica na Constituição de 1988. Interpretação e Crítica*. São Paulo: Revista dos Tribunais, 1991.

_____. *O Direito Posto e o Direito Pressuposto*. São Paulo: Malheiros, 2005.

GREENSPAN, Alan. *The Age of Turbulence: Adventures in a New World*.

http://www.panzertruppen.org/ebooks/27.pdf

GUASTINI, Ricardo. *Das Fontes às Normas*. São Paulo: Quartier Latin, 2005.

GUDIN, Eugênio. *Princípios de Economia Monetária*. Rio de Janeiro: Agir, 1979.

GUERRA FILHO, Willis Santiago. *Dos Direitos Huma-*

nos aos Direitos Fundamentais. Porto Alegre: Livraria do Advogado, 1997.

_____. *Teoria Política do Direito. Uma Introdução Política ao Direito.* Brasília: Brasília Jurídica, 2000.

HART, Hebert L. A. *O Conceito de Direito.* Lisboa: Fundação Calouste Gulbenkian, 2001.

HEATH, Joseph. *Lucro Sujo.* Rio de Janeiro: Elsevier, 2009.

HESSE, Konrad. *A Força Normativa da Constituição.* Porto Alegre: Sérgio Antonio Fabris Editor, 1991.

KANT, Immanuel. *Crítica da Razão Pura.* São Paulo: Martim Claret, 2005.

LAMBERTON, D. M. *Teoria do Lucro.* Rio de Janeiro: Bloch Editores, 1967.

LEAL, Leogevildo Pereira. *Marxismo e Socialismo. Análise Crítica da Revolução Cubana.* Belo Horizonte: Editora Fórum, 2008.

LEITE, Carlos Henrique Bezerra. *Direitos Humanos.* Rio de Janeiro: Lumen Juris, 2010.

LEWIS, Gregory. *O Preço do Lucro.* Lisboa: Lyon Multimedia Edições, 1992.

LIMA, Paulo Rogério dos Santos. *Responsabilidade Social. A Experiência do Selo da Empresa Cidadã na Cidade de São Paulo.* São Paulo: Editora PUC-SP, 2005.

LISBOA, Roberto Senise. Dignidade e Solidariedade Civil-Constitucional. In: *Revista de Direito Privado,* 2010, n° 42 e 30.

LUCCA, Newton de. *Da Ética Geral à Ética Empresarial.* São Paulo: Quartier Latin, 2009.

MACHADO, Mariângela Campos. *Fraternidade.* São Paulo: Editora Diretriz, 2004.

MANDOLFO, Rodolfo. *El Humanismo de Marx*. México: Fondo de Cultura Económica Editora, 1973.

MARITAIN, Jacques. *Humanismo Integral*. São Paulo: Dominus Editora S/A, 1962.

MARTINS, Ana Maria Guerra. *Direito Internacional dos Direitos Humanos*. Coimbra: Almedina, 2006.

MARTINS, Sérgio Pinto. *Participação dos Empregados nos Lucros das Empresas*. São Paulo: Atlas, 2009.

MARX, Karl. *O Capital: Crítica da Economia Política*. Tradução de Gabriel Deville. São Paulo: Edipro, 2008.

MEIRELES, Manuel. *O Lucro: Esboço para uma Teoria do Lucro como Fruto da Alavancagem Tecnológica do Capital*. São Paulo: Editora Arte & Ciência Villipress, 2000.

MELGARÉ, Plínio. *Dignidade da Pessoa Humana - Fundamentos e Critérios Interpretativos*. São Paulo: Malheiros, 2010.

MELLO, Celso Antônio Bandeira. *Conteúdo Jurídico do Princípio da Igualdade*. São Paulo: Malheiros, 1998.

_____. *Eficácia das Normas Constitucionais e Direitos Sociais*. São Paulo: Malheiros, 2009.

MILL, John Stuart. *Ensaio sobre a Liberdade*. São Paulo: Editora Escala, 2006.

_____. *Sistema e Lógica Dedutiva e Indutiva e Outros Textos*. São Paulo: Editor Victor Civita, 1979.

MIRANDA, Pontes de. *Tratado de Direito Privado. Parte Especial*. Tomo XXVI. São Paulo: Bookseller, 2003.

_____. *Tratado de Direito Privado. Parte Especial*. Tomo II. São Paulo: Bookseller, 2000.

MORAIS, Luis Fernando Lobão. *A Função Social do Lucro e a Sociedade Pós-Capitalista*. São Paulo: Emopi, 2008.

MOREIRA, Vital. *A Ordem Jurídica do Capitalismo -*

Perspectiva Jurídica. Coimbra: Centelha, 1973.

NAVES, Marcio Bilharinho. *Marx - Ciência e Revolução.* São Paulo: Quartier Latin, 2008.

_____. *Marxismo e Direito: Um Estudo sobre Pachukanis.* São Paulo: Boitempo Editorial, 2000.

NAZAR, Nelson. *Direito Econômico.* São Paulo: Edipro, 2009.

NOGARE, Pedro Dalle. *Humanismos e Anti-Humanismos - Introdução à Antropologia Filosófica.* Rio de Janeiro: Editora Vozes, 1990.

PEDUZZI, Maria Cristina Irigoyen. *O Princípio da Dignidade da Pessoa Humana na Perspectiva do Direito como Integridade.* São Paulo: Editora Ltr, 2009.

PIOVESAN, Flávia. *Direitos Humanos e o Direito Constitucional Internacional.* São Paulo: Max Limonad Editora, 1997.

_____. *Direitos Humanos, Globalização Econômica e Integração Regional. Desafios do Direito Constitucional Internacional.* São Paulo: Max Limonad Editora, 2002.

_____. *Temas de Direitos Humanos.* São Paulo: Saraiva, 2009.

POLONIO, Wilson Alves. *Manual das Sociedades Cooperativas.* São Paulo: Atlas, 2001.

PORTO, José Luiz de Almeida Nogueira. *Contribuição para a Teoria do Lucro.* São Paulo: Edição Própria, 1954.

POSNER, Richard A. *Problemas de Filosofia de Direito.* São Paulo: Martins Fontes, 2007.

_____. *The Economics of Justice.* Boston: Harvard University Press, 1983.

RÁO, Vicente. *O Direito e a Vida dos Direitos. Noções Gerais. Direito Positivo. Direito Objetivo. Teoria Geral de Direito Subjetivo. Análise dos Elementos que Constituem os Direitos Sub-*

jetivos. São Paulo: Revista dos Tribunais, 2005.

REQUIÃO, Rubens. *Curso de Direito Comercial*. Volume II. São Paulo: Saraiva, 1988.

RODRIGUEZ, Martius Vicente. *Ética e Responsabilidade Social nas Empresas*. Rio de Janeiro: Elsevier, 2005.

SANTOS, Francisco Araújo. *Lucro & Ética*. São Leopoldo: Editora Unisinos, 2003.

SARLET, Ingo Wolfgang. *Dignidade da Pessoa Humana e Direitos Fundamentais*. Porto Alegre: Livraria do Advogado, 2009.

_____. *A Eficácia dos Direitos Fundamentais. Uma Teoria Geral dos Direitos Fundamentais na Perspectiva Constitucional*. Porto Alegre: Livraria do Advogado, 2009.

SAVITZ, Andrew W. *The Triple Bottom Line: How Today's Best-Run Companies Are Achieving Economic, Social, and Environmental Success — and How You Can Too*

http://pro-ex.org/books/archive/files/b76eaa14ccc-6578769babbe61aeaca39.pdf

SAYEG, Ricardo H.; BALERA, Wagner. *O Capitalismo Humanista: Filosofia Humanista de Direito Econômico*. Petrópolis: KBR, 2011.

SILVA, José Afonso da. *Curso de Direito Constitucional Positivo*. 16ª Ed. São Paulo: Malheiros, 1999.

SINGER, Paul. *Introdução à Economia Solidária*. São Paulo: Editora Fundação Perseu Abramo, 2010.

_____. *O Capitalismo: sua evolução, sua lógica e sua dinâmica*. São Paulo: Moderna, 1987.

SORTINO, Dorival. *Uma Fraternidade e seus Princípios Básicos*. Edição Própria, 1993.

SZTAJN, Rachel. *Direito & Economia. Análise Econômica do Direito e das Organizações*. Rio de Janeiro: Elsevier, 2005.

TAUSSIG, F. W. *Princípios de Economia*. Tomos I e II. Buenos Aires: Espasa Calpe, 1945.

TAVARES, André Ramos. *Direito Constitucional Econômico*. São Paulo. Editora Método, 2011.

TEIXEIRA, J. H. Meirelles. *Curso de Direito Constitucional*. Rio de Janeiro: Forense Universitária, 1991.

TELLES JUNIOR, Goffredo. *A Criação do Direito*. São Paulo: Juarez de Oliveira, 2004.

THOMAS, Ann Van Wynen. *O Comunismo contra o Direito Internacional*. São Paulo: Saraiva, 1958.

VIEHWEG, Theodor. *Tópica e Jurisprudência: uma contribuição à investigação dos fundamentos jurídico-científicos*. Porto Alegre: Sérgio Antonio Fabris Editor, 2008.

VILANOVA, Lourival. *As Estruturas Lógicas e o Sistema do Direito Positivo*. Belo Horizonte: Max Limonad Editora, 1997.

WEIS, Carlos. *Direitos Humanos Contemporâneos*. São Paulo: Malheiros, 2011.

WEYNE, Gastão Rúbio de Sá. *Marxismo e Práticas Socialistas no Direito Inglês*. São Paulo: Scortecci, 2007.

WOOD, Adrian. *Uma Teoria de Lucros*. Rio de Janeiro: Editora Paz e Terra, 1980.

XAVIER, Alberto. *Direito Tributário Internacional do Brasil*. Rio de Janeiro: Forense, 2007.

YUNUS, Muhammad. *Um Mundo sem Pobreza: A empresa social e o futuro do capitalismo*. São Paulo: Ática, 2009.

APPENDIX

Human Rights Treaties Mentioned in This Book

APPENDIX A

DECLARATION OF THE RIGHTS OF MAN
1789[100]

APPROVED BY THE NATIONAL ASSEMBLY OF FRANCE, AUGUST 26, 1789

The representatives of the French people, organized as a National Assembly, believing that the ignorance, neglect, or contempt of the rights of man are the sole cause of public calamities and of the corruption of governments, have determined to set forth in a solemn declaration the natural, unalienable, and sacred rights of man, in order that this declaration, being constantly before all the members of the Social body, shall remind them continually of their rights and duties; in order that the acts of the legislative power, as well as those of the executive power, may be compared at any moment with the objects and purposes of all political institutions and may thus be more respected, and, lastly, in order that the grievances of the citizens, based hereafter upon simple and incontestable principles, shall tend to the maintenance of the constitution and redound to the happiness of all. Therefore the National Assembly recognizes and proclaims, in the presence and under the auspices of the Supreme Being, the following rights of man and of the citizen:

---

100 Source: http://avalon.law.yale.edu/18th_century/rightsof.asp

Articles:

1. Men are born and remain free and equal in rights. Social distinctions may be founded only upon the general good.

2. The aim of all political association is the preservation of the natural and imprescriptible rights of man. These rights are liberty, property, security, and resistance to oppression.

3. The principle of all sovereignty resides essentially in the nation. No body nor individual may exercise any authority which does not proceed directly from the nation.

4. Liberty consists in the freedom to do everything which injures no one else; hence the exercise of the natural rights of each man has no limits except those which assure to the other members of the society the enjoyment of the same rights. These limits can only be determined by law.

5. Law can only prohibit such actions as are hurtful to society. Nothing may be prevented which is not forbidden by law, and no one may be forced to do anything not provided for by law.

6. Law is the expression of the general will. Every citizen has a right to participate personally, or through his representative, in its foundation. It must be the same for all, whether it protects or punishes. All citizens, being equal in the eyes of the law, are equally eligible to all dignities and to all public positions and occupations, according to their abilities, and without distinction except that of their virtues and talents.

7. No person shall be accused, arrested, or imprisoned except in the cases and according to the forms prescribed by law. Any one soliciting, transmitting, executing, or causing to be executed, any arbitrary order, shall be punished. But any citizen summoned or arrested in virtue of the law shall submit without delay, as resistance constitutes an offense.

8. The law shall provide for such punishments only as are strictly and obviously necessary, and no one shall suffer punishment except it be legally inflicted in virtue of a law passed and promulgated before the commission of the offense.

9. As all persons are held innocent until they shall have been declared guilty, if arrest shall be deemed indispensable, all harshness not essential to the securing of the prisoner's person shall be severely repressed by law.

10. No one shall be disquieted on account of his opinions, including his religious views, provided their manifestation does not disturb the public order established by law.

11. The free communication of ideas and opinions is one of the most precious of the rights of man. Every citizen may, accordingly, speak, write, and print with freedom, but shall be responsible for such abuses of this freedom as shall be defined by law.

12. The security of the rights of man and of the citizen requires public military forces. These forces are, therefore, established for the good of all and not for the personal advantage of those to whom they shall be entrusted.

13. A common contribution is essential for the maintenance of the public forces and for the cost of administration. This should be equitably distributed among all the citizens in proportion to their means.

14. All the citizens have a right to decide, either personally or by their representatives, as to the necessity of the public contribution; to grant this freely; to know to what uses it is put; and to fix the proportion, the mode of assessment and of collection and the duration of the taxes.

15. Society has the right to require of every public agent an account of his administration.

16. A society in which the observance of the law is not assured, nor the separation of powers defined, has no constitution at all.

17. Since property is an inviolable and sacred right, no one shall be deprived thereof except where public necessity, legally determined, shall clearly demand it, and then only on condition that the owner shall have been previously and equitably indemnified.

APPENDIX B

UNIVERSAL DECLARATION OF HUMAN RIGHTS[101]

INTERNATIONAL COVENANT ON CIVIL AND POLITICAL RIGHTS DECREE 592 OF JULY 6, 1992

Preamble

Whereas recognition of the inherent dignity and of the equal and inalienable rights of all members of the human family is the foundation of freedom, justice and peace in the world,

Whereas disregard and contempt for human rights have resulted in barbarous acts which have outraged the conscience of Mankind, and the advent of a world in which human beings shall enjoy freedom of speech and belief and freedom from fear and want has been proclaimed as the highest aspiration of the common people,

Whereas it is essential, if man is not to be compelled to have recourse, as a last resort, to rebellion against tyranny and oppression, that human rights should be protected by the rule of law,

Whereas it is essential to promote the development of friendly relations between nations,

Whereas the peoples of the United Nations have in the Charter reaffirmed their faith in fundamental human rights, in the dignity and worth of the human person and in the equal rights of men and women and have determined to promote social progress and better standards of life in larger freedom,

---

101 Source: http://www.un.org/en/documents/udhr/

Whereas Member States have pledged themselves to achieve, in co-operation with the United Nations, the promotion of universal respect for and observance of human rights and fundamental freedoms,

Whereas a common understanding of these rights and freedoms is of the greatest importance for the full realization of this pledge,

Now, Therefore THE GENERAL ASSEMBLY proclaims THIS UNIVERSAL DECLARATION OF HUMAN RIGHTS as a common standard of achievement for all peoples and all nations, to the end that every individual and every organ of society, keeping this Declaration constantly in mind, shall strive by teaching and education to promote respect for these rights and freedoms and by progressive measures, national and international, to secure their universal and effective recognition and observance, both among the peoples of Member States themselves and among the peoples of territories under their jurisdiction.

Articles:

1. All human beings are born free and equal in dignity and rights. They are endowed with reason and conscience and should act towards one another in a spirit of brotherhood.

2. Everyone is entitled to all the rights and freedoms set forth in this Declaration, without distinction of any kind, such as race, color, sex, language, religion, political or other opinion, national or social origin, property, birth or other status. Furthermore, no distinction shall be made on the basis of the political, jurisdictional or international status of the country or territory to which a person belongs, whether it be independent, trust, non-self-governing or under any other limitation of sovereignty.

3. Everyone has the right to life, liberty and security of person.

4. No one shall be held in slavery or servitude; slavery and the slave trade shall be prohibited in all their forms.

5. No one shall be subjected to torture or to cruel, inhuman or degrading treatment or punishment.

6. Everyone has the right to recognition everywhere as a person before the law.

7. All are equal before the law and are entitled without any discrimination to equal protection of the law. All are entitled to equal protection against any discrimination in violation of this Declaration and against any incitement to such discrimination.

8. Everyone has the right to an effective remedy by the competent national tribunals for acts violating the fundamental rights granted him by the constitution or by law.

9. No one shall be subjected to arbitrary arrest, detention or exile.

10. Everyone is entitled in full equality to a fair and public hearing by an independent and impartial tribunal, in the determination of his rights and obligations and of any criminal charge against him.

11. (1) Everyone charged with a penal offence has the right to be presumed innocent until proved guilty according to law in a public trial at which he has had all the guarantees necessary for his defense.

(2) No one shall be held guilty of any penal offence on account of any act or omission which did not constitute a penal offence, under national or international law, at the time when it was committed. Nor shall a heavier penalty be imposed than the one that was applicable at the time the penal offence was committed.

12. No one shall be subjected to arbitrary interference with his privacy, family, home or correspondence, nor to attacks upon his honor and reputation. Everyone has the right to the protection of the law against such interference or attacks.

13. (1) Everyone has the right to freedom of movement and residence within the borders of each state.

(2) Everyone has the right to leave any country, including his own, and to return to his country.

14. (1) Everyone has the right to seek and to enjoy in other countries asylum from persecution.

(2) This right may not be invoked in the case of prosecutions genuinely arising from non-political crimes or from acts contrary to the purposes and principles of the United Nations.

15. (1) Everyone has the right to a nationality.

(2) No one shall be arbitrarily deprived of his nationality nor denied the right to change his nationality.

16. (1) Men and women of full age, without any limitation due to race, nationality or religion, have the right to marry and to found a family. They are entitled to equal rights as to marriage, during marriage and at its dissolution.

(2) Marriage shall be entered into only with the free and full consent of the intending spouses.

(3) The family is the natural and fundamental group unit of society and is entitled to protection by society and the State.

17. (1) Everyone has the right to own property alone as well as in association with others.

(2) No one shall be arbitrarily deprived of his property.

18. Everyone has the right to freedom of thought, conscience and religion; this right includes freedom to change his religion or belief, and freedom, either alone or in community with others and in public or private, to manifest his religion or belief in teaching, practice, worship and observance.

19. Everyone has the right to freedom of opinion and expression; this right includes freedom to hold opinions without interference and to seek, receive and impart information and ideas through any media and regardless of frontiers.

20. (1) Everyone has the right to freedom of peaceful assembly and association.

(2) No one may be compelled to belong to an association.

21. (1) Everyone has the right to take part in the government of his country, directly or through freely chosen representatives.

(2) Everyone has the right of equal access to public service in his country.

(3) The will of the people shall be the basis of the authority of government; this will shall be expressed in periodic and genuine elections, which shall be by universal and equal suffrage and shall be held by secret vote or by equivalent free voting procedures.

22. Everyone, as a member of society, has the right to social security and is entitled to realization, through national effort and international co-operation and in accordance with the organization and resources of each State, of the economic, social and cultural rights indispensable for his dignity and the free development of his personality.

23. (1) Everyone has the right to work, to free choice of employment, to just and favorable conditions of work and to protection against unemployment.

(2) Everyone, without any discrimination, has the right to equal pay for equal work.

(3) Everyone who works has the right to just and favorable remuneration ensuring for himself and his family an existence worthy of human dignity, and supplemented, if necessary, by other means of social protection.

(4) Everyone has the right to form and to join trade unions for the protection of his interests.

24. Everyone has the right to rest and leisure, including reasonable limitation of working hours and periodic holidays with pay.

25. (1) Everyone has the right to a standard of living adequate for the health and well-being of himself and of his family, including food, clothing, housing and medical care and necessary social services, and the right to security in the event of unemployment, sickness, disability, widowhood, old age or other lack of livelihood in circumstances beyond his control.

(2) Motherhood and childhood are entitled to special care and assistance. All children, whether born in or out of wedlock, shall enjoy the same social protection.

26. (1) Everyone has the right to education. Education shall be free, at least in the elementary and fundamental stages. Elementary education shall be compulsory. Technical and professional education shall be made generally available and higher education shall be equally accessible to all on the basis of merit.

(2) Education shall be directed to the full development of the human personality and to the strengthening of respect for human rights and fundamental freedoms. It shall promote understanding, tolerance and friendship among all nations, racial or religious groups, and shall further the activities of the United Nations for the maintenance of peace.

(3) Parents have a prior right to choose the kind of education that shall be given to their children.

27. (1) Everyone has the right freely to participate in the cultural life of the community, to enjoy the arts and to share in scientific advancement and its benefits.

(2) Everyone has the right to the protection of the moral

and material interests resulting from any scientific, literary or artistic production of which he is the author.

28. Everyone is entitled to a social and international order in which the rights and freedoms set forth in this Declaration can be fully realized.

29. (1) Everyone has duties to the community in which alone the free and full development of his personality is possible.

(2) In the exercise of his rights and freedoms, everyone shall be subject only to such limitations as are determined by law solely for the purpose of securing due recognition and respect for the rights and freedoms of others and of meeting the just requirements of morality, public order and the general welfare in a democratic society.

(3) These rights and freedoms may in no case be exercised contrary to the purposes and principles of the United Nations.

30. Nothing in this Declaration may be interpreted as implying for any State, group or person any right to engage in any activity or to perform any act aimed at the destruction of any of the rights and freedoms set forth herein.

APPENDIX C

INTERNATIONAL COVENANT ON CIVIL AND POLITICAL RIGHTS[102]

ADOPTED AND OPENED FOR SIGNATURE, RATIFICATION AND ACCESSION BY GENERAL ASSEMBLY RESOLUTION 2200A (XXI) OF 16 DECEMBER 1966 ENTRY INTO FORCE 23 MARCH 1976, IN ACCORDANCE WITH ARTICLE 49

Preamble

The States Parties to the present Covenant,

Considering that, in accordance with the principles proclaimed in the Charter of the United Nations, recognition of the inherent dignity and of the equal and inalienable rights of all members of the human family is the foundation of freedom, justice and peace in the world,

Recognizing that these rights derive from the inherent dignity of the human person,

Recognizing that, in accordance with the Universal Declaration of Human Rights, the ideal of free human beings enjoying civil and political freedom and freedom from fear and want can only be achieved if conditions are created whereby everyone may enjoy his civil and political rights, as well as his economic, social and cultural rights,

---

102 Source: http://www.ohchr.org/en/professionalinterest/pages/ccpr.aspx

Considering the obligation of States under the Charter of the United Nations to promote universal respect for, and observance of, human rights and freedoms,

Realizing that the individual, having duties to other individuals and to the community to which he belongs, is under a responsibility to strive for the promotion and observance of the rights recognized in the present Covenant,

Agree upon the following articles:

PART I

Article 1

1. All peoples have the right of self-determination. By virtue of that right they freely determine their political status and freely pursue their economic, social and cultural development.

2. All peoples may, for their own ends, freely dispose of their natural wealth and resources without prejudice to any obligations arising out of international economic co-operation, based upon the principle of mutual benefit, and international law. In no case may a people be deprived of its own means of subsistence.

3. The States Parties to the present Covenant, including those having responsibility for the administration of Non-Self-Governing and Trust Territories, shall promote the realization of the right of self-determination, and shall respect that right, in conformity with the provisions of the Charter of the United Nations.

PART II

Article 2

1. Each State Party to the present Covenant undertakes to respect and to ensure to all individuals within its territory and subject to its jurisdiction the rights recognized in the present Covenant, without distinction of any kind, such as race, color, sex, language, religion, political or other opinion, national or social origin, property, birth or other status.

2. Where not already provided for by existing legislative or other measures, each State Party to the present Covenant undertakes to take the necessary steps, in accordance with its constitutional processes and with the provisions of the present Covenant, to adopt such laws or other measures as may be necessary to give effect to the rights recognized in the present Covenant.

3. Each State Party to the present Covenant undertakes:

(a) To ensure that any person whose rights or freedoms as herein recognized are violated shall have an effective remedy, notwithstanding that the violation has been committed by persons acting in an official capacity;

(b) To ensure that any person claiming such a remedy shall have his right thereto determined by competent judicial, administrative or legislative authorities, or by any other competent authority provided for by the legal system of the State, and to develop the possibilities of judicial remedy;

(c) To ensure that the competent authorities shall enforce such remedies when granted.

Article 3

The States Parties to the present Covenant undertake to ensure the equal right of men and women to the enjoyment of all civil and political rights set forth in the present Covenant.

Article 4

1. In time of public emergency which threatens the life of the nation and the existence of which is officially proclaimed, the States Parties to the present Covenant may take measures derogating from their obligations under the present Covenant to the extent strictly required by the exigencies of the situation, provided that such measures are not inconsistent with their other obligations under international law and do not involve discrimination solely on the ground of race, color, sex, language, religion or social origin.

2. No derogation from articles 6, 7, 8 (paragraphs 1 and 2), 11, 15, 16 and 18 may be made under this provision.

3. Any State Party to the present Covenant availing itself of the right of derogation shall immediately inform the other States Parties to the present Covenant, through the intermediary of the Secretary-General of the United Nations, of the provisions from which it has derogated and of the reasons by which it was actuated. A further communication shall be made, through the same intermediary, on the date on which it terminates such derogation.

Article 5

1. Nothing in the present Covenant may be interpreted as implying for any State, group or person any right to engage in any activity or perform any act aimed at the destruction of any of the rights and freedoms recognized herein or at their limitation to a greater extent than is provided for in the present Covenant.

2. There shall be no restriction upon or derogation from any of the fundamental human rights recognized or existing in any State Party to the present Covenant pursuant to law, conventions, regulations or custom on the pretext that the present Covenant does not recognize such rights or that it recognizes them to a lesser extent.

PART III

Article 6

1. Every human being has the inherent right to life. This right shall be protected by law. No one shall be arbitrarily deprived of his life.

2. In countries which have not abolished the death penalty, sentence of death may be imposed only for the most serious crimes in accordance with the law in force at the time of the commission of the crime and not contrary to the provisions of the present Covenant and to the Convention on the Prevention and Punishment of the Crime of Genocide. This penalty can only be carried out pursuant to a final judgment rendered by a competent court.

3. When deprivation of life constitutes the crime of genocide, it is understood that nothing in this article shall authorize any State Party to the present Covenant to derogate in any way from any obligation assumed under the provisions of the Convention on the Prevention and Punishment of the Crime of Genocide.

4. Anyone sentenced to death shall have the right to seek pardon or commutation of the sentence. Amnesty, pardon or commutation of the sentence of death may be granted in all cases.

5. Sentence of death shall not be imposed for crimes committed by persons below eighteen years of age and shall not be carried out on pregnant women.

6. Nothing in this article shall be invoked to delay or to prevent the abolition of capital punishment by any State Party to the present Covenant.

Article 7

No one shall be subjected to torture or to cruel, inhuman or degrading treatment or punishment. In particular, no one shall be subjected without his free consent to medical or scientific experimentation.

Article 8

1. No one shall be held in slavery; slavery and the slave-trade in all their forms shall be prohibited.

2. No one shall be held in servitude.

3. (a) No one shall be required to perform forced or compulsory labor;

(b) Paragraph 3 (a) shall not be held to preclude, in countries where imprisonment with hard labor may be imposed as a punishment for a crime, the performance of hard labor in pursuance of a sentence to such punishment by a competent court;

(c) For the purpose of this paragraph the term "forced or compulsory labor" shall not include:

(i) Any work or service, not referred to in subparagraph (b), normally required of a person who is under detention in consequence of a lawful order of a court, or of a person during conditional release from such detention;

(ii) Any service of a military character and, in countries where conscientious objection is recognized, any national service required by law of conscientious objectors;

(iii) Any service exacted in cases of emergency or calamity threatening the life or well-being of the community;

(iv) Any work or service which forms part of normal civil obligations.

Article 9

1. Everyone has the right to liberty and security of person. No one shall be subjected to arbitrary arrest or detention. No one shall be deprived of his liberty except on such grounds and in accordance with such procedure as are established by law.

2. Anyone who is arrested shall be informed, at the time of arrest, of the reasons for his arrest and shall be promptly informed of any charges against him.

3. Anyone arrested or detained on a criminal charge shall be brought promptly before a judge or other officer authorized by law to exercise judicial power and shall be entitled to trial within a reasonable time or to release. It shall not be the general rule that persons awaiting trial shall be detained in custody, but release may be subject to guarantees to appear for trial, at any other stage of the judicial proceedings, and, should occasion arise, for execution of the judgment.

4. Anyone who is deprived of his liberty by arrest or detention shall be entitled to take proceedings before a court, in order that that court may decide without delay on the lawfulness of his detention and order his release if the detention is not lawful.

5. Anyone who has been the victim of unlawful arrest or detention shall have an enforceable right to compensation.

Article 10

1. All persons deprived of their liberty shall be treated with humanity and with respect for the inherent dignity of the human person.

2. (a) Accused persons shall, save in exceptional circumstances, be segregated from convicted persons and shall be subject to separate treatment appropriate to their status as non-convicted persons;

(b) Accused juvenile persons shall be separated from adults and brought as speedily as possible for adjudication.

3. The penitentiary system shall comprise treatment of prisoners the essential aim of which shall be their reformation and social rehabilitation. Juvenile offenders shall be segregated from adults and be accorded treatment appropriate to their age and legal status.

Article 11
No one shall be imprisoned merely on the ground of inability to fulfil a contractual obligation.

Article 12
1. Everyone lawfully within the territory of a State shall, within that territory, have the right to liberty of movement and freedom to choose his residence.

2. Everyone shall be free to leave any country, including his own.

3. The above-mentioned rights shall not be subject to any restrictions except those which are provided by law, are necessary to protect national security, public order (*ordre public*), public health or morals or the rights and freedoms of others, and are consistent with the other rights recognized in the present Covenant.

4. No one shall be arbitrarily deprived of the right to enter his own country.

Article 13
An alien lawfully in the territory of a State Party to the present Covenant may be expelled therefrom only in pursuance of a decision reached in accordance with law and shall, except where compelling reasons of national security otherwise require, be allowed to submit the reasons against his expulsion and to have his case reviewed by, and be represented for the purpose before, the competent authority or a person or persons especially designated by the competent authority.

Article 14
1. All persons shall be equal before the courts and tribunals. In the determination of any criminal charge against him, or of his rights and obligations in a suit at law, everyone shall be entitled to a fair and public hearing by a competent, independent and impartial tribunal established by law. The press and the public may be excluded from all or part of a trial for reasons of morals, public order (*ordre public*) or national security in a democratic society, or when the interest of the private lives of the parties so requires, or to the extent strictly necessary in the opinion of the court in special circumstances where publicity would prejudice the interests of justice; but any judg-

ment rendered in a criminal case or in a suit at law shall be made public except where the interest of juvenile persons otherwise requires or the proceedings concern matrimonial disputes or the guardianship of children.

2. Everyone charged with a criminal offence shall have the right to be presumed innocent until proved guilty according to law.

3. In the determination of any criminal charge against him, everyone shall be entitled to the following minimum guarantees, in full equality: (a) To be informed promptly and in detail in a language which he understands of the nature and cause of the charge against him; (b) To have adequate time and facilities for the preparation of his defense and to communicate with counsel of his own choosing; (c) To be tried without undue delay; (d) To be tried in his presence, and to defend himself in person or through legal assistance of his own choosing; to be informed, if he does not have legal assistance, of this right; and to have legal assistance assigned to him, in any case where the interests of justice so require, and without payment by him in any such case if he does not have sufficient means to pay for it; (e) To examine, or have examined, the witnesses against him and to obtain the attendance and examination of witnesses on his behalf under the same conditions as witnesses against him; (f) To have the free assistance of an interpreter if he cannot understand or speak the language used in court; (g) Not to be compelled to testify against himself or to confess guilt.

4. In the case of juvenile persons, the procedure shall be such as will take account of their age and the desirability of promoting their rehabilitation.

5. Everyone convicted of a crime shall have the right to his conviction and sentence being reviewed by a higher tribunal according to law.

6. When a person has by a final decision been convicted of a criminal offence and when subsequently his conviction has been reversed or he has been pardoned on the ground that a new or newly discovered fact shows conclusively that there has been a miscarriage of justice, the person who has suffered punishment as a result of such conviction shall be compensated according to law, unless it is proved that the non-disclosure of the unknown fact in time is wholly or partly attributable to him.

7. No one shall be liable to be tried or punished again for an offence for which he has already been finally convicted or acquitted in accordance with the law and penal procedure of each country.

Article 15

1. No one shall be held guilty of any criminal offence on account of any act or omission which did not constitute a criminal offence, under national or international law, at the time when it was committed. Nor shall a heavier penalty be imposed than the one that was applicable at the time when the criminal offence was committed. If, subsequent to the commission of the offence, provision is made by law for the imposition of the lighter penalty, the offender shall benefit thereby.

2. Nothing in this article shall prejudice the trial and punishment of any person for any act or omission which, at the time when it was committed, was criminal according to the general principles of law recognized by the community of nations.

Article 16

Everyone shall have the right to recognition everywhere as a person before the law.

Article 17

1. No one shall be subjected to arbitrary or unlawful interference with his privacy, family, home or correspondence, nor to unlawful attacks on his honor and reputation.

2. Everyone has the right to the protection of the law against such interference or attacks.

Article 18

1. Everyone shall have the right to freedom of thought, conscience and religion. This right shall include freedom to have or to adopt a religion or belief of his choice, and freedom, either individually or in community with others and in public or private, to manifest his religion or belief in worship, observance, practice and teaching.

2. No one shall be subject to coercion, which would impair his freedom to have or to adopt a religion or belief of his choice.

3. Freedom to manifest one's religion or beliefs may be subject only to such limitations as are prescribed by law and are necessary to protect public safety, order, health, or morals or the fundamental rights and freedoms of others.

4. The States Parties to the present Covenant undertake to have respect for the liberty of parents and, when applicable, legal guardians to ensure the religious and moral education of their children in conformity with their own convictions.

Article 19

1. Everyone shall have the right to hold opinions without interference.

2. Everyone shall have the right to freedom of expression; this right shall include freedom to seek, receive and impart information and ideas of all kinds, regardless of frontiers, either orally, in writing or in print, in the form of art, or through any other media of his choice.

3. The exercise of the rights provided for in paragraph 2 of this article carries with it special duties and responsibilities. It may therefore be subject to certain restrictions, but these shall only be such as are provided by law and are necessary:

(a) For respect of the rights or reputations of others;

(b) For the protection of national security or of public order (*ordre public*), or of public health or morals.

Article 20

1. Any propaganda for war shall be prohibited by law.

2. Any advocacy of national, racial or religious hatred that constitutes incitement to discrimination, hostility or violence shall be prohibited by law.

Article 21

The right of peaceful assembly shall be recognized. No restrictions may be placed on the exercise of this right other than those imposed in conformity with the law and which are necessary in a democratic society in the interests of national security or public safety, public order (*ordre public*), the protection of public health or morals or the protection of the rights and freedoms of others.

Article 22

1. Everyone shall have the right to freedom of association with others, including the right to form and join trade unions for the protection of his interests.

2. No restrictions may be placed on the exercise of this right other than those which are prescribed by law and which are necessary in a democratic society in the interests of national security or public safety, public order (*ordre public*), the protection of public health or morals or the protection of the rights and freedoms of others. This article shall not prevent the imposition of lawful restrictions on members of the armed forces and of the police in their exercise of this right.

3. Nothing in this article shall authorize States Parties to the International Labor Organization Convention of 1948 concerning Freedom of Association and Protection of the Right to Organize to take legislative measures which would prejudice, or to apply the law in such a manner as to prejudice, the guarantees provided for in that Convention.

Article 23

1. The family is the natural and fundamental group unit of society and is entitled to protection by society and the State.

2. The right of men and women of marriageable age to marry and to found a family shall be recognized.

3. No marriage shall be entered into without the free and full consent of the intending spouses.

4. States Parties to the present Covenant shall take appropriate steps to ensure equality of rights and responsibilities of spouses as to marriage, during marriage and at its dissolution. In the case of dissolution, provision shall be made for the necessary protection of any children.

Article 24

1. Every child shall have, without any discrimination as to race, color, sex, language, religion, national or social origin, property or birth, the right to such measures of protection as are required by his status as a minor, on the part of his family, society and the State.

2. Every child shall be registered immediately after birth and shall have a name.

3. Every child has the right to acquire a nationality.

Article 25
Every citizen shall have the right and the opportunity, without any of the distinctions mentioned in article 2 and without unreasonable restrictions:

(a) To take part in the conduct of public affairs, directly or through freely chosen representatives;

(b) To vote and to be elected at genuine periodic elections which shall be by universal and equal suffrage and shall be held by secret ballot, guaranteeing the free expression of the will of the electors;

(c) To have access, on general terms of equality, to public service in his country.

Article 26
All persons are equal before the law and are entitled without any discrimination to the equal protection of the law. In this respect, the law shall prohibit any discrimination and guarantee to all persons equal and effective protection against discrimination on any ground such as race, color, sex, language, religion, political or other opinion, national or social origin, property, birth or other status.

Article 27
In those States in which ethnic, religious or linguistic minorities exist, persons belonging to such minorities shall not be denied the right, in community with the other members of their group, to enjoy their own culture, to profess and practice their own religion, or to use their own language.

PART IV

Article 28
1. There shall be established a Human Rights Committee (hereafter referred to in the present Covenant as the Committee). It shall consist of eighteen members and shall carry out the functions

hereinafter provided.

2. The Committee shall be composed of nationals of the States Parties to the present Covenant who shall be persons of high moral character and recognized competence in the field of human rights, consideration being given to the usefulness of the participation of some persons having legal experience.

3. The members of the Committee shall be elected and shall serve in their personal capacity.

Article 29

1. The members of the Committee shall be elected by secret ballot from a list of persons possessing the qualifications prescribed in article 28 and nominated for the purpose by the States Parties to the present Covenant.

2. Each State Party to the present Covenant may nominate not more than two persons. These persons shall be nationals of the nominating State.

3. A person shall be eligible for re-nomination.

Article 30

1. The initial election shall be held no later than six months after the date of the entry into force of the present Covenant.

2. At least four months before the date of each election to the Committee, other than an election to fill a vacancy declared in accordance with article 34, the Secretary-General of the United Nations shall address a written invitation to the States Parties to the present Covenant to submit their nominations for membership of the Committee within three months.

3. The Secretary-General of the United Nations shall prepare a list in alphabetical order of all the persons thus nominated, with an indication of the States Parties which have nominated them, and shall submit it to the States Parties to the present Covenant no later than one month before the date of each election.

4. Elections of the members of the Committee shall be held at a meeting of the States Parties to the present Covenant convened by the Secretary General of the United Nations at the Headquarters of the United Nations. At that meeting, for which two thirds of the States Parties to the present Covenant shall constitute a quorum, the persons elected to the Committee shall be those nominees who obtain the largest number of votes and an absolute majority of the votes of the representatives of States Parties present and voting.

Article 31

1. The Committee may not include more than one national of the same State.

2. In the election of the Committee, consideration shall be given to equitable geographical distribution of membership and to the representation of the different forms of civilization and of the principal legal systems.

Article 32

1. The members of the Committee shall be elected for a term of four years. They shall be eligible for re-election if re-nominated. However, the terms of nine of the members elected at the first election shall expire at the end of two years; immediately after the first election, the names of these nine members shall be chosen by lot by the Chairman of the meeting referred to in article 30, paragraph 4.

2. Elections at the expiry of office shall be held in accordance with the preceding articles of this part of the present Covenant.

Article 33

1. If, in the unanimous opinion of the other members, a member of the Committee has ceased to carry out his functions for any cause other than absence of a temporary character, the Chairman of the Committee shall notify the Secretary-General of the United Nations, who shall then declare the seat of that member to be vacant.

2. In the event of the death or the resignation of a member of the Committee, the Chairman shall immediately notify the Secretary-General of the United Nations, who shall declare the seat vacant from the date of death or the date on which the resignation takes effect.

Article 34

1. When a vacancy is declared in accordance with article 33 and if the term of office of the member to be replaced does not expire within six months of the declaration of the vacancy, the Secretary-General of the United Nations shall notify each of the States Parties to the present Covenant, which may within two months submit nominations in accordance with article 29 for the purpose of filling the vacancy.

2. The Secretary-General of the United Nations shall prepare a list in alphabetical order of the persons thus nominated and shall submit it to the States Parties to the present Covenant. The election to fill the vacancy shall then take place in accordance with the relevant provisions of this part of the present Covenant.

3. A member of the Committee elected to fill a vacancy declared in accordance with article 33 shall hold office for the remainder of the term of the member who vacated the seat on the Committee under the provisions of that article.

Article 35

The members of the Committee shall, with the approval of the General Assembly of the United Nations, receive emoluments from United Nations resources on such terms and conditions as the General Assembly may decide, having regard to the importance of the Committee's responsibilities.

Article 36

The Secretary-General of the United Nations shall provide the necessary staff and facilities for the effective performance of the functions of the Committee under the present Covenant.

Article 37

1. The Secretary-General of the United Nations shall convene the initial meeting of the Committee at the Headquarters of the United Nations.

2. After its initial meeting, the Committee shall meet at such times as shall be provided in its rules of procedure.

3. The Committee shall normally meet at the Headquarters of the United Nations or at the United Nations Office at Geneva.

Article 38

Every member of the Committee shall, before taking up his duties, make a solemn declaration in open committee that he will perform his functions impartially and conscientiously.

Article 39

1. The Committee shall elect its officers for a term of two years. They may be re-elected.

2. The Committee shall establish its own rules of procedure, but these rules shall provide, inter alia, that:

(a) Twelve members shall constitute a quorum;

(b) Decisions of the Committee shall be made by a majority vote of the members present.

Article 40

1. The States Parties to the present Covenant undertake to submit reports on the measures they have adopted which give effect to the rights recognized herein and on the progress made in the enjoyment of those rights: (a) Within one year of the entry into force of the present Covenant for the States Parties concerned;

(b) Thereafter whenever the Committee so requests.

2. All reports shall be submitted to the Secretary-General of the United Nations, who shall transmit them to the Committee for consideration. Reports shall indicate the factors and difficulties, if any, affecting the implementation of the present Covenant.

3. The Secretary-General of the United Nations may, after consultation with the Committee, transmit to the specialized agencies concerned copies of such parts of the reports as may fall within their field of competence.

4. The Committee shall study the reports submitted by the States Parties to the present Covenant. It shall transmit its reports, and such general comments as it may consider appropriate, to the States Parties. The Committee may also transmit to the Economic and Social Council these comments along with the copies of the reports it has received from States Parties to the present Covenant.

5. The States Parties to the present Covenant may submit to the Committee observations on any comments that may be made in accordance with paragraph 4 of this article.

Article 41

1. A State Party to the present Covenant may at any time declare under this article that it recognizes the competence of the Committee to receive and consider communications to the effect that a State Party claims that another State Party is not fulfilling its obligations under the present Covenant. Communications under this article may be received and considered only if submitted by a State Party which has made a declaration recognizing in regard to itself the competence of the Committee. No communication shall be received by the Committee if it concerns a State Party which has not made such a declaration. Communications received under this article shall be dealt with in accordance with the following procedure:

(a) If a State Party to the present Covenant considers that another State Party is not giving effect to the provisions of the present Covenant, it may, by written communication, bring the matter to the attention of that State Party. Within three months after the receipt of the communication the receiving State shall afford the State which sent the communication an explanation, or any other statement in writing clarifying the matter which should include, to the extent possible and pertinent, reference to domestic procedures and remedies taken, pending, or available in the matter;

(b) If the matter is not adjusted to the satisfaction of both States Parties concerned within six months after the receipt by the receiving State of the initial communication, either State shall have the right to refer the matter to the Committee, by notice given to the Committee and to the other State;

(c) The Committee shall deal with a matter referred to it only after it has ascertained that all available domestic remedies have been invoked and exhausted in the matter, in conformity with the generally recognized principles of international law. This shall not be the rule where the application of the remedies is unreasonably prolonged;

(d) The Committee shall hold closed meetings when examining communications under this article;

(e) Subject to the provisions of subparagraph (c), the Committee shall make available its good offices to the States Parties concerned with a view to a friendly solution of the matter on the basis of respect for human rights and fundamental freedoms as recognized in the present Covenant;

(f) In any matter referred to it, the Committee may call upon the States Parties concerned, referred to in subparagraph (b), to supply any relevant information;

(g) The States Parties concerned, referred to in subparagraph (b), shall have the right to be represented when the matter is being considered in the Committee and to make submissions orally and/or in writing;

(h) The Committee shall, within twelve months after the date of receipt of notice under subparagraph (b), submit a report:

(i) If a solution within the terms of subparagraph (e) is reached, the Committee shall confine its report to a brief statement of the facts and of the solution reached;

(ii) If a solution within the terms of subparagraph (e) is not reached, the Committee shall confine its report to a brief statement of the facts; the written submissions and record of the oral submissions made by the States Parties concerned shall be attached to the report. In every matter, the report shall be communicated to the States Parties concerned.

2. The provisions of this article shall come into force when ten States Parties to the present Covenant have made declarations under paragraph I of this article. Such declarations shall be deposited by the States Parties with the Secretary-General of the United Nations, who shall transmit copies thereof to the other States Parties. A declaration may be withdrawn at any time by notification to the Secretary-General. Such a withdrawal shall not prejudice the consideration of any matter which is the subject of a communication already transmitted under this article; no further communication by any State Party shall be received after the notification of withdrawal of the declaration has been received by the Secretary-General, unless the State Party concerned has made a new declaration.

Article 42

1. (a) If a matter referred to the Committee in accordance with article 41 is not resolved to the satisfaction of the States Parties concerned, the Committee may, with the prior consent of the States Parties concerned, appoint an ad hoc Conciliation Commission (hereinafter referred to as the Commission). The good offices of the Commission shall be made available to the States Parties concerned with a view to an amicable solution of the matter on the basis of respect for the present Covenant;

      (b) The Commission shall consist of five persons acceptable to the States Parties concerned. If the States Parties concerned fail to reach agreement within three months on all or part of the composition of the Commission, the members of the Commission concerning whom no agreement has been reached shall be elected by secret ballot by a two-thirds majority vote of the Committee from among its members.

      2. The members of the Commission shall serve in their personal capacity. They shall not be nationals of the States Parties concerned, or of a State not Party to the present Covenant, or of a State Party which has not made a declaration under article 41.

      3. The Commission shall elect its own Chairman and adopt its own rules of procedure.

      4. The meetings of the Commission shall normally be held at the Headquarters of the United Nations or at the United Nations Office at Geneva. However, they may be held at such other convenient places as the Commission may determine in consultation with the Secretary-General of the United Nations and the States Parties concerned.

      5. The secretariat provided in accordance with article 36 shall also service the commissions appointed under this article.

      6. The information received and collated by the Committee shall be made available to the Commission and the Commission may call upon the States Parties concerned to supply any other relevant information.

      7. When the Commission has fully considered the matter, but in any event not later than twelve months after having been seized of the matter, it shall submit to the Chairman of the Committee a report for communication to the States Parties concerned:

      (a) If the Commission is unable to complete its consideration of the matter within twelve months, it shall confine its report to a brief statement of the status of its consideration of the matter;

      (b) If an amicable solution to the matter on the basis of respect for human rights as recognized in the present Covenant is reached, the Commission shall confine its report to a brief statement of the facts and of the solution reached;

(c) If a solution within the terms of subparagraph (b) is not reached, the Commission's report shall embody its findings on all questions of fact relevant to the issues between the States Parties concerned, and its views on the possibilities of an amicable solution of the matter. This report shall also contain the written submissions and a record of the oral submissions made by the States Parties concerned;

(d) If the Commission's report is submitted under subparagraph (c), the States Parties concerned shall, within three months of the receipt of the report, notify the Chairman of the Committee whether or not they accept the contents of the report of the Commission.

8. The provisions of this article are without prejudice to the responsibilities of the Committee under article 41.

9. The States Parties concerned shall share equally all the expenses of the members of the Commission in accordance with estimates to be provided by the Secretary-General of the United Nations.

10. The Secretary-General of the United Nations shall be empowered to pay the expenses of the members of the Commission, if necessary, before reimbursement by the States Parties concerned, in accordance with paragraph 9 of this article.

Article 43

The members of the Committee, and of the ad hoc conciliation commissions which may be appointed under article 42, shall be entitled to the facilities, privileges and immunities of experts on mission for the United Nations as laid down in the relevant sections of the Convention on the Privileges and Immunities of the United Nations.

Article 44

The provisions for the implementation of the present Covenant shall apply without prejudice to the procedures prescribed in the field of human rights by or under the constituent instruments and the conventions of the United Nations and of the specialized agencies and shall not prevent the States Parties to the present Covenant from having recourse to other procedures for settling a dispute in accordance with general or special international agreements in force between them.

Article 45
The Committee shall submit to the General Assembly of the United Nations, through the Economic and Social Council, an annual report on its activities.

PART V

Article 46
Nothing in the present Covenant shall be interpreted as impairing the provisions of the Charter of the United Nations and of the constitutions of the specialized agencies, which define the respective responsibilities of the various organs of the United Nations and of the specialized agencies in regard to the matters dealt with in the present Covenant.

Article 47
Nothing in the present Covenant shall be interpreted as impairing the inherent right of all peoples to enjoy and utilize fully and freely their natural wealth and resources.

PART VI

Article 48
1. The present Covenant is open for signature by any State Member of the United Nations or member of any of its specialized agencies, by any State Party to the Statute of the International Court of Justice, and by any other State which has been invited by the General Assembly of the United Nations to become a Party to the present Covenant.

2. The present Covenant is subject to ratification. Instruments of ratification shall be deposited with the Secretary-General of the United Nations.

3. The present Covenant shall be open to accession by any State referred to in paragraph 1 of this article.

4. Accession shall be effected by the deposit of an instrument of accession with the Secretary-General of the United Nations.

5. The Secretary-General of the United Nations shall inform all States which have signed this Covenant or acceded to it of the deposit of each instrument of ratification or accession.

Article 49

1. The present Covenant shall enter into force three months after the date of the deposit with the Secretary-General of the United Nations of the thirty-fifth instrument of ratification or instrument of accession.

2. For each State ratifying the present Covenant or acceding to it after the deposit of the thirty-fifth instrument of ratification or instrument of accession, the present Covenant shall enter into force three months after the date of the deposit of its own instrument of ratification or instrument of accession.

Article 50

The provisions of the present Covenant shall extend to all parts of federal States without any limitations or exceptions.

Article 51

1. Any State Party to the present Covenant may propose an amendment and file it with the Secretary-General of the United Nations. The Secretary-General of the United Nations shall thereupon communicate any proposed amendments to the States Parties to the present Covenant with a request that they notify him whether they favor a conference of States Parties for the purpose of considering and voting upon the proposals. In the event that at least one third of the States Parties favors such a conference, the Secretary-General shall convene the conference under the auspices of the United Nations. Any amendment adopted by a majority of the States Parties present and voting at the conference shall be submitted to the General Assembly of the United Nations for approval.

2. Amendments shall come into force when they have been approved by the General Assembly of the United Nations and accepted by a two-thirds majority of the States Parties to the present Covenant in accordance to their respective constitutional processes.

3. When amendments come into force, they shall be binding on those States Parties, which have accepted them, other States Parties still being bound by the provisions of the present Covenant and any earlier amendment which they have accepted.

Article 52

1. Irrespective of the notifications made under article 48, paragraph 5, the Secretary-General of the United Nations shall inform all States referred to in paragraph I of the same article of the following particulars:

(a) Signatures, ratifications and accessions under article 48;

(b) The date of the entry into force of the present Covenant under article 49 and the date of the entry into force of any amendments under article 51.

Article 53

1. The present Covenant, of which the Chinese, English, French, Russian and Spanish texts are equally authentic, shall be deposited in the archives of the United Nations.

2. The Secretary-General of the United Nations shall transmit certified copies of the present Covenant to all States referred to in article 48.

APPENDIX D

INTERNATIONAL COVENANT ON ECONOMIC, SOCIAL AND CULTURAL RIGHTS[103]

ADOPTED AND OPENED FOR SIGNATURE, RATIFICATION AND ACCESSION BY GENERAL ASSEMBLY RESOLUTION 2200A (XXI) OF 16 DECEMBER 1966 ENTRY INTO FORCE 3 JANUARY 1976, IN ACCORDANCE WITH ARTICLE 27

Preamble

The States Parties to the present Covenant,

Considering that, in accordance with the principles proclaimed in the Charter of the United Nations, recognition of the inherent dignity and of the equal and inalienable rights of all members of the human family is the foundation of freedom, justice and peace in the world,

Recognizing that these rights derive from the inherent dignity of the human person,

Recognizing that, in accordance with the Universal Declaration of Human Rights, the ideal of free human beings enjoying freedom from fear and want can only be achieved if conditions are created whereby everyone may enjoy his economic, social and cultural rights, as well as his civil and political rights,

---

103 Source: http://www.ohchr.org/EN/ProfessionalInterest/Pages/CESCR.aspx

Considering the obligation of States under the Charter of the United Nations to promote universal respect for, and observance of, human rights and freedoms,

Realizing that the individual, having duties to other individuals and to the community to which he belongs, is under a responsibility to strive for the promotion and observance of the rights recognized in the present Covenant,

Agree upon the following articles:

PART I

Article 1

1. All peoples have the right of self-determination. By virtue of that right they freely determine their political status and freely pursue their economic, social and cultural development.

2. All peoples may, for their own ends, freely dispose of their natural wealth and resources without prejudice to any obligations arising out of international economic co-operation, based upon the principle of mutual benefit, and international law. In no case may a people be deprived of its own means of subsistence.

3. The States Parties to the present Covenant, including those having responsibility for the administration of Non-Self-Governing and Trust Territories, shall promote the realization of the right of self-determination, and shall respect that right, in conformity with the provisions of the Charter of the United Nations.

PART II

Article 2

1. Each State Party to the present Covenant undertakes to take steps, individually and through international assistance and co-operation, especially economic and technical, to the maximum of its available resources, with a view to achieving progressively the full realization of the rights recognized in the present Covenant by all appropriate means, including particularly the adoption of legislative measures.

2. The States Parties to the present Covenant undertake to guarantee that the rights enunciated in the present Covenant will be exercised without discrimination of any kind as to race, color, sex, language, religion, political or other opinion, national or social origin, property, birth or other status.

3. Developing countries, with due regard to human rights and their national economy, may determine to what extent they would guarantee the economic rights recognized in the present Covenant to non-nationals.

Article 3

The States Parties to the present Covenant undertake to ensure the equal right of men and women to the enjoyment of all economic, social and cultural rights set forth in the present Covenant.

Article 4

The States Parties to the present Covenant recognize that, in the enjoyment of those rights provided by the State in conformity with the present Covenant, the State may subject such rights only to such limitations as are determined by law only in so far as this may be compatible with the nature of these rights and solely for the purpose of promoting the general welfare in a democratic society.

Article 5

1. Nothing in the present Covenant may be interpreted as implying for any State, group or person any right to engage in any activity or to perform any act aimed at the destruction of any of the rights or freedoms recognized herein, or at their limitation to a greater extent than is provided for in the present Covenant.

2. No restriction upon or derogation from any of the fundamental human rights recognized or existing in any country in virtue of law, conventions, regulations or custom shall be admitted on the pretext that the present Covenant does not recognize such rights or that it recognizes them to a lesser extent.

PART III

Article 6

1. The States Parties to the present Covenant recognize the right to work, which includes the right of everyone to the opportunity to gain his living by work which he freely chooses or accepts, and will take appropriate steps to safeguard this right.

2. The steps to be taken by a State Party to the present Covenant to achieve the full realization of this right shall include technical and vocational guidance and training programs, policies and techniques to achieve steady economic, social and cultural development and full and productive employment under conditions safeguarding fundamental political and economic freedoms to the individual.

Article 7

The States Parties to the present Covenant recognize the right of everyone to the enjoyment of just and favorable conditions of work, which ensure, in particular:

(a) Remuneration, which provides all workers, as a minimum, with:

(i) Fair wages and equal remuneration for work of equal value without distinction of any kind, in particular women being guaranteed conditions of work not inferior to those enjoyed by men, with equal pay for equal work;

(ii) A decent living for themselves and their families in accordance with the provisions of the present Covenant;

(b) Safe and healthy working conditions;

(c) Equal opportunity for everyone to be promoted in his employment to an appropriate higher level, subject to no considerations other than those of seniority and competence;

(d) Rest, leisure and reasonable limitation of working hours and periodic holidays with pay, as well as remuneration for public holidays

Article 8

1. The States Parties to the present Covenant undertake to ensure:

(a) The right of everyone to form trade unions and join the

trade union of his choice, subject only to the rules of the organization concerned, for the promotion and protection of his economic and social interests. No restrictions may be placed on the exercise of this right other than those prescribed by law and which are necessary in a democratic society in the interests of national security or public order or for the protection of the rights and freedoms of others;

(b) The right of trade unions to establish national federations or confederations and the right of the latter to form or join international trade-union organizations;

(c) The right of trade unions to function freely subject to no limitations other than those prescribed by law and which are necessary in a democratic society in the interests of national security or public order or for the protection of the rights and freedoms of others;

(d) The right to strike, provided that it is exercised in conformity with the laws of the particular country.

2. This article shall not prevent the imposition of lawful restrictions on the exercise of these rights by members of the armed forces or of the police or of the administration of the State.

3. Nothing in this article shall authorize States Parties to the International Labor Organization Convention of 1948 concerning Freedom of Association and Protection of the Right to Organize to take legislative measures which would prejudice, or apply the law in such a manner as would prejudice, the guarantees provided for in that Convention.

Article 9

The States Parties to the present Covenant recognize the right of everyone to social security, including social insurance.

Article 10

The States Parties to the present Covenant recognize that:

1. The widest possible protection and assistance should be accorded to the family, which is the natural and fundamental group unit of society, particularly for its establishment and while it is responsible for the care and education of dependent children. Marriage must be entered into with the free consent of the intending spouses.

2. Special protection should be accorded to mothers during a reasonable period before and after childbirth. During such period working mothers should be accorded paid leave or leave with adequate social security benefits.

3. Special measures of protection and assistance should be taken on behalf of all children and young persons without any discrimination for reasons of parentage or other conditions. Children and young persons should be protected from economic and social exploitation. Their employment in work harmful to their morals or health or dangerous to life or likely to hamper their normal development should be punishable by law. States should also set age limits below which the paid employment of child labor should be prohibited and punishable by law.

Article 11

1. The States Parties to the present Covenant recognize the right of everyone to an adequate standard of living for himself and his family, including adequate food, clothing and housing, and to the continuous improvement of living conditions. The States Parties will take appropriate steps to ensure the realization of this right, recognizing to this effect the essential importance of international co-operation based on free consent.

2. The States Parties to the present Covenant, recognizing the fundamental right of everyone to be free from hunger, shall take, individually and through international co-operation, the measures, including specific programs, which are needed:

(a) To improve methods of production, conservation and distribution of food by making full use of technical and scientific knowledge, by disseminating knowledge of the principles of nutrition and by developing or reforming agrarian systems in such a way as to achieve the most efficient development and utilization of natural resources;

(b) Taking into account the problems of both food-importing and food-exporting countries, to ensure an equitable distribution of world food supplies in relation to need.

Article 12

1. The States Parties to the present Covenant recognize the right of everyone to the enjoyment of the highest attainable standard of physical and mental health.

2. The steps to be taken by the States Parties to the present Covenant to achieve the full realization of this right shall include those necessary for:

(a) The provision for the reduction of the stillbirth-rate and of infant mortality and for the healthy development of the child;

(b) The improvement of all aspects of environmental and industrial hygiene;

(c) The prevention, treatment and control of epidemic, endemic, occupational and other diseases;

(d) The creation of conditions, which would assure to all medical service and medical attention in the event of sickness.

Article 13

1. The States Parties to the present Covenant recognize the right of everyone to education. They agree that education shall be directed to the full development of the human personality and the sense of its dignity, and shall strengthen the respect for human rights and fundamental freedoms. They further agree that education shall enable all persons to participate effectively in a free society, promote understanding, tolerance and friendship among all nations and all racial, ethnic or religious groups, and further the activities of the United Nations for the maintenance of peace.

2. The States Parties to the present Covenant recognize that, with a view to achieving the full realization of this right:

(a) Primary education shall be compulsory and available free to all;

(b) Secondary education in its different forms, including technical and vocational secondary education, shall be made generally available and accessible to all by every appropriate means, and in particular by the progressive introduction of free education;

(c) Higher education shall be made equally accessible to all, on the basis of capacity, by every appropriate means, and in particular by the progressive introduction of free education;

(d) Fundamental education shall be encouraged or intensified as far as possible for those persons who have not received or completed the whole period of their primary education;

(e) The development of a system of schools at all levels shall be actively pursued, an adequate fellowship system shall be established, and the material conditions of teaching staff shall be continuously improved.

3. The States Parties to the present Covenant undertake to have respect for the liberty of parents and, when applicable, legal guardians to choose for their children schools, other than those established by the public authorities, which conform to such minimum educational standards as may be laid down or approved by the State and to ensure the religious and moral education of their children in conformity with their own convictions.

4. No part of this article shall be construed so as to interfere with the liberty of individuals and bodies to establish and direct educational institutions, subject always to the observance of the principles set forth in paragraph 1 of this article and to the requirement that the education given in such institutions shall conform to such minimum standards as may be laid down by the State.

Article 14

Each State Party to the present Covenant which, at the time of becoming a Party, has not been able to secure in its metropolitan territory or other territories under its jurisdiction compulsory primary education, free of charge, undertakes, within two years, to work out and adopt a detailed plan of action for the progressive implementation, within a reasonable number of years, to be fixed in the plan, of the principle of compulsory education free of charge for all.

Article 15

1. The States Parties to the present Covenant recognize the right of everyone:

(a) To take part in cultural life;

(b) To enjoy the benefits of scientific progress and its applications;

(c) To benefit from the protection of the moral and material interests resulting from any scientific, literary or artistic production of which he is the author.

2. The steps to be taken by the States Parties to the present Covenant to achieve the full realization of this right shall include those necessary for the conservation, the development and the diffusion of science and culture.

3. The States Parties to the present Covenant undertake to respect the freedom indispensable for scientific research and creative activity.

4. The States Parties to the present Covenant recognize the benefits to be derived from the encouragement and development of international contacts and co-operation in the scientific and cultural fields.

PART IV

Article 16

1. The States Parties to the present Covenant undertake to submit in conformity with this part of the Covenant reports on the measures, which they have adopted and the progress made in achieving the observance of the rights recognized herein.

2. (a) All reports shall be submitted to the Secretary-General of the United Nations, who shall transmit copies to the Economic and Social Council for consideration in accordance with the provisions of the present Covenant;

(b) The Secretary-General of the United Nations shall also transmit to the specialized agencies copies of the reports, or any relevant parts therefrom, from States Parties to the present Covenant which are also members of these specialized agencies in so far as these reports, or parts therefrom, relate to any matters which fall within the responsibilities of the said agencies in accordance with their constitutional instruments.

Article 17

1. The States Parties to the present Covenant shall furnish their reports in stages, in accordance with a program to be established by the Economic and Social Council within one year of the entry into

force of the present Covenant after consultation with the States Parties and the specialized agencies concerned.

2. Reports may indicate factors and difficulties affecting the degree of fulfilment of obligations under the present Covenant.

3. Where relevant information has previously been furnished to the United Nations or to any specialized agency by any State Party to the present Covenant, it will not be necessary to reproduce that information, but a precise reference to the information so furnished will suffice.

Article 18

Pursuant to its responsibilities under the Charter of the United Nations in the field of human rights and fundamental freedoms, the Economic and Social Council may make arrangements with the specialized agencies in respect of their reporting to it on the progress made in achieving the observance of the provisions of the present Covenant falling within the scope of their activities. These reports may include particulars of decisions and recommendations on such implementation adopted by their competent organs.

Article 19

The Economic and Social Council may transmit to the Commission on Human Rights for study and general recommendation or, as appropriate, for information, the reports concerning human rights submitted by States in accordance with articles 16 and 17, and those concerning human rights submitted by the specialized agencies in accordance with article 18.

Article 20

The States Parties to the present Covenant and the specialized agencies concerned may submit comments to the Economic and Social Council on any general recommendation under article 19 or reference to such general recommendation in any report of the Commission on Human Rights or any documentation referred to therein.

Article 21

The Economic and Social Council may submit from time to time to the General Assembly reports with recommendations of a general nature and a summary of the information received from the States Parties to the present Covenant and the specialized agencies on the measures taken and the progress made in achieving general observance of the rights recognized in the present Covenant.

Article 22

The Economic and Social Council may bring to the attention of other organs of the United Nations, their subsidiary organs and specialized agencies concerned with furnishing technical assistance any matters arising out of the reports referred to in this part of the present Covenant which may assist such bodies in deciding, each within its field of competence, on the advisability of international measures likely to contribute to the effective progressive implementation of the present Covenant.

Article 23

The States Parties to the present Covenant agree that international action for the achievement of the rights recognized in the present Covenant includes such methods as the conclusion of conventions, the adoption of recommendations, the furnishing of technical assistance and the holding of regional meetings and technical meetings for the purpose of consultation and study organized in conjunction with the Governments concerned.

Article 24

Nothing in the present Covenant shall be interpreted as impairing the provisions of the Charter of the United Nations and of the constitutions of the specialized agencies, which define the respective responsibilities of the various organs of the United Nations and of the specialized agencies in regard to the matters dealt with in the present Covenant.

Article 25

Nothing in the present Covenant shall be interpreted as

impairing the inherent right of all peoples to enjoy and utilize fully and freely their natural wealth and resources.

PART V

Article 26
1. The present Covenant is open for signature by any State Member of the United Nations or member of any of its specialized agencies, by any State Party to the Statute of the International Court of Justice, and by any other State which has been invited by the General Assembly of the United Nations to become a party to the present Covenant.

2. The present Covenant is subject to ratification. Instruments of ratification shall be deposited with the Secretary-General of the United Nations.

3. The present Covenant shall be open to accession by any State referred to in paragraph 1 of this article.

4. Accession shall be effected by the deposit of an instrument of accession with the Secretary-General of the United Nations.

5. The Secretary-General of the United Nations shall inform all States which have signed the present Covenant or acceded to it of the deposit of each instrument of ratification or accession.

Article 27
1. The present Covenant shall enter into force three months after the date of the deposit with the Secretary-General of the United Nations of the thirty-fifth instrument of ratification or instrument of accession.

2. For each State ratifying the present Covenant or acceding to it after the deposit of the thirty-fifth instrument of ratification or instrument of accession, the present Covenant shall enter into force three months after the date of the deposit of its own instrument of ratification or instrument of accession.

Article 28
The provisions of the present Covenant shall extend to all parts of federal States without any limitations or exceptions.

Article 29

1. Any State Party to the present Covenant may propose an amendment and file it with the Secretary-General of the United Nations. The Secretary-General shall thereupon communicate any proposed amendments to the States Parties to the present Covenant with a request that they notify him whether they favor a conference of States Parties for the purpose of considering and voting upon the proposals. In the event that at least one third of the States Parties favors such a conference, the Secretary-General shall convene the conference under the auspices of the United Nations. Any amendment adopted by a majority of the States Parties present and voting at the conference shall be submitted to the General Assembly of the United Nations for approval.

2. Amendments shall come into force when they have been approved by the General Assembly of the United Nations and accepted by a two-thirds majority of the States Parties to the present Covenant in accordance with their respective constitutional processes.

3. When amendments come into force they shall be binding on those States Parties, which have accepted them, other States Parties still being bound by the provisions of the present Covenant and any earlier amendment which they have accepted.

Article 30

Irrespective of the notifications made under article 26, paragraph 5, the Secretary-General of the United Nations shall inform all States referred to in paragraph I of the same article of the following particulars:

(a) Signatures, ratifications and accessions under article 26;

(b) The date of the entry into force of the present Covenant under article 27 and the date of the entry into force of any amendments under article 29.

Article 31

1. The present Covenant, of which the Chinese, English, French, Russian and Spanish texts are equally authentic, shall be deposited in the archives of the United Nations.

2. The Secretary-General of the United Nations shall transmit certified copies of the present Covenant to all States referred to in article 26.

APPENDIX E

AMERICAN CONVENTION ON HUMAN RIGHTS "PACT OF SAN JOSE, COSTA RICA[104]

Preamble

The American states signatory to the present Convention,

Reaffirming their intention to consolidate in this hemisphere, within the framework of democratic institutions, a system of personal liberty and social justice based on respect for the essential rights of man;

Recognizing that the essential rights of man are not derived from one's being a national of a certain state, but are based upon attributes of the human personality, and that they therefore justify international protection in the form of a convention reinforcing or complementing the protection provided by the domestic law of the American states;

Considering that these principles have been set forth in the Charter of the Organization of American States, in the American Declaration of the Rights and Duties of Man, and in the Universal Declaration of Human Rights, and that they have been reaffirmed and refined in other international instruments, worldwide as well as regional in scope;

Reiterating that, in accordance with the Universal Declaration of Human Rights, the ideal of free men enjoying freedom from fear and want can be achieved only if conditions are created whereby everyone may enjoy his economic, social, and cultural rights, as well as his civil and political rights; and

---

104 Source: http://www.oas.org/dil/treaties_B-32_American_Convention_on_Human_Rights.htm

Considering that the Third Special Inter-American Conference (Buenos Aires, 1967) approved the incorporation into the Charter of the Organization itself of broader standards with respect to economic, social, and educational rights and resolved that an inter-American convention on human rights should determine the structure, competence, and procedure of the organs responsible for these matters,

Have agreed upon the following:

PART I - STATE OBLIGATIONS AND RIGHTS PROTECTED

CHAPTER I - GENERAL OBLIGATIONS

Article 1. Obligation to Respect Rights

1. The States Parties to this Convention undertake to respect the rights and freedoms recognized herein and to ensure to all persons subject to their jurisdiction the free and full exercise of those rights and freedoms, without any discrimination for reasons of race, color, sex, language, religion, political or other opinion, national or social origin, economic status, birth, or any other social condition.

2. For the purposes of this Convention, "person" means every human being.

Article 2. Domestic Legal Effects

Where the exercise of any of the rights or freedoms referred to in Article 1 is not already ensured by legislative or other provisions, the States Parties undertake to adopt, in accordance with their constitutional processes and the provisions of this Convention, such legislative or other measures as may be necessary to give effect to those rights or freedoms.

CHAPTER II - CIVIL AND POLITICAL RIGHTS

Article 3. Right to Juridical Personality

Every person has the right to recognition as a person before the law.

Article 4. Right to Life

1. Every person has the right to have his life respected. This right shall be protected by law and, in general, from the moment of conception. No one shall be arbitrarily deprived of his life.

2. In countries that have not abolished the death penalty, it may be imposed only for the most serious crimes and pursuant to a final judgment rendered by a competent court and in accordance with a law establishing such punishment, enacted prior to the commission of the crime. The application of such punishment shall not be extended to crimes to which it does not presently apply.

3. The death penalty shall not be reestablished in states that have abolished it.

4. In no case shall capital punishment be inflicted for political offenses or related common crimes.

5. Capital punishment shall not be imposed upon persons who, at the time the crime was committed, were under 18 years of age or over 70 years of age; nor shall it be applied to pregnant women.

6. Every person condemned to death shall have the right to apply for amnesty, pardon, or commutation of sentence, which may be granted in all cases. Capital punishment shall not be imposed while such a petition is pending decision by the competent authority.

Article 5. Right to Humane Treatment

1. Every person has the right to have his physical, mental, and moral integrity respected.

2. No one shall be subjected to torture or to cruel, inhuman, or degrading punishment or treatment. All persons deprived of their liberty shall be treated with respect for the inherent dignity of the human person.

3. Punishment shall not be extended to any person other than the criminal.

4. Accused persons shall, save in exceptional circumstances, be segregated from convicted persons, and shall be subject to separate treatment appropriate to their status as non-convicted persons.

5. Minors while subject to criminal proceedings shall be separated from adults and brought before specialized tribunals, as speedily as possible, so that they may be treated in accordance with their status as minors.

6. Punishments consisting of deprivation of liberty shall have as an essential aim the reform and social re-adaptation of the prisoners.

Article 6. Freedom from Slavery

1. No one shall be subject to slavery or to involuntary servitude, which are prohibited in all their forms, as are the slave trade and traffic in women.

2. No one shall be required to perform forced or compulsory labor. This provision shall not be interpreted to mean that, in those countries in which the penalty established for certain crimes is deprivation of liberty at forced labor, the carrying out of such a sentence imposed by a competent court is prohibited. Forced labor shall not adversely affect the dignity or the physical or intellectual capacity of the prisoner.

3. For the purposes of this article, the following do not constitute forced or compulsory labor:

a. work or service normally required of a person imprisoned in execution of a sentence or formal decision passed by the competent judicial authority. Such work or service shall be carried out under the supervision and control of public authorities, and any persons performing such work or service shall not be placed at the disposal of any private party, company, or juridical person;

b. military service and, in countries in which conscientious objectors are recognized, national service that the law may provide for in lieu of military service;

c. service exacted in time of danger or calamity that threatens the existence or the well-being of the community; or

d. work or service that forms part of normal civic obligations.

Article 7. Right to Personal Liberty

1. Every person has the right to personal liberty and security.

2. No one shall be deprived of his physical liberty except for the reasons and under the conditions established beforehand by the constitution of the State Party concerned or by a law established pursuant thereto.

3. No one shall be subject to arbitrary arrest or imprisonment.

4. Anyone who is detained shall be informed of the reasons for his detention and shall be promptly notified of the charge or charges against him.

5. Any person detained shall be brought promptly before a judge or other officer authorized by law to exercise judicial power and shall be entitled to trial within a reasonable time or to be released without prejudice to the continuation of the proceedings. His release may be subject to guarantees to assure his appearance for trial.

6. Anyone who is deprived of his liberty shall be entitled to recourse to a competent court, in order that the court may decide without delay on the lawfulness of his arrest or detention and order his release if the arrest or detention is unlawful. In States Parties whose laws provide that anyone who believes himself to be threatened with deprivation of his liberty is entitled to recourse to a competent court in order that it may decide on the lawfulness of such threat, this remedy may not be restricted or abolished. The interested party or another person in his behalf is entitled to seek these remedies.

7. No one shall be detained for debt. This principle shall not limit the orders of a competent judicial authority issued for nonfulfillment of duties of support.

Article 8. Right to a Fair Trial

1. Every person has the right to a hearing, with due guarantees and within a reasonable time, by a competent, independent, and impartial tribunal, previously established by law, in the substantiation of any accusation of a criminal nature made against him or for the determination of his rights and obligations of a civil, labor, fiscal, or any other nature.

2. Every person accused of a criminal offense has the right to be presumed innocent so long as his guilt has not been proven according to law. During the proceedings, every person is entitled, with full equality, to the following minimum guarantees:

a. the right of the accused to be assisted without charge by a translator or interpreter, if he does not understand or does not speak the language of the tribunal or court;

b. prior notification in detail to the accused of the charges against him;

c. adequate time and means for the preparation of his defense;

d. the right of the accused to defend himself personally or to be assisted by legal counsel of his own choosing, and to communicate freely and privately with his counsel;

e. the inalienable right to be assisted by counsel provided by the state, paid or not as the domestic law provides, if the accused does not defend himself personally or engage his own counsel within the time period established by law;

f. the right of the defense to examine witnesses present in the court and to obtain the appearance, as witnesses, of experts or other persons who may throw light on the facts;

g. the right not to be compelled to be a witness against himself or to plead guilty; and

h. the right to appeal the judgment to a higher court.

3. A confession of guilt by the accused shall be valid only if it is made without coercion of any kind.

4. An accused person acquitted by a non-appealable judgment shall not be subjected to a new trial for the same cause.

5. Criminal proceedings shall be public, except insofar as may be necessary to protect the interests of justice.

Article 9. Freedom from Ex Post Facto Laws

No one shall be convicted of any act or omission that did not constitute a criminal offense, under the applicable law, at the time it was committed. A heavier penalty shall not be imposed than the one that was applicable at the time the criminal offense was committed. If subsequent to the commission of the offense the law provides for the imposition of a lighter punishment, the guilty person shall benefit therefrom.

Article 10. Right to Compensation

Every person has the right to be compensated in accordance with the law in the event he has been sentenced by a final judgment through a miscarriage of justice.

Article 11. Right to Privacy

1. Everyone has the right to have his honor respected and his dignity recognized.

2. No one may be the object of arbitrary or abusive interference with his private life, his family, his home, or his correspondence, or of unlawful attacks on his honor or reputation.

3. Everyone has the right to the protection of the law against such interference or attacks.

Article 12. Freedom of Conscience and Religion

1. Everyone has the right to freedom of conscience and of religion. This right includes freedom to maintain or to change one's religion or beliefs, and freedom to profess or disseminate one's religion or beliefs, either individually or together with others, in public or in private.

2. No one shall be subject to restrictions that might impair his freedom to maintain or to change his religion or beliefs.

3. Freedom to manifest one's religion and beliefs may be subject only to the limitations prescribed by law that are necessary to protect public safety, order, health, or morals, or the rights or freedoms of others.

4. Parents or guardians, as the case may be, have the right to provide for the religious and moral education of their children or wards that is in accord with their own convictions.

Article 13. Freedom of Thought and Expression

1. Everyone has the right to freedom of thought and expression. This right includes freedom to seek, receive, and impart information and ideas of all kinds, regardless of frontiers, either orally, in writing, in print, in the form of art, or through any other medium of one's choice.

2. The exercise of the right provided for in the foregoing paragraph shall not be subject to prior censorship but shall be subject to subsequent imposition of liability, which shall be expressly established by law to the extent necessary to ensure:

a. respect for the rights or reputations of others; or

b. the protection of national security, public order, or public health or morals.

3. The right of expression may not be restricted by indirect methods or means, such as the abuse of government or private controls over newsprint, radio broadcasting frequencies, or equipment used in the dissemination of information, or by any other means tending to impede the communication and circulation of ideas and opinions.

4. Notwithstanding the provisions of paragraph 2 above, public entertainments may be subject by law to prior censorship for the sole purpose of regulating access to them for the moral protection of childhood and adolescence.

5. Any propaganda for war and any advocacy of national, racial, or religious hatred that constitute incitements to lawless violence or to any other similar action against any person or group of persons on any grounds including those of race, color, religion, language, or national origin shall be considered as offenses punishable by law.

Article 14. Right of Reply

1. Anyone injured by inaccurate or offensive statements or ideas disseminated to the public in general by a legally regulated medium of communication has the right to reply or to make a correction using the same communications outlet, under such conditions as the law may establish.

2. The correction or reply shall not in any case remit other legal liabilities that may have been incurred.

3. For the effective protection of honor and reputation, every publisher, and every newspaper, motion picture, radio, and television company, shall have a person responsible who is not protected by immunities or special privileges.

Article 15. Right of Assembly

The right of peaceful assembly, without arms, is recognized. No restrictions may be placed on the exercise of this right other than those imposed in conformity with the law and necessary in a democratic society in the interest of national security, public safety or public order, or to protect public health or morals or the rights or freedom of others.

Article 16. Freedom of Association

1. Everyone has the right to associate freely for ideological, religious, political, economic, labor, social, cultural, sports, or other purposes.

2. The exercise of this right shall be subject only to such restrictions established by law as may be necessary in a democratic society, in the interest of national security, public safety or public order, or to protect public health or morals or the rights and freedoms of others.

3. The provisions of this article do not bar the imposition of legal restrictions, including even deprivation of the exercise of the right of association, on members of the armed forces and the police.

Article 17. Rights of the Family

1. The family is the natural and fundamental group unit of society and is entitled to protection by society and the state.

2. The right of men and women of marriageable age to marry and to raise a family shall be recognized, if they meet the conditions required by domestic laws, insofar as such conditions do not affect the principle of nondiscrimination established in this Convention.

3. No marriage shall be entered into without the free and full consent of the intending spouses.

4. The States Parties shall take appropriate steps to ensure the equality of rights and the adequate balancing of responsibilities of the spouses as to marriage, during marriage, and in the event of its dissolution. In case of dissolution, provision shall be made for the necessary protection of any children solely on the basis of their own best interests.

5. The law shall recognize equal rights for children born out of wedlock and those born in wedlock.

Article 18. Right to a Name

Every person has the right to a given name and to the surnames of his parents or that of one of them. The law shall regulate the manner in which this right shall be ensured for all, by the use of assumed names if necessary.

Article 19. Rights of the Child

Every minor child has the right to the measures of protection required by his condition as a minor on the part of his family, society, and the state.

Article 20. Right to Nationality

1. Every person has the right to a nationality.

2. Every person has the right to the nationality of the state in whose territory he was born if he does not have the right to any other nationality.

3. No one shall be arbitrarily deprived of his nationality or of the right to change it.

Article 21. Right to Property

1. Everyone has the right to the use and enjoyment of his property. The law may subordinate such use and enjoyment to the interest of society.

2. No one shall be deprived of his property except upon payment of just compensation, for reasons of public utility or social interest, and in the cases and according to the forms established by law.

3. Usury and any other form of exploitation of man by man shall be prohibited by law.

Article 22. Freedom of Movement and Residence

1. Every person lawfully in the territory of a State Party has the right to move about in it, and to reside in it subject to the provisions of the law.

2. Every person has the right to leave any country freely, including his own.

3. The exercise of the foregoing rights may be restricted only pursuant to a law to the extent necessary in a democratic society to prevent crime or to protect national security, public safety, public order, public morals, public health, or the rights or freedoms of others.

4. The exercise of the rights recognized in paragraph 1 may also be restricted by law in designated zones for reasons of public interest.

5. No one can be expelled from the territory of the state of which he is a national or be deprived of the right to enter it.

6. An alien lawfully in the territory of a State Party to this Convention may be expelled from it only pursuant to a decision reached in accordance with law.

7. Every person has the right to seek and be granted asylum in a foreign territory, in accordance with the legislation of the state and international conventions, in the event he is being pursued for political offenses or related common crimes.

8. In no case may an alien be deported or returned to a country, regardless of whether or not it is his country of origin, if in that country his right to life or personal freedom is in danger of being violated because of his race, nationality, religion, social status, or political opinions.

9. The collective expulsion of aliens is prohibited.

Article 23. Right to Participate in Government

1. Every citizen shall enjoy the following rights and opportunities:

a. to take part in the conduct of public affairs, directly or through freely chosen representatives;

b. to vote and to be elected in genuine periodic elections, which shall be by universal and equal suffrage and by secret ballot that guarantees the free expression of the will of the voters; and

c. to have access, under general conditions of equality, to the public service of his country.

2. The law may regulate the exercise of the rights and opportunities referred to in the preceding paragraph only on the basis of age, nationality, residence, language, education, civil and mental capacity, or sentencing by a competent court in criminal proceedings.

Article 24. Right to Equal Protection

All persons are equal before the law. Consequently, they are entitled, without discrimination, to equal protection of the law.

Article 25. Right to Judicial Protection

1. Everyone has the right to simple and prompt recourse, or any other effective recourse, to a competent court or tribunal for protection against acts that violate his fundamental rights recognized by the constitution or laws of the state concerned or by this Convention, even though such violation may have been committed by persons acting in the course of their official duties.

2. The States Parties undertake:

a. to ensure that any person claiming such remedy shall have his rights determined by the competent authority provided for by the legal system of the state;

    b. to develop the possibilities of judicial remedy; and

    c. to ensure that the competent authorities shall enforce such remedies when granted.

CHAPTER III - ECONOMIC, SOCIAL, AND CULTURAL RIGHTS

Article 26. Progressive Development

The States Parties undertake to adopt measures, both internally and through international cooperation, especially those of an economic and technical nature, with a view to achieving progressively, by legislation or other appropriate means, the full realization of the rights implicit in the economic, social, educational, scientific, and cultural standards set forth in the Charter of the Organization of American States as amended by the Protocol of Buenos Aires.

CHAPTER IV - SUSPENSION OF GUARANTEES, INTERPRETATION, AND APPLICATION

Article 27. Suspension of Guarantees

1. In time of war, public danger, or other emergency that threatens the independence or security of a State Party, it may take measures derogating from its obligations under the present Convention to the extent and for the period of time strictly required by the exigencies of the situation, provided that such measures are not inconsistent with its other obligations under international law and do not involve discrimination on the ground of race, color, sex, language, religion, or social origin.

2. The foregoing provision does not authorize any suspension of the following articles: Article 3 (Right to Juridical Personality), Article 4 (Right to Life), Article 5 (Right to Humane Treatment), Article 6 (Freedom from Slavery), Article 9 (Freedom from Ex Post Facto Laws), Article 12 (Freedom of Conscience and Religion), Article 17 (Rights of the Family), Article 18 (Right to a Name), Article 19 (Rights of the Child), Article 20 (Right to Nationality), and Article 23 (Right to Participate in Government), or of the judicial guarantees essential for the protection of such rights.

3. Any State Party availing itself of the right of suspension shall immediately inform the other States Parties, through the Secretary General of the Organization of American States, of the provisions the application of which it has suspended, the reasons that gave rise to the suspension, and the date set for the termination of such suspension.

Article 28. Federal Clause

1. Where a State Party is constituted as a federal state, the national government of such State Party shall implement all the provisions of the Convention over whose subject matter it exercises legislative and judicial jurisdiction.

2. With respect to the provisions over whose subject matter the constituent units of the federal state have jurisdiction, the national government shall immediately take suitable measures, in accordance with its constitution and its laws, to the end that the competent authorities of the constituent units may adopt appropriate provisions for the fulfillment of this Convention.

3. Whenever two or more States Parties agree to form a federation or other type of association, they shall take care that the resulting federal or other compact contains the provisions necessary for continuing and rendering effective the standards of this Convention in the new state that is organized.

Article 29. Restrictions Regarding Interpretation

No provision of this Convention shall be interpreted as:

a. permitting any State Party, group, or person to suppress the enjoyment or exercise of the rights and freedoms recognized in this Convention or to restrict them to a greater extent than is provided for herein;

b. restricting the enjoyment or exercise of any right or freedom recognized by virtue of the laws of any State Party or by virtue of another convention to which one of the said states is a party;

c. precluding other rights or guarantees that are inherent in the human personality or derived from representative democracy as a form of government; or

    d. excluding or limiting the effect that the American Declaration of the Rights and Duties of Man and other international acts of the same nature may have.

Article 30. Scope of Restrictions

The restrictions that, pursuant to this Convention, may be placed on the enjoyment or exercise of the rights or freedoms recognized herein may not be applied except in accordance with laws enacted for reasons of general interest and in accordance with the purpose for which such restrictions have been established.

Article 31. Recognition of Other Rights

Other rights and freedoms recognized in accordance with the procedures established in Articles 76 and 77 may be included in the system of protection of this Convention.

CHAPTER V - PERSONAL RESPONSIBILITIES

Article 32. Relationship between Duties and Rights

1. Every person has responsibilities to his family, his community, and Mankind.

2. The rights of each person are limited by the rights of others, by the security of all, and by the just demands of the general welfare, in a democratic society.

PART II - MEANS OF PROTECTION

CHAPTER VI - COMPETENT ORGANS

Article 33

The following organs shall have competence with respect to matters relating to the fulfillment of the commitments made by the States Parties to this Convention:

    a. the Inter-American Commission on Human Rights, referred to as "The Commission;" and

b. the Inter-American Court of Human Rights, referred to as "The Court."

CHAPTER VII - INTER-AMERICAN COMMISSION ON HUMAN RIGHTS

Section 1. Organization

Article 34
The Inter-American Commission on Human Rights shall be composed of seven members, who shall be persons of high moral character and recognized competence in the field of human rights.

Article 35
The Commission shall represent all the member countries of the Organization of American States.

Article 36
1. The members of the Commission shall be elected in a personal capacity by the General Assembly of the Organization from a list of candidates proposed by the governments of the member states.
2. Each of those governments may propose up to three candidates, who may be nationals of the states proposing them or of any other member state of the Organization of American States. When a slate of three is proposed, at least one of the candidates shall be a national of a state other than the one proposing the slate.

Article 37
1. The members of the Commission shall be elected for a term of four years and may be reelected only once, but the terms of three of the members chosen in the first election shall expire at the end of two years. Immediately following that election the General Assembly shall determine the names of those three members by lot.
2. No two nationals of the same state may be members of the Commission.

Article 38

Vacancies that may occur on the Commission for reasons other than the normal expiration of a term shall be filled by the Permanent Council of the Organization in accordance with the provisions of the Statute of the Commission.

Article 39

The Commission shall prepare its Statute, which it shall submit to the General Assembly for approval. It shall establish its own Regulations.

Article 40

Secretariat services for the Commission shall be furnished by the appropriate specialized unit of the General Secretariat of the Organization. This unit shall be provided with the resources required to accomplish the tasks assigned to it by the Commission.

Section 2. Functions

Article 41

The main function of the Commission shall be to promote respect for and defense of human rights. In the exercise of its mandate, it shall have the following functions and powers:

a. to develop an awareness of human rights among the peoples of America;

b. to make recommendations to the governments of the member states, when it considers such action advisable, for the adoption of progressive measures in favor of human rights within the framework of their domestic law and constitutional provisions as well as appropriate measures to further the observance of those rights;

c. to prepare such studies or reports as it considers advisable in the performance of its duties;

d. to request the governments of the member states to supply it with information on the measures adopted by them in matters of human rights;

e. to respond, through the General Secretariat of the Organization of American States, to inquiries made by the member states on matters related to human rights and, within the limits of its possibilities, to provide those states with the advisory services they request;

f. to take action on petitions and other communications pursuant to its authority under the provisions of Articles 44 through 51 of this Convention; and

g. to submit an annual report to the General Assembly of the Organization of American States.

Article 42

The States Parties shall transmit to the Commission a copy of each of the reports and studies that they submit annually to the Executive Committees of the Inter-American Economic and Social Council and the Inter-American Council for Education, Science, and Culture, in their respective fields, so that the Commission may watch over the promotion of the rights implicit in the economic, social, educational, scientific, and cultural standards set forth in the Charter of the Organization of American States as amended by the Protocol of Buenos Aires.

Article 43

The States Parties undertake to provide the Commission with such information as it may request of them as to the manner in which their domestic law ensures the effective application of any provisions of this Convention.

Section 3. Competence

Article 44

Any person or group of persons, or any nongovernmental entity legally recognized in one or more member states of the Organization, may lodge petitions with the Commission containing denunciations or complaints of violation of this Convention by a State Party.

Article 45

1. Any State Party may, when it deposits its instrument of rat-

ification of or adherence to this Convention, or at any later time, declare that it recognizes the competence of the Commission to receive and examine communications in which a State Party alleges that another State Party has committed a violation of a human right set forth in this Convention.

2. Communications presented by virtue of this article may be admitted and examined only if they are presented by a State Party that has made a declaration recognizing the aforementioned competence of the Commission. The Commission shall not admit any communication against a State Party that has not made such a declaration.

3. A declaration concerning recognition of competence may be made to be valid for an indefinite time, for a specified period, or for a specific case.

4. Declarations shall be deposited with the General Secretariat of the Organization of American States, which shall transmit copies thereof to the member states of that Organization.

Article 46

1. Admission by the Commission of a petition or communication lodged in accordance with Articles 44 or 45 shall be subject to the following requirements:

a. that the remedies under domestic law have been pursued and exhausted in accordance with generally recognized principles of international law;

b. that the petition or communication is lodged within a period of six months from the date on which the party alleging violation of his rights was notified of the final judgment;

c. that the subject of the petition or communication is not pending in another international proceeding for settlement; and

d. that, in the case of Article 44, the petition contains the name, nationality, profession, domicile, and signature of the person or persons or of the legal representative of the entity lodging the petition.

2. The provisions of paragraphs 1.a and 1.b of this article shall not be applicable when:

a. the domestic legislation of the state concerned does not afford due process of law for the protection of the right or rights that have allegedly been violated;

b. the party alleging violation of his rights has been denied access to the remedies under domestic law or has been prevented from exhausting them; or

c. there has been unwarranted delay in rendering a final judgment under the aforementioned remedies.

Article 47

The Commission shall consider inadmissible any petition or communication submitted under Articles 44 or 45 if:

a. any of the requirements indicated in Article 46 has not been met;

b. the petition or communication does not state facts that tend to establish a violation of the rights guaranteed by this Convention;

c. the statements of the petitioner or of the state indicate that the petition or communication is manifestly groundless or obviously out of order; or

d. the petition or communication is substantially the same as one previously studied by the Commission or by another international organization.

Section 4. Procedure

Article 48

1. When the Commission receives a petition or communication alleging violation of any of the rights protected by this Convention, it shall proceed as follows:

a. If it considers the petition or communication admissible, it shall request information from the government of the state indicated as being responsible for the alleged violations and shall furnish that government a transcript of the pertinent portions of the petition or communication. This information shall be submitted within a reasonable period to be determined by the Commission in accordance with the circumstances of each case.

b. After the information has been received, or after the period established has elapsed and the information has not been received, the Commission shall ascertain whether the grounds for the petition or communication still exist. If they do not, the Commission shall order the record to be closed.

c. The Commission may also declare the petition or communication inadmissible or out of order on the basis of information or evidence subsequently received.

d. If the record has not been closed, the Commission shall, with the knowledge of the parties, examine the matter set forth in the petition or communication in order to verify the facts. If necessary and advisable, the Commission shall carry out an investigation, for the effective conduct of which it shall request, and the states concerned shall furnish to it, all necessary facilities.

e. The Commission may request the states concerned to furnish any pertinent information and, if so requested, shall hear oral statements or receive written statements from the parties concerned.

f. The Commission shall place itself at the disposal of the parties concerned with a view to reaching a friendly settlement of the matter on the basis of respect for the human rights recognized in this Convention.

2. However, in serious and urgent cases, only the presentation of a petition or communication that fulfills all the formal requirements of admissibility shall be necessary in order for the Commission to conduct an investigation with the prior consent of the state in whose territory a violation has allegedly been committed.

Article 49

If a friendly settlement has been reached in accordance with paragraph 1.f of Article 48, the Commission shall draw up a report, which shall be transmitted to the petitioner and to the States Parties to this Convention, and shall then be communicated to the Secretary General of the Organization of American States for publication. This report shall contain a brief statement of the facts and of the solution reached. If any party in the case so requests, the fullest possible information shall be provided to it.

Article 50

1. If a settlement is not reached, the Commission shall, within the time limit established by its Statute, draw up a report setting forth the facts and stating its conclusions. If the report, in whole or in part, does not represent the unanimous agreement of the members of the Commission, any member may attach to it a separate opinion. The written and oral statements made by the parties in accordance with paragraph 1.e of Article 48 shall also be attached to the report.

2. The report shall be transmitted to the states concerned, which shall not be at liberty to publish it.

3. In transmitting the report, the Commission may make such proposals and recommendations as it sees fit.

Article 51

1. If, within a period of three months from the date of the transmittal of the report of the Commission to the states concerned, the matter has not either been settled or submitted by the Commission or by the state concerned to the Court and its jurisdiction accepted, the Commission may, by the vote of an absolute majority of its members, set forth its opinion and conclusions concerning the question submitted for its consideration.

2. Where appropriate, the Commission shall make pertinent recommendations and shall prescribe a period within which the state is to take the measures that are incumbent upon it to remedy the situation examined.

3. When the prescribed period has expired, the Commission shall decide by the vote of an absolute majority of its members whether the state has taken adequate measures and whether to publish its report.

CHAPTER VIII - INTER-AMERICAN COURT OF HUMAN RIGHTS

Section 1. Organization

Article 52

1. The Court shall consist of seven judges, nationals of the member states of the Organization, elected in an individual capacity from among jurists of the highest moral authority and of recognized competence in the field of human rights, who possess the qualifications required for the exercise of the highest judicial functions in conformity with the law of the state of which they are nationals or of the state that proposes them as candidates.

2. No two judges may be nationals of the same state.

Article 53

1. The judges of the Court shall be elected by secret ballot by an absolute majority vote of the States Parties to the Convention, in the General Assembly of the Organization, from a panel of candidates proposed by those states.

2. Each of the States Parties may propose up to three candidates, nationals of the state that proposes them or of any other member state of the Organization of American States. When a slate of three is proposed, at least one of the candidates shall be a national of a state other than the one proposing the slate.

Article 54

1. The judges of the Court shall be elected for a term of six years and may be reelected only once. The term of three of the judges chosen in the first election shall expire at the end of three years. Immediately after the election, the names of the three judges shall be determined by lot in the General Assembly.

2. A judge elected to replace a judge whose term has not expired shall complete the term of the latter.

3. The judges shall continue in office until the expiration of their term. However, they shall continue to serve with regard to cases that they have begun to hear and that are still pending, for which purposes they shall not be replaced by the newly elected judges.

Article 55

1. If a judge is a national of any of the States Parties to a case submitted to the Court, he shall retain his right to hear that case.

2. If one of the judges called upon to hear a case should be a national of one of the States Parties to the case, any other State Party in the case may appoint a person of its choice to serve on the Court as an *ad hoc* judge.

3. If among the judges called upon to hear a case none is a national of any of the States Parties to the case, each of the

latter may appoint an *ad hoc* judge.

4. An *ad hoc* judge shall possess the qualifications indicated in Article 52.

5. If several States Parties to the Convention should have the same interest in a case, they shall be considered as a single party for purposes of the above provisions. In case of doubt, the Court shall decide.

Article 56

Five judges shall constitute a quorum for the transaction of business by the Court.

Article 57

The Commission shall appear in all cases before the Court.

Article 58

1. The Court shall have its seat at the place determined by the States Parties to the Convention in the General Assembly of the Organization; however, it may convene in the territory of any member state of the Organization of American States when a majority of the Court considers it desirable, and with the prior consent of the state concerned. The seat of the Court may be changed by the States Parties to the Convention in the General Assembly by a two-thirds vote.

2. The Court shall appoint its own Secretary.

3. The Secretary shall have his office at the place where the Court has its seat and shall attend the meetings that the Court may hold away from its seat.

Article 59

The Court shall establish its Secretariat, which shall function under the direction of the Secretary of the Court, in accordance with the administrative standards of the General Secretariat of the Organization in all respects not incompatible with the independence of the Court. The staff of the Court's Secretariat shall be appointed by the Secretary General of the Organization, in consultation with the Secretary of the Court.

Article 60

The Court shall draw up its Statute, which it shall submit to the General Assembly for approval. It shall adopt its own Rules of Procedure.

Section 2. Jurisdiction and Functions

Article 61

1. Only the States Parties and the Commission shall have the right to submit a case to the Court.

2. In order for the Court to hear a case, it is necessary that the procedures set forth in Articles 48 and 50 shall have been completed.

Article 62

1. A State Party may, upon depositing its instrument of ratification or adherence to this Convention, or at any subsequent time, declare that it recognizes as binding, *ipso facto,* and not requiring special agreement, the jurisdiction of the Court on all matters relating to the interpretation or application of this Convention.

2. Such declaration may be made unconditionally, on the condition of reciprocity, for a specified period, or for specific cases. It shall be presented to the Secretary General of the Organization, who shall transmit copies thereof to the other member states of the Organization and to the Secretary of the Court.

3. The jurisdiction of the Court shall comprise all cases concerning the interpretation and application of the provisions of this Convention that are submitted to it, provided that the States Parties to the case recognize or have recognized such jurisdiction, whether by special declaration pursuant to the preceding paragraphs, or by a special agreement.

Article 63

1. If the Court finds that there has been a violation of a right or freedom protected by this Convention, the Court shall rule that the injured party be ensured the enjoyment of his right or freedom that was violated. It shall also rule, if appropriate, that the consequences of the measure or situation that constituted the breach of such right or freedom be remedied and that fair compensation be paid to the injured party.

2. In cases of extreme gravity and urgency, and when necessary to avoid irreparable damage to persons, the Court shall adopt such provisional measures as it deems pertinent in matters it has under consideration. With respect to a case not yet submitted to the Court, it may act at the request of the Commission.

Article 64

1. The member states of the Organization may consult the Court regarding the interpretation of this Convention or of other treaties concerning the protection of human rights in the American states. Within their spheres of competence, the organs listed in Chapter X of the Charter of the Organization of American States, as amended by the Protocol of Buenos Aires, may in like manner consult the Court.

2. The Court, at the request of a member state of the Organization, may provide that state with opinions regarding the compatibility of any of its domestic laws with the aforesaid international instruments.

Article 65

To each regular session of the General Assembly of the Organization of American States the Court shall submit, for the Assembly's consideration, a report on its work during the previous year. It shall specify, in particular, the cases in which a state has not complied with its judgments, making any pertinent recommendations.

Section 3. Procedure

Article 66

1. Reasons shall be given for the judgment of the Court.

2. If the judgment does not represent in whole or in part the unanimous opinion of the judges, any judge shall be entitled to have his dissenting or separate opinion attached to the judgment.

Article 67

The judgment of the Court shall be final and not subject to appeal. In case of disagreement as to the meaning or scope of the judgment, the Court shall interpret it at the request of any of the parties, provided the request is made within ninety days from the date of notification of the judgment.

Article 68

1. The States Parties to the Convention undertake to comply with the judgment of the Court in any case to which they are parties.

2. That part of a judgment that stipulates compensatory damages may be executed in the country concerned in accordance with domestic procedure governing the execution of judgments against the state.

Article 69

The parties to the case shall be notified of the judgment of the Court and it shall be transmitted to the States Parties to the Convention.

CHAPTER IX - COMMON PROVISIONS

Article 70

1. The judges of the Court and the members of the Commission shall enjoy, from the moment of their election and throughout their term of office, the immunities extended to diplomatic agents in accordance with international law. During the exercise of their official function they shall, in addition, enjoy the diplomatic privileges necessary for the performance of their duties.

2. At no time shall the judges of the Court or the members of the Commission be held liable for any decisions or opinions issued in the exercise of their functions.

Article 71

The position of judge of the Court or member of the Commission is incompatible with any other activity that might affect the independence or impartiality of such judge or member, as determined in the respective statutes.

Article 72

The judges of the Court and the members of the Commission shall receive emoluments and travel allowances in the form and under the conditions set forth in their statutes, with due regard for the importance and independence of their office. Such emoluments and travel allowances shall be determined in the budget of the Organization of American States, which shall also include the expenses of the Court and its Secretariat. To this end, the Court shall draw up its own budget and submit it for approval to the General Assembly through the General Secretariat. The latter may not introduce any changes in it.

Article 73

The General Assembly may, only at the request of the Commission or the Court, as the case may be, determine sanctions to be applied against members of the Commission or judges of the Court when there are justifiable grounds for such action as set forth in the respective statutes. A vote of a two-thirds majority of the member states of the Organization shall be required for a decision in the case of members of the Commission and, in the case of judges of the Court, a two-thirds majority vote of the States Parties to the Convention shall also be required.

PART III - GENERAL AND TRANSITORY PROVISIONS

CHAPTER X - SIGNATURE, RATIFICATION, RESERVATIONS, AMENDMENTS, PROTOCOLS, AND DENUNCIATION

Article 74

1. This Convention shall be open for signature and ratification by or adherence of any member state of the Organization of American States.

2. Ratification of or adherence to this Convention shall be made by the deposit of an instrument of ratification or adherence with the General Secretariat of the Organization of American States.

As soon as eleven states have deposited their instruments of ratification or adherence, the Convention shall enter into force. With respect to any state that ratifies or adheres thereafter, the Convention shall enter into force on the date of the deposit of its instrument of ratification or adherence.

3. The Secretary General shall inform all member states of the Organization of the entry into force of the Convention.

Article 75
This Convention shall be subject to reservations only in conformity with the provisions of the Vienna Convention on the Law of Treaties signed on May 23, 1969.

Article 76
1. Proposals to amend this Convention may be submitted to the General Assembly for the action it deems appropriate by any State Party directly, and by the Commission or the Court through the Secretary General.

2. Amendments shall enter into force for the States ratifying them on the date when two-thirds of the States Parties to this Convention have deposited their respective instruments of ratification. With respect to the other States Parties, the amendments shall enter into force on the dates on which they deposit their respective instruments of ratification.

Article 77
1. In accordance with Article 31, any State Party and the Commission may submit proposed protocols to this Convention for consideration by the States Parties at the General Assembly with a view to gradually including other rights and freedoms within its system of protection.

2. Each protocol shall determine the manner of its entry into force and shall be applied only among the States Parties to it.

Article 78
1. The States Parties may denounce this Convention at the expiration of a five-year period from the date of its entry into force and

by means of notice given one year in advance. Notice of the denunciation shall be addressed to the Secretary General of the Organization, who shall inform the other States Parties.

2. Such a denunciation shall not have the effect of releasing the State Party concerned from the obligations contained in this Convention with respect to any act that may constitute a violation of those obligations and that has been taken by that state prior to the effective date of denunciation.

CHAPTER XI - TRANSITORY PROVISIONS

Section 1. Inter-American Commission on Human Rights

Article 79

Upon the entry into force of this Convention, the Secretary General shall, in writing, request each member state of the Organization to present, within ninety days, its candidates for membership on the Inter-American Commission on Human Rights. The Secretary General shall prepare a list in alphabetical order of the candidates presented, and transmit it to the member states of the Organization at least thirty days prior to the next session of the General Assembly.

Article 80

The members of the Commission shall be elected by secret ballot of the General Assembly from the list of candidates referred to in Article 79. The candidates who obtain the largest number of votes and an absolute majority of the votes of the representatives of the member states shall be declared elected. Should it become necessary to have several ballots in order to elect all the members of the Commission, the candidates who receive the smallest number of votes shall be eliminated successively, in the manner determined by the General Assembly.

Section 2. Inter-American Court of Human Rights

Article 81

Upon the entry into force of this Convention, the Secretary

General shall, in writing, request each State Party to present, within ninety days, its candidates for membership on the Inter-American Court of Human Rights. The Secretary General shall prepare a list in alphabetical order of the candidates presented and transmit it to the States Parties at least thirty days prior to the next session of the General Assembly.

Article 82
The judges of the Court shall be elected from the list of candidates referred to in Article 81, by secret ballot of the States Parties to the Convention in the General Assembly. The candidates who obtain the largest number of votes and an absolute majority of the votes of the representatives of the States Parties shall be declared elected. Should it become necessary to have several ballots in order to elect all the judges of the Court, the candidates who receive the smallest number of votes shall be eliminated successively, in the manner determined by the States Parties.

APPENDIX F

THE VIRGINIA DECLARATION OF RIGHTS[105]

Virginia's Declaration of Rights was drawn upon by Thomas Jefferson for the opening paragraphs of the Declaration of Independence. It was widely copied by the other colonies and became the basis of the Bill of Rights. Written by George Mason, it was adopted by the Virginia Constitutional Convention on June 12, 1776.

A DECLARATION OF RIGHTS made by the representatives of the good people of Virginia, assembled in full and free convention which rights do pertain to them and their posterity, as the basis and foundation of government .

Section 1. That all men are by nature equally free and independent and have certain inherent rights, of which, when they enter into a state of society, they cannot, by any compact, deprive or divest their posterity; namely, the enjoyment of life and liberty, with the means of acquiring and possessing property, and pursuing and obtaining happiness and safety.

Section 2. That all power is vested in, and consequently derived from, the people; that magistrates are their trustees and servants and at all times amenable to them.

Section 3. That government is, or ought to be, instituted for the common benefit, protection, and security of the people, nation, or community; of all the various modes and forms of government, that is best which is capable of producing the greatest degree of happi-

---

105 Source: http://www.archives.gov/exhibits/charters/virginia_declaration_of_rights.html

ness and safety and is most effectually secured against the danger of maladministration. And that, when any government shall be found inadequate or contrary to these purposes, a majority of the community has an indubitable, inalienable, and indefeasible right to reform, alter, or abolish it, in such manner as shall be judged most conducive to the public weal.

Section 4. That no man, or set of men, is entitled to exclusive or separate emoluments or privileges from the community, but in consideration of public services; which, nor being descendible, neither ought the offices of magistrate, legislator, or judge to be hereditary.

Section 5. That the legislative and executive powers of the state should be separate and distinct from the judiciary; and that the members of the two first may be restrained from oppression, by feeling and participating the burdens of the people, they should, at fixed periods, be reduced to a private station, return into that body from which they were originally taken, and the vacancies be supplied by frequent, certain, and regular elections, in which all, or any part, of the former members, to be again eligible, or ineligible, as the laws shall direct.

Section 6. That elections of members to serve as representatives of the people, in assembly ought to be free; and that all men, having sufficient evidence of permanent common interest with, and attachment to, the community, have the right of suffrage and cannot be taxed or deprived of their property for public uses without their own consent or that of their representatives so elected, nor bound by any law to which they have not, in like manner, assembled for the public good.

Section 7. That all power of suspending laws, or the execution of laws, by any authority, without consent of the representatives of the people, is injurious to their rights and ought not to be exercised.

Section 8. That in all capital or criminal prosecutions a man has a right to demand the cause and nature of his accusation, to be confronted with the accusers and witnesses, to call for evidence in his favor, and to a speedy trial by an impartial jury of twelve men of his vicinage, without whose unanimous consent he cannot be found guilty; nor can he be compelled to give evidence against himself; that no man be deprived of his liberty except by the law of the land or the judgment of his peers.

Section 9. That excessive bail ought not to be required, nor excessive fines imposed, nor cruel and unusual punishments inflicted.

Section 10. That general warrants, whereby an officer or messenger may be commanded to search suspected places without evidence of a fact committed, or to seize any person or persons not named, or whose offense is not particularly described and supported by evidence, are grievous and oppressive and ought not to be granted.

Section 11. That in controversies respecting property and in suits between man and man, the ancient trial by jury is preferable to any other and ought to be held sacred.

Section 12. That the freedom of the press is one of the great bulwarks of liberty, and can never be restrained but by despotic governments.

Section 13. That a well-regulated militia, composed of the body of the people, trained to arms, is the proper, natural, and safe defense of a free state; that standing armies, in time of peace, should be avoided as dangerous to liberty; and that in all cases the military should be under strict subordination to, and governed by, the civil power.

Section 14. That the people have a right to uniform government; and, therefore, that no government separate from or independent of the government of Virginia ought to be erected or established within the limits thereof.

Section 15. That no free government, or the blessings of liberty, can be preserved to any people but by a firm adherence to justice, moderation, temperance, frugality, and virtue and by frequent recurrence to fundamental principles.

Section 16. That religion, or the duty which we owe to our Creator, and the manner of discharging it, can be directed only by reason and conviction, not by force or violence; and therefore all men are equally entitled to the free exercise of religion, according to the dictates of conscience; and that it is the mutual duty of all to practice Christian forbearance, love, and charity toward each other.

APPENDIX G

UNIVERSAL ISLAMIC DECLARATION OF HUMAN RIGHTS[106]

His is a declaration for Mankind, a guidance and instruction to those who fear God.
(Al Qur'an, Al-Imran 3:138)

Foreword
Islam gave to Mankind an ideal code of human rights fourteen centuries ago. These rights aim at conferring honor and dignity on Mankind and eliminating exploitation, oppression and injustice.

Human rights in Islam are firmly rooted in the belief that God, and God alone, is the Law Giver and the Source of all human rights. Due to their Divine origin, no ruler, government, assembly or authority can curtail or violate in any way the human rights conferred by God, nor can they be surrendered.

Human rights in Islam are an integral part of the overall Islamic order and it is obligatory on all Muslim governments and organs of society to implement them in letter and in spirit within the framework of that order.

It is unfortunate that human rights are being trampled upon with impunity in many countries of the world, including some Muslim countries. Such violations are a matter of serious concern and are arousing the conscience of more and more people throughout the world.

I sincerely hope that this *Declaration of Human Rights* will give

---

106 Source: http://www.alhewar.com/ISLAMDECL.html

a powerful impetus to the Muslim peoples to stand firm and defend resolutely and courageously the rights conferred on them by God.

This *Declaration of Human Rights* is the second fundamental document proclaimed by the Islamic Council to mark the beginning of the 15th Century of the Islamic era, the first being the *Universal Islamic Declaration* announced at the International Conference on The Prophet Muhammad (peace and blessings be upon him) and his Message, held in London from 12 to 15 April 1980.

The *Universal Islamic Declaration of Human Rights* is based on the Qur'an and the Sunnah and has been compiled by eminent Muslim scholars, jurists and representatives of Islamic movements and thought. May God reward them all for their efforts and guide us along the right path.

Paris 21 Dhul Qaidah 1401 Salem Azzam
19th September 1981 *Secretary General.*

O men! Behold, We have created you all out of a male and a female, and have made you into nations and tribes, so that you might come to know one another. Verily, the noblest of you in the sight of God is the one who is most deeply conscious of Him. Behold, God is all-knowing, all aware.
(Al Qur'an, Al-Hujurat 49:13)

Preamble

WHEREAS the age-old human aspiration for a just world order wherein people could live, develop and prosper in an environment free from fear, oppression, exploitation and deprivation, remains largely unfulfilled;

WHEREAS the Divine Mercy unto Mankind reflected in its having been endowed with super-abundant economic sustenance is being wasted, or unfairly or unjustly withheld from the inhabitants of the earth;

WHEREAS Allah (God) has given Mankind through His revelations in the Holy Qur'an and the Sunnah of His Blessed Prophet Muhammad an abiding legal and moral framework within which to establish and regulate human institutions and relationships;

WHEREAS the human rights decreed by the Divine Law aim at conferring dignity and honor on Mankind and are designed to eliminate oppression and injustice;

WHEREAS by virtue of their Divine source and sanction these rights can neither be curtailed, abrogated or disregarded by authorities, assemblies or other institutions, nor can they be surrendered or alienated;

Therefore we, as Muslims, who believe

a) in God, the Beneficent and Merciful, the Creator, the Sustainer, the Sovereign, the sole Guide of Mankind and the Source of all Law;

b) in the vice-ruling (*Khilafah*) of man who has been created to fulfill the Will of God on earth;

c) in the wisdom of Divine guidance brought by the Prophets, whose mission found its culmination in the final Divine message that was conveyed by the Prophet Muhammad (Peace be upon him) to all Mankind;

d) that rationality by itself without the light of revelation from God can neither be a sure guide in the affairs of Mankind nor provide spiritual nourishment to the human soul, and, knowing that the teachings of Islam represent the quintessence of Divine guidance in its final and perfect form, feel duty-bound to remind man of the high status and dignity bestowed on him by God;

e) in inviting all Mankind to the message of Islam;

f) that by the terms of our primeval covenant with God our duties and obligations have priority over our rights, and that each one of us is under a bounden duty to spread the teachings of Islam by word, deed, and indeed in all gentle ways, and to make them effective not only in our individual lives but also in the society around us;

g) in our obligation to establish an Islamic order:

i) wherein all human beings shall be equal and none shall enjoy a privilege or suffer a disadvantage or discrimination by reason of race, color, sex, origin or language;

ii) wherein all human beings are born free;

iii) wherein slavery and forced labor are abhorred;

iv) wherein conditions shall be established such that the institution of family shall be preserved, protected and honored as the basis of all social life;

v) wherein the rulers and the ruled alike are subject to, and equal before, the Law;

vi) wherein obedience shall be rendered only to those commands that are in consonance with the Law;

vii) wherein all worldly power shall be considered as a sacred trust, to be exercised within the limits prescribed by the Law and in a manner approved by it, and with due regard for the priorities fixed by it;

viii) wherein all economic resources shall be treated as Divine blessings bestowed upon Mankind, to be enjoyed by all in accordance with the rules and the values set out in the Qur'an and the Sunnah;

ix) wherein all public affairs shall be determined and conducted, and the authority to administer them shall be exercised after mutual consultation *(Shura)* between the believers qualified to contribute to a decision which would accord well with the Law and the public good;

x) wherein everyone shall undertake obligations proportionate to his capacity and shall be held responsible pro rata for his deeds;

xi) wherein everyone shall, in case of an infringement of his rights, be assured of appropriate remedial measures in accordance with the Law;

xii) wherein no one shall be deprived of the rights assured to him by the Law except by its authority and to the extent permitted by it;

xiii) wherein every individual shall have the right to bring legal action against anyone who commits a crime against society as a whole or against any of its members;

xiv) wherein every effort shall be made to

(a) secure unto Mankind deliverance from every type of exploitation, injustice and oppression,

(b) ensure to everyone security, dignity and liberty in terms set out and by methods approved and within the limits set by the Law;

Do hereby, as servants of Allah and as members of the Universal Brotherhood of Islam, at the beginning of the Fifteenth Century of the Islamic Era, affirm our commitment to uphold the following inviolable and inalienable human rights that we consider are enjoined by Islam.

I - Right to Life

a) Human life is sacred and inviolable and every effort shall be made to protect it. In particular, no one shall be exposed to injury or death, except under the authority of the Law.

b) Just as in life, so also after death, the sanctity of a person's body shall be inviolable. It is the obligation of believers to see that a deceased person's body is handled with due solemnity.

II - Right to Freedom

a) Man is born free. No inroads shall be made on his right to liberty except under the authority and in due process of the Law.

b) Every individual and every people has the inalienable right to freedom in all its forms ¾ physical, cultural, economic and political — and shall be entitled to struggle by all available means against any infringement or abrogation of this right; and every oppressed individual or people has a legitimate claim to the support of other individuals and/or peoples in such a struggle.

III - Right to Equality and Prohibition Against Impermissible Discrimination

a) All persons are equal before the Law and are entitled to equal opportunities and protection of the Law.

b) All persons shall be entitled to equal wage for equal work.

c) No person shall be denied the opportunity to work or be discriminated against in any manner or exposed to greater physical risk by reason of religious belief, color, race, origin, sex or language.

IV - Right to Justice

a) Every person has the right to be treated in accordance with the Law, and only in accordance with the Law.

b) Every person has not only the right but also the obligation to protest against injustice; to recourse to remedies provided by the Law in respect of any unwarranted personal injury or loss; to self-defense against any charges that are preferred against him and to obtain fair adjudication before an independent judicial tribunal in any dispute with public authorities or any other person.

c) It is the right and duty of every person to defend the rights of any other person and the community in general *(Hisbah)*.

d) No person shall be discriminated against while seeking to defend private and public rights.

e) It is the right and duty of every Muslim to refuse to obey any command, which is contrary to the Law, no matter by whom it may be issued.

V - Right to Fair Trial

a) No person shall be adjudged guilty of an offence and made liable to punishment except after proof of his guilt before an independent judicial tribunal.

b) No person shall be adjudged guilty except after a fair trial and after reasonable opportunity for defense has been provided to him.

c) Punishment shall be awarded in accordance with the Law, in proportion to the seriousness of the offence and with due consideration of the circumstances under which it was committed.

d) No act shall be considered a crime unless it is stipulated as such in the clear wording of the Law.

e) Every individual is responsible for his actions. Responsibility for a crime cannot be vicariously extended to other members of his family or group, who are not otherwise directly or indirectly involved in the commission of the crime in question.

VI - Right to Protection Against Abuse of Power

Every person has the right to protection against harassment by official agencies. He is not liable to account for himself except for making a defense to the charges made against him or where he is found in a situation wherein a question regarding suspicion of his involvement in a crime could be *reasonably* raised

VII - Right to Protection Against Torture

No person shall be subjected to torture in mind or body, or degraded, or threatened with injury either to himself or to anyone related to or held dear by him, or forcibly made to confess to the commission of a crime, or forced to consent to an act, which is injurious to his interests.

VIII - Right to Protection of Honor and Reputation

Every person has the right to protect his honor and reputation against calumnies, groundless charges or deliberate attempts at defamation and blackmail.

IX - Right to Asylum

a) Every persecuted or oppressed person has the right to seek refuge and asylum. This right is guaranteed to every human being irrespective of race, religion, color and sex.

b) Al Masjid Al Haram (the sacred house of Allah) in Mecca is a sanctuary for all Muslims.

X - Rights of Minorities

a) The Qur'anic principle "There is no compulsion in religion" shall govern the religious rights of non-Muslim minorities.

b) In a Muslim country religious minorities shall have the choice to be governed in respect of their civil and personal matters by Islamic Law, or by their own laws.

XI - Right and Obligation to Participate in the Conduct and Management of Public Affairs

a) Subject to the Law, every individual in the community *(Ummah)* is entitled to assume public office.

b) Process of free consultation *(Shura)* is the basis of the administrative relationship between the government and the people. People also have the right to choose and remove their rulers in accordance with this principle.

XII - Right to Freedom of Belief, Thought and Speech

a) Every person has the right to express his thoughts and beliefs so long as he remains within the limits prescribed by the Law. No one, however, is entitled to disseminate falsehood or to circulate reports, which may outrage public decency, or to indulge in slander, innuendo or to cast defamatory aspersions on other persons.

b) Pursuit of knowledge and search after truth is not only a right but a duty of every Muslim.

c) It is the right and duty of every Muslim to protest and strive (within the limits set out by the Law) against oppression even if it involves challenging the highest authority in the state.

d) There shall be no bar on the dissemination of information provided it does not endanger the security of the society or the state and is confined within the limits imposed by the Law.

e) No one shall hold in contempt or ridicule the religious beliefs of others or incite public hostility against them; respect for the religious feelings of others is obligatory on all Muslims.

XIII - Right to Freedom of Religion

Every person has the right to freedom of conscience and worship in accordance with his religious beliefs.

XIV - Right to Free Association

a) Every person is entitled to participate individually and collectively in the religious, social, cultural and political life of his community and to establish institutions and agencies meant to enjoin what is right *(ma'roof)* and to prevent what is wrong *(munkar)*.

b) Every person is entitled to strive for the establishment of institutions where under an enjoyment of these rights would be made possible. Collectively, the community is obliged to establish conditions so as to allow its members full development of their personalities.

XV - The Economic Order and the Rights Evolving Therefrom

a) In their economic pursuits, all persons are entitled to the full benefits of nature and all its resources. These are blessings bestowed by God for the benefit of Mankind as a whole.

b) All human beings are entitled to earn their living according to the Law.

c) Every person is entitled to own property individually or in association with others. State ownership of certain economic resources in the public interest is legitimate.

d) The poor have the right to a prescribed share in the wealth of the rich, as fixed by Zakah, levied and collected in accordance with the Law.

e) All means of production shall be utilized in the interest of the community *(Ummah)* as a whole, and may not be neglected or misused.

f) In order to promote the development of a balanced economy and to protect society from exploitation, Islamic Law forbids monopolies, unreasonable restrictive trade practices, usury, the use of coercion in the making of contracts and the publication of misleading advertisements.

g) All economic activities are permitted provided they are not detrimental to the interests of the community *(Ummah)* and do not violate Islamic laws and values.

XVI - Right to Protection of Property
No property may be expropriated except in the public interest and on payment of fair and adequate compensation.

XVII - Status and Dignity of Workers
Islam honors work and the worker and enjoins Muslims not only to treat the worker justly but also generously. He is not only to be paid his earned wages promptly, but is also entitled to adequate rest and leisure.

XVIII - Right to Social Security
Every person has the right to food, shelter, clothing, education and medical care consistent with the resources of the community. This obligation of the community extends in particular to all individuals who cannot take care of themselves due to some temporary or permanent disability.

XIX - Right to Found a Family and Related Matters
a) Every person is entitled to marry, to found a family and to bring up children in conformity with his religion, traditions and culture. Every spouse is entitled to such rights and privileges and carries such obligations as are stipulated by the Law.

b) Each of the partners in a marriage is entitled to respect and consideration from the other.

c) Every husband is obligated to maintain his wife and children according to his means.

d) Every child has the right to be maintained and properly brought up by its parents, it being forbidden that children are made to work at an early age or that any burden is put on them, which would arrest or harm their natural development.

e) If parents are for some reason unable to discharge their obligations towards a child it becomes the responsibility of the community to fulfill these obligations at public expense.

f) Every person is entitled to material support, as well as care and protection, from his family during his childhood, old age or incapacity. Parents are entitled to material support as well as care and protection from their children.

g) Motherhood is entitled to special respect, care and assistance on the part of the family and the public organs of the community *(Ummah)*.

h) Within the family, men and women are to share in their obligations and responsibilities according to their sex, their natural endowments, talents and inclinations, bearing in mind their common responsibilities toward their progeny and their relatives.

i) No person may be married against his or her will, or lose or suffer diminution of legal personality on account of marriage.

XX - Rights of Married Women

Every married woman is entitled to:

a) live in the house in which her husband lives;

b) receive the means necessary for maintaining a standard of living which is not inferior to that of her spouse, and, in the event of divorce, receive during the statutory period of waiting *(iddah)* means of maintenance commensurate with her husband's resources, for herself as well as for the children she nurses or keeps, irrespective of her own financial status, earnings, or property that she may hold in her own rights;

c) seek and obtain dissolution of marriage *(Khul'a)* in accordance with the terms of the Law. This right is in addition to her right to seek divorce through the courts.

d) inherit from her husband, her parents, her children and other relatives according to the Law;

e) strict confidentiality from her spouse, or ex-spouse if divorced, with regard to any information that he may have obtained about her, the disclosure of which could prove detrimental to her interests. A similar responsibility rests upon her in respect of her spouse or ex-spouse.

XXI - Right to Education
a) Every person is entitled to receive education in accordance with his natural capabilities.

b) Every person is entitled to a free choice of profession and career and to the opportunity for the full development of his natural endowments.

XXII - Right of Privacy
Every person is entitled to the protection of his privacy.

XXIII - Right to Freedom of Movement and Residence
a) In view of the fact that the World of Islam is veritably *Ummah Islamia*, every Muslim shall have the right to freely move in and out of any Muslim country.

b) No one shall be forced to leave the country of his residence, or be arbitrarily deported therefrom without recourse to due process of Law.

Explanatory Notes
1. In the above formulation of Human Rights, unless the context provides otherwise:

a) the term 'person' refers to both the male and female sexes.

b) the term 'Law' denotes the *Shari'ah*, i.e. the totality of ordinances derived from the Qur'an and the Sunnah and any other laws that are deduced from these two sources by methods considered valid in Islamic jurisprudence.

2. Each one of the Human Rights enunciated in this declaration carries a corresponding duty.

3. In the exercise and enjoyment of the rights referred to above every person shall be subject only to such limitations as are enjoined by the Law for the purpose of securing the due recognition of, and respect for, the rights and the freedom of others and of meeting

the just requirements of morality, public order and the general welfare of the Community *(Ummah)*.

The Arabic text of this *Declaration* is the original.

Glossary of Arabic Terms

SUNNAH - The example or way of life of the Prophet (peace be upon him), embracing what he said, did or agreed to.

KHALIFAH - The vice-ruler of man on earth or succession to the Prophet, transliterated into English as the Caliphate.

HISBAH- Public vigilance, an institution of the Islamic State enjoined to observe and facilitate the fulfillment of right norms of public behavior. The "Hisbah" consists in public vigilance as well as an opportunity to private individuals to seek redress through it.

MA'ROOF - Good act.

MUNKAR - Reprehensible deed.

ZAKAH - The 'purifying' tax on wealth, one of the five pillars of Islam obligatory on Muslims.

IDDAH - The waiting period of a widowed or divorced woman during which she is not to re-marry.

KHUL'A - Divorce a woman obtains at her own request.

UMMAH ISLAMIA - *World Muslim community.*

SHARI'AH - Islamic Law.

APPENDIX H

UNIVERSAL DECLARATION OF THE COLLECTIVE RIGHTS OF PEOPLES (CONSEU)[107]
1990

(SEE ARTICLE 9 FOR LANGUAGE DISPOSITIONS)

Preamble

Bearing in mind the progress achieved, especially in the last two hundred years, since the "Declaration of the Rights of Man and Citizen" in raising awareness of equality of all human beings;

Bearing in mind that one of the greatest contributions to the understanding of this equality has been the recognition of the difference among human beings because of language, culture, belonging to a specific people. As stated in the "Universal Declaration of Human Rights" proclaimed by the United Nations Organization in 1948;

Bearing in mind that individual rights to equality and difference can only be completely fulfilled within the framework of specific peoples in relation to which every individual identifies;

Bearing in mind that each people is fundamentally the holder of its own collective and unalienable rights to equality and difference;

Bearing in mind that the Charter of the United Nations has stated and recognized in its article 1.2 the need to "develop friendly relations among nations based on respect for the principle of equal rights and self-determination of peoples"; that other UN texts such as the several International Pacts relative to political, social, economical, cultural rights, etc. require to be included in the scope of collective

---

107 Source: http://www.slmc.uottawa.ca/?q=int_rights_cesn

rights; those documents which are at present being dealt with in the UN itself, such as the "Declaration on the Rights of Indigenous Peoples", lead us to interpret all individual rights, in order to fully grasp their meaning, in the light of collective rights.

Considering that, pursuant to these principles, numerous peoples can not only exercise their right to self-determination and take their corresponding sovereignty and independence, but also to deepen their internal cohesion and their solidarity among other peoples;

In view of the fact that other collective rights have not yet been recognized or sufficiently developed and throughout the world there persist conflicts and confrontations resulting from the denial or limitation of the exercise of the collective rights of all peoples;

In view that these situations have legal as well as political consequences in the organization of society which, in international law, institutionalize inequality and discrimination among peoples, and that this organization is essentially at the mercy of constituted states and the bodies created and controlled by them;

In view of the fact that international relations have become more and more the monopoly of constituted states which as a consequence have granted themselves the power to of determining the degree of sovereignty of each people even though the peoples themselves are the only subjects and source of rights in all collective dimensions;

In view of the fact that in order to assure their domination and their international powers of decision over determinate geographical areas, the constituted states have imposed institutional models in which citizenship and the act of belonging to a specific people are confused, thus allowing them to deny the existence of peoples and, by means of various legal statues (autonomy, regionalization and so on), to submit them to limitations on their sovereignty or situations of dependence;

In view of the fact that during the last few years efforts have been made on the part of the civil society in order to promote the recognition of the rights of peoples, specially after the "Declaration of the Rights of Peoples" published in Algiers on July 4th, 1976;

In view of the fact that nonetheless the initiatives aimed at this objective still allow restrictions to collective rights of peoples on conditioning them to the supremacy of constituted states, particularly through the idea of minority;

In view of the fact that in order to arrive at a new stage in creating and understanding among peoples, and thus to contribute to world peace, it is essential to define, in a complete and intrinsic way, the collective rights of peoples and the method for exercising them regardless of current political and legal situations;

The General Assembly of the "Conference of European Stateless Nations" (CONSEU) proposes to all humanity and to competent international organizations that they adopt and put into practice this "Universal Declaration of the Collective Rights of Peoples".

Preliminaries

The absence of a unanimously accepted definition of the concept of "people" shows that it is a dynamic rather than a static notion. History demonstrates that certain communities recognized as peoples have appeared and disappeared, or reappeared, on the international scene under other names. However, the evolutions or regressions of these communities or peoples cannot in any way be the grounds for the acceptance, denial or limitation of the due respect for the collective and individual rights of the persons that form them. Objectively, the rights of peoples always maintain the proper and same identity. It is up to these same communities to set themselves up as peoples along the course of history and, therefore, become subjects of collective rights.

Taking all this into account, this Declaration proposes to define the collective rights of peoples and clearly state therewith the concept of people.

Section I. Peoples and Nations

Art. 1. - Any group of persons who have a common reference to a culture and their own historical tradition, developed within a determinate geographical territory or other environments, constitute a people.

Art. 2. - Any people has the right to identify itself as such. No other instance can substitute for defining it.

Art. 3. - Any people has the right to set itself up as a nation.

The existence of a nation is consequence of the will shared by the members of a people to organize itself politically and institutionally.

Art. 4. - Any people has the benefit of the imprescriptible and unalienable collective rights and prerogatives mentioned in this Declaration.

Section II. National Rights of Peoples

Art. 5. - Any people has the right to exist freely whatever its demographic size may be.

Art. 6. - Any people has the right to self-determination in an independent and sovereign way.

Art. 7. - Any people has the right to self-government, in accordance with the democratic options of its members.

Art. 8.1. - Any people has the right to the free exercise of its sovereignty in the whole of its own territory.

Art. 8.2. - Any people that has been forced to leave its territory has the right to return to that territory to settle and exercise its sovereignty, respecting the rights of other persons belonging to other peoples who may be possibly living there.

Art. 8.3. - Any people that may be object of a division as consequence of an interstate or intrastate partition has the right to recover its territorial, political and institutional unity.

Art. 8.4. - Any itinerant people that has historically developed its national consciousness in accordance with this means of existence has the right to guarantee its free circulation.

Art. 9.1. - Any people has the right to express and develop its culture, its language and its organizational forms and, in order to do so, to provide for its own political, educational, communications and public administrational structures within the framework of its sovereignty.

Art. 9.2. - Any people which might be under the conditions described in article 8.2, or be the victim of other decisions that may arbitrarily divide it, has the right to reestablish its linguistic, cultural unity and the rest of prerogatives that distinguish it.

Art. 10. - Any people has the right to dispose of the natural resources in its own territory and, where applicable, territorial waters included therein, and to value them for the development, progress and well-being of its members, in accordance with articles 16, 17 and 18 of this Declaration, related to ecological and solidary requirements.

Art. 11. - All peoples are and remain free and equal in rights whatever the nature of their international relations may be.

Art. 12. - Any people has the right to be fully recognized as such by the international community and to participate with equal voice and vote in the work and decisions of all international organizations representative of sovereign wills.

Art. 13. - Any people has the right to freely establish with each of the other peoples relations suitable to both parties and in the way they have jointly determined.

Art. 14. - Any people has the right to join together with other peoples, to form confederations or the like, always retaining the right to freely and unilaterally break agreements without any prejudice to the rights of other peoples.

Art. 15. - Any people has the right to benefit fairly from the natural resources of this planet and the universe, technological advances, scientific progress and ecological balance which constitute the common patrimony of humanity.

Art. 16. - Any people has the right to solidarity which involves mutual cooperation among peoples, the explicit recognition of the identities that distinguish them, the application of the principles of equity and reciprocity, exchanges of the national wealth and technological advances and economic and social progress, as well as of other goods which are to be shared.

Art. 17. - Any people has the right to prevent the use of natural wealth and technological advances for purposes and in conditions that endanger the health and safety of other peoples or jeopardize the ecological balance of the environment.

Art. 18. - Any people has the right to the legitimate recovery of its own property as well as an adequate reparation if it is completely or partially despoiled of its natural wealth or affected in its sovereignty or in the ecological balance of its environment.

Art. 19. - Any people has the right to direct recourse before the international courts in which those responsible must be elected democratically by all peoples and the arbiter chosen and agreed upon by the parties in the litigation.

Section IV. The Rights of Members of Peoples

Art. 20. - Any person, whether living among his own people or not, has the right to fully exercise the individual rights recognized by the various international declarations, conventions and pacts, in the light of the collective rights mentioned herein.

Section V. Transitional Provisions

Art. 21. - In compliance with the norms of International Law, which are to be completed with the principles of the present Declaration, any people that has been deprived of any of its collective rights by force of arms or by means of other constrictions, has the right of resistance by using the means they consider necessary for their legal defense and its full re-establishment.

Art. 22. - Any people, even if it is recognized, as far as it is subjected to trust situations or those which involve discrimination, colonization in all sense or other limitations to its sovereignty, has the right to put into practice the means and resources specified in Article 21 to gain its independence and the full exercise of rights belonging to every people.

Section VI. Final Clauses

Art. 23. - The application of this Declaration implies the disappearance of all situation which are negative or limiting to the collective rights of peoples and the expiry of all state and international juridical provisions that attack them.

Art. 24. - The signatories of this Declaration commit themselves to winning recognition for all peoples and their collective rights by the competent international organizations and that all the peoples attain their own representation in them. These organizations will therefore have the mission of insuring the respect of the collective rights of peoples defined herein and to intervene in order to solve any violations, which could attack them.